The Official XTree®
MS-DOS & Hard Disk
Companion

Second Edition

BY BETH WOODS

Cartoons by
Rich Tennant

D0761550

IDG Books Worldwide, Inc.
San Mateo, California 94402

Published by
IDG Books Worldwide, Inc.
An International Data Group Company
155 Bovet Road, Suite 730
San Mateo, CA 94402
(415) 358-1250

Edited by Jan Altman, The Express Train
Produced by Michael McCarthy, Editor-in-Chief,
Jeremy Judson, Associate Book Editor, Christine Strehlo,
and Steve Finerty
Interior design by Mark Houts and Beth Woods & Michael Cahlin

A Cahlin/Williams Communications Product

Copyright © 1990, 1991 by IDG Books Worldwide, Inc. All rights
reserved. No part of this book may be reproduced or transmitted in any
form, by any means (electronic, photocopying, recording, or otherwise)
without the prior written permission of the publisher.

Library of Congress Catalog Card No.: 91-071239
ISBN 1-878058-22-3

Printed in the United States of America

10 9 8 7 6 5 4 3 2 1

Distributed in the United States by IDG Books Worldwide, Inc.
Distributed in Canada by Macmillan of Canada, a Division of Canada
Publishing Corporation.
Distributed in the United Kingdom and Ireland by Computer Bookshops.
For information on translations and availability in other countries, contact
IDG Books Worldwide.
For sales inquiries and special prices for bulk quantities, write to the
address above or call IDG Books Worldwide at (415) 358-1250.

Trademarks: XTree is a registered trademark, and XTreePro, XTreePro
Gold, XTreeNet, 1WORD, and XTree Company are trademarks of
Executive Systems, Inc. Other brand names are trademarks of their
respective holders.

Limits of Liability/Disclaimer of Warranty: The authors and publisher
of this book have used their best efforts in preparing this book and its
contents. IDG Books Worldwide, Inc. makes no representation or
warranties with respect to the accuracy or completeness of the contents
hereof and specifically disclaim any implied warranties or merchantability
or fitness for any particular purpose.

Acknowledgements

We would like to thank:

Therese Solimeno, Rick James, Chris Clancy, Joe Raftery, Jan Altman, Steve Laff, the Wayniac, Bob Kimball, Todd Walker (for the Q&A's from the tech department), Chris Williams, Michael Chuises, Tracey Immel, and Carey Williams-Cahlin.

Special thanks to Bill Murphy, without whom this book would not have been possible.

CONTENTS

Foreword 9
Introduction 17

PART 1: MS-DOS CONCEPTS
What is DOS?..21
Drives 23
Directories 24
System Prompt..26
Files 28
Copy..35

PART 2: XTREE BASICS
Introducing XTree, XTreePro, and XTreePro Gold.......39
Global XTree Basics 41

PART 3: QUICK REFERENCE GUIDE
Applications Menu...50
Attributes...53
Batch Files 55
Cancel..60
Command Shell 61
Configuration 66
Copy..70
Date & Time Stamp 80
Delete 82
Directory 86
Directory Window...96
Edit..97
Execute 102
File Display 106
File Window 108
Filespec 108
Find 114
Format a Disk..117
Function Keys..120
Global..124
Graft 125
Help 125

PART 3: QUICK REFERENCE GUIDE (CONT.)

Hide/Unhide 130
History 130
Invert 133
Laptop Configuration 133
Log 137
Memory 139
Mouse Commands...140
Move..141
No Files! 147
Open (and Associate) 148
Print 148
Quit...151
Rename...152
Security..155
Showall Window...159
Sort Criteria..161
Split/Unsplit 163
Statistics...165
Substitute..168
Tag/Untag...169
View 177

PART 4: HARD DISK MANAGEMENT IN A NUTSHELL

Hard Disk Optimization...183
Backup...191
Delete Unneeded Files 195

PART 5: QUICK UPDATE GUIDE TO XTREEGOLD, XTREE EASY

Comments by King Lee, President, XTree..................199
Introduction 204
Application Menu...205
Archiving 213
Avail..213
Branch File Window 213
Compare...214
Copy..216
Dir Empty/Dir Not Logged 217

PART 5: QUICK UPDATE GUIDE (CONT.)

Filespec 217
Function Keys 217
History 217
Laptop Configuration 217
Log 222
Menu 224
Move 224
No Files! 225
Oops! 225
Open 228
Pull-Down Menus 228
XTreeMenu 231
View 231
Wiggle 233

PART 6: XTREENET: NETWORKS MADE EASY

Attach/Detach 238
Attributes (Directory) 238
Attributes (File) 239
Tag/Untag Branch 240
Tag/Untag by Attributes 240
Map 241
Volume 241

PART 7: SHORTCUTS:
COMMAND KEYS/ FUNCTION KEYS

XTree 245
XTreePro 247
XTreePro Gold 249
XTreeGold 252
XTree Easy 256
XTreeNet 258

APPENDICES

A. Archiving—The Shocking Truth! 263
B. XTree Tech Support Q&A 276
C. Where To Go From Here (Resources) 285
D. Answers To Pop Quizzes 288

INDEX 290

"I'LL BE WITH YOU AS SOON AS I EXECUTE A FEW MORE COMMANDS."

Foreword

An Unapologetic History Of XTree

by Jeff Johnson
Co-creator of XTree

I'D LIKE TO tell you that we had it all planned. That in 1983, the creative geniuses at Executive Systems Inc. (ESI) sat down and, probing the depths of our programming and engineering knowledge, peered into the future and said, "Ah-ha! Hard disks." Then in a round-the-clock hacker frenzy of pepperoni pizzas and classic Cokes, created XTree.

I'd like to say that.

I'd like to tell you it's going to be a movie and Tom Cruise is playing me.

But, like many great products and inventions, what you now know as XTree just sorta happened while we were involved in other projects. Think of it as a hi-tech version of Woody Allen's statement that life is what happens to you while you're out doing something else.

IT WAS 1983, a critical, pivotal year for the computer industry, and for me. Saying 1983 to someone who really knows the computer industry is like saying 1929 to a stock broker, or 1960 to a Yankees fan.

At the end of 1983, three important events took place: MS-DOS began its ascent as the dominant computer operating system replacing CP/M; IBM's PCjr, a computer recently cited by an industry magazine as "arguably (IBM's) biggest failure of the 1980's," was pronounced D.O.A. by everyone in the computer industry; and ESI gave me a try as an independent contractor. After a month, they hired me as a full-time employee, and I've been part of the company ever since. At the time, ESI was writing the BIOS and utilities for the Epson QX-10.

1984 rolled in and Epson asked Henry Hernandez, one of ESI's founders, if we could design utilities for their new PC DOS computers. Now Henry is this great big bear of a guy. Loveable, fun to work with and for, and not one to let a little thing like not knowing any better get in the way, said "Sure."

So we got the job and everybody (I mean everybody) at ESI was involved in the project; Dale Sinor, Tom Smith, and Henry (the owners), Ken Broomfield and me (the full-time programmers) and Claire Johnson (who did everything to run the company) put in 16-hour days. Three weeks and no sleep later, we delivered half a dozen utilities to Epson. They thanked us and gave us more work — a lot more work.

A couple of months later we had hundreds of floppy disks and several hard disks crammed packed with files and no idea where anything was. We had no way to manage all the files — and there hangs the tale.

You see nobody had a way of managing files. At least not any reasonably easy way. There just weren't any utilities to do it. There was a utility for CP/M written by a friend of ours, Mike Karas, that we had been using, and some "command line" oriented programs, but none of them addressed the concept of managing a directory structure. You know, paths and stuff like that.

Which made us all say, "Hmmmm?"

SO WE THOUGHT about it. We talked about it. We shouted over it. We threatened one another with ancient Klingon curses. In other words, we sat down like adults and reasoned the thing out.

We discussed different kinds of tree structures, recursive processing, and other technical stuff. Drawings and diagrams came and went like the kitchen trash.

Among the subjects discussed were *how* the program would represent the DOS directory structure on the screen, and *what* the screen might look like. I drew a picture of this outline on a white board. It looked like a tree that needed water. It was a swell picture but no one thought it could be done. "Impossible," they said.

Famous last words.

I went home on a Friday, programmed like mad until Sunday, and showed it to Henry on Monday. A week later we decided to try out the "tree" display in a backup program we were writing for Epson. They liked it. And we had the beginnings of a product.

In December of 1984, we really began working on what you now know as XTree. Our feature list was huge, and a lot of these features didn't make it into the original version of XTree, but were added later in XTreePro and XTreePro Gold. I was working full time on the program, Ken worked on it between other tasks, and everyone else chipped in as needed. When enough of the program was written so it could be used, we used it ourselves. We felt that if other people were going to rely on the program, it had to be rock solid for everyday use, easy to learn, and a cinch to operate.

If it's not yet obvious, I don't want you to think that I'm some kind of mad genius and created XTree all by myself. Far from it. Whenever you're trying to do something that's never been done before, lotsa people are involved.

That's the way it was with XTree. Dale made sure it had plenty of whiz-bang features. Henry made sure we didn't write any bad code. Tom made sure the user interface was consistent. (His unrelenting efforts to maintain consistency in the interface really weren't appreciated until the hundreds of reviews and millions of users began expressing their pleasure at how easy XTree is to use. Of course, back then, every time we thought XTree was ready, Tom had "just one more small revision." Right.) Finally, there was Ken, bug catcher supreme.

ALL THAT WAS left was a name.

Arletta, my wife, gets credit for that one. We had been throwing names around the office for months and no one could agree on anything. One night, late at night, very late at night, she suggested, "Xtree. You know, like Xtree, Xtree read all about it!"

Pretty stupid, I thought, but jotted it down.

When I mentioned it to everyone at the office the next day, they said, "Pretty stupid," and before you knew it we had a name — XTree.

Okay, we've got a name, we've got a program, we've also

got a problem; how do we get it into the stores so people like you can buy it and we can make ba-zillions of dollars? At the time, we had two choices: we could either publish it ourselves or find someone who knew more about software publishing than we did — and in early 1985 there weren't a lot of people to choose from.

On March 1st, 1985, we made the decision to publish XTree ourselves. Which is when Dale took charge and in a moment of sheer insanity vowed to have XTree ready to sell at the West Coast Computer Faire in San Francisco on April 1st, 1985. Dale promised to have XTree packaged; the manual completed, written and printed; and all the hundreds other details required to bring a product to market ready . . . in 30 days. As this was a seemingly impossible task, we thought April Fools' Day was an appropriate choice for our premiere.

What we didn't know was Dale had an ace up his sleeve. . . Michael Cahlin, president of Cahlin/Williams Communications.

In the next four weeks, Cahlin had the product packaged; the cover designed and printed; created press materials and had them in the hands of the industry's most influential reviewers and syndicated columnists; wrote, produced, and printed the first "XTree, XTree, Read All About It" brochure, and, along with Dale Sinor and Judy Mason, even set up XTree's booth at the West Coast Computer Faire. (Rumor has it that when Cahlin hired Bob Cabeen to actually design the first XTree package, he gave Bob only seven days to create it. When Bob protested, Cahlin is alleged to have said, "Look, Bob, God created the Universe in six days — all I want is a package design." When Bob came through in five days, the rumor continues, he replied, "Show *that* to God!")

Of course, Dale had his own miracles to perform. Two days before the show, he went to the typesetters to pick up the final proofs for the manual and discovered the typesetter had been evicted and was ducking everyone. Dale finally tracked him down, but the guy would only exchange the proofs for cash — something we weren't exactly knee-deep in. While the countdown to the West Coast Computer Faire continued, Dale found the cash, got the proofs, rushed them to the printer, then to the bindery, and waited for them, refusing to let them out of his sight. He left Los Angeles at 1:30 a.m. Four hours later, he pulled into Moscone Center, in San Francisco, carried the boxes of manuals, software cases, cover inserts, and brochures inside, and calmly began assembling the booth. The show opened at 9:00 a.m.

And so it goes.

THE ORIGINAL XTREE was officially, and ironically, introduced on April 1, 1985, at The West Coast Computer Faire, which at the time, was one of the most popular computer shows in the country. I hate to sound like your father, but this was back in the old days when computer shows were a far cry from the slick conventions you see today. These were *end*-user shows, and there were so many silicon-type bargains at these shows that they made the twenty-four bucks the Indians paid for Manhattan seem a bit high.

We sold XTree Version 1.0 for only $39.95 at that show, and we were literally selling them from the front of the booth while frantically putting the software packages together in the back! (And now they're a bonafide collectors item.) We shared a 10x10 booth with a small software publisher, who, as fate would have it, almost published the original XTree. The president's name was Pete Ryan, and knowing a good thing when he saw one, he became XTree's Product Manager six months later, and eventually worked his way up to Marketing Vice President and Chief Wheeler-Dealer.

Within weeks after the show, XTree was in the hands of John Dvorak, Jerry Pournelle, and all those other demigods of hi-tech who decide the fate of products. Dvorak, et al, loved the product and positive reviews appeared one after another. Near as I can figure, XTree was quite simply the right product, at the right price, at the right time: inexpensive software that solved a common problem and was easy to use. A rare beast in those days, or any days. In November '85, *PC Magazine* gave XTree their prestigious "Editor's Choice" Award. (XTreePro, released in 1987, received the same award, as did XTreePro Gold in 1990.) Other reviews and awards followed, and following them were orders from distributors and retailers.

. . . And the rest is software history.

XTreePro and XTreePro Gold were developed as more and more features were added. Gold is now translated into Dutch, French, German, Italian, and Spanish, to name a few. With more than three million copies in use, all versions of XTree are well-recognized industry standards for disk management. And that "impossible" tree structure has been copied by almost everyone who has made a hard disk management system since.

As for the future, the XTree program will continue to grow and expand its capabilities as it has in the past. Our main concern is answering the needs of our customers. We read your letters. We listen to your concerns. And we appreciate your support.

This time we have it all planned.

Right.

Jeff Johnson
September 1990

P.S. To my wife Arletta and our children, Tari, Dan, and Arynn, for putting up with my long workdays: I love you.

"OUR XTREE HANDBOOK HAS US MAINTAINING OUR HARD DISK THROUGH A MORE COMPREHENSIVE DOS-SHELL, AND YOU ASK WHY WE'RE DANCING?"

Introduction

■ MS-DOS & Hard Disk Management — Are We Having Fun Yet?

Granted, on the "fun meter," MS-DOS and Hard Disk Management generally register somewhere below flossing your teeth and remembering to put more fiber in your diet.

A lot less fun, however, is wasting your time with arcane MS-DOS commands when you could be taking full advantage of terrific tools contained in the XTree product line.

Unfortunately, every version of XTree has presented a bizarre paradox: XTree encourages you to forget about traditional MS-DOS commands — yet you need a decent working knowledge of MS-DOS to get the most out of it. In other words, to figure out how to use XTree, you have to know how to get along without it!

The bad news

The good news is that you don't have to earn a black belt in MS-DOS to use XTree. Far from it. You are actually only a few MS-DOS concepts away from doing power-user stuff with XTree.

The good news

The Official XTree MS-DOS & Hard Disk Companion bridges the gap between the desire and the *power*.

The plan is simple. The *Companion* begins at the very beginning by covering six important "MS-DOS Concepts." This section is not intended as a comprehensive DOS command guide. It simply covers the topics you need to be familiar with if you intend to utilize XTree to its fullest benefit. If you already feel comfortable with DOS, you can jump ahead to the "XTree Basics" section.

The solution

Next, the "Quick Reference Guide" will show you how you can effortlessly copy files, create directories, format disks, and back up whenever the mood should strike. You'll also learn (depending on which version of XTree you have) how to search through your whole hard disk for a "lost" file, or a file that contains a certain piece of text. You'll be able to use a "mouse," create a menu system to automate frequently used commands, and learn lots of other timesaving, power-user tricks.

"Hard Disk Management In a Nutshell" follows the "Quick Reference Guide." This covers what you need to know to keep your hard disk healthy. There's a section that answers the question, "What's the least amount of maintenance I can get by with?"

Since the first edition of this book, the ever-restless programmers at XTree Corp. have added not one but three new versions: XTree Easy, a revamping of the basic XTree product; XTreeGold, an update to XTreePro Gold; and XTreeNet, a special version just for network users. Since these new versions add only a handful of refinements, and rather than try to juggle *six* shaded bars in the Quick Reference Guide, we bring you up to date in Part 5, the "Quick Update Guide." If you've just bought one of the new versions, take a look there to see what's new, then refer to the Quick Reference Guide for your day-to-day work.

As long as we were adding stuff, we also put at the end of Part 5 a shortcut list of commands and function keys for when you've mastered XTree and just want to take a quick peek at the command list as a refresher.

The "Appendices" include additional topics like archiving and, from XTree Company's technical support staff, "The Most Commonly Asked Questions About XTreePro Gold."

Finally, the *Companion's* "Index Section" contains the equivalent of a "misspeller's dictionary." So even if you're unsure about the proper terminology, look it up as best you can, and you'll be guided to the appropriate place.

The purpose of *The Official XTree MS-DOS & Hard Disk Companion* is to help you harness the power of XTree to make hard disk maintenance simple and, perhaps, even fun. The idea is to always be prepared for the inevitable hard disk crash.

The *inevitable* hard disk crash?

Better safe than you-know-what

Of course, inevitable. Remember, a hard disk is nothing more than an ordinary piece of machinery assembled by human beings right here on good ol' planet Earth. Hard disks are subject to the same laws of Murphy and entropy as refrigerators, cars, and marriages. In other words, you should live like there's no tomorrow when it comes to the life of your hard disk.

Which brings us to the most important XTree benefit. . . peace of mind.

Ladies and Gentlemen, start your engines.

The 5th Wave

"RESPONSE TIME SEEMS A BIT SLOW."

MS-DOS Concepts

1

To be sure, this section is not a comprehensive course in DOS. In fact, it covers no real DOS commands. It's XTree's job to send the right commands to DOS. However, knowing a few DOS principles will make it possible to tap XTree's power. Plus, what you learn here about DOS will be surprisingly useful when you're using other programs.

If you already know DOS, you can skim (or skip) this section. The margin headings will pick out the major points for you and there are pop quizzes along the way.

Note: Any DOS command may be entered in either upper or lowercase letters. It doesn't matter.

■ *What is MS-DOS?*

Basically, MS-DOS (an acronym for Microsoft Disk Operating System) is a program (software) entrusted with the critical task of telling your computer how to behave like a proper computer.

Operating system

You may have assumed that when you bought your computer, it already knew how to be a computer. It didn't. Without DOS, a computer is as useful as a tape player without a tape. What you actually got was a box with tremendous potential.

What your computer *does* know how to do, is seek out the operating system every time you turn it on. Within a few seconds of powering up, your computer automatically finds DOS (right there on your hard disk where you or your dealer put it) and transforms itself into a fully functional computer, eagerly awaiting your command.

A major part of what an operating system does goes on invisibly. Behind the scene, DOS quietly processes dozens of functions to keep the computer running. (Much like the autonomic part of your body's own operating system which pumps blood, grows toenails, breathes, etc., all without any conscious effort on your part.)

Another level of DOS activities, like formatting a disk, deleting files, and so forth, requires your *conscious* interaction with DOS in the form of a typed command. (Much like jogging requires tremendous conscious will.)

These DOS commands must be entered using a particular set of words in a precise order. Most people get frustrated with DOS because they don't speak the language very well (or at all).

In general, then, the term "DOS" means both the autonomic and conscious portions of the computer's disk operating system.

The term "DOS" is also used in a couple of other ways.

A place on the hard disk

Most people give the name "DOS" to the *place* on their hard disk where the DOS accessory programs are stored. This is a convenient way to keep DOS files separate from other program files. We'll learn more about this in the section on directories.

Not in a program

Another thing DOS can mean is *not in a program*. When you're finished working with a particular software application and you press the "quit command," you may be questioned about your intentions to "exit to DOS." (The reason you're asked if you're "sure" you want to exit, is not because the program feels you should re-think your decision. Rather, it's just double-checking that you didn't hit the "quit command" by accident.) Once you confirm your decision to exit, you're dumped out of your program and you're back at the operating system level. You're not in a program, you're *in DOS*.

Now this is not the same thing as being in the place (directory area) on your hard disk named DOS where all your DOS files are stored as described previously. In this case DOS simply means *not in a program*.

What are the three things DOS can mean?

For the answer, go to page 288.

Pop Quiz

■ Drives

A "drive" in a computer is a device that records and plays back information. A hard disk stores information on a special piece of metal (hence, "hard"). A floppy drive stores information on something like videotape (which would be very "floppy" if it weren't in a special jacket).

Both hard and floppy disk drives work a lot like a VCR or tape player that also uses "heads" to record (save) and play back. A disk *drive* works similarly — a disk spins and a head reads the magnetic impulses.

The hard disk, which can store a tremendous amount of information, is where DOS, your programs, and your work are kept.

By comparison, the floppy disk can only hold a small amount of information. But the floppy drive's main job is to act as your hard disk's link to the outside world. You can copy *from* the hard disk to the floppy, or *to* the hard disk from the floppy.

However, when it's time to copy something to or from a hard disk, you can't ask DOS to copy the file to "that drive on the top." You have to know DOS's name (or *address)* for that drive.

Drive names

The address for the first floppy drive is "A:". The address for the first hard disk is "C:". Don't forget the colon. It's that little colon (:) that tells DOS that you're talking about a *drive* named "A" rather than a file named "A". (If you forget the colon, you could find the files you want to copy mushed together in a giant file called "A"!)

Current drive As you work with your computer, one of your drives is the designated, or *current,* drive. This drive is where DOS expects to find the next program you want to use. Usually the current drive is your hard drive (C:). If you want to make a different drive the current drive, you need to type the drive's name and hit the enter key on your keyboard (e.g., type **A:** and press **<ENTER>** to make drive A the current drive.) You'll see how this works later when the issue of the *current drive* becomes important.

• •

What does the colon (:) mean when you see "A:" and "C:"?

For the answer, go to page 288 .

Pop Quiz •

■ Directories

Tree When "they" invented hard disks that could hold thousands of files, they probably soon realized that dumping thousands of files onto one hard disk would create chaos. (Imagine trying to find one file among a list of a thousand!) A method had to be created to organize files on a hard disk. Thus, the venerable "Inverted Tree Hierarchical Structure" was born.

You may ask, "What is an Inverted Tree Hierarchical Structure, and why do I have to know about it?" You have to know about it because it's the backbone of your computer system. So let's break it down into comfortable bite-sized pieces.

Okay, first, an "inverted tree" is nothing more than an upside-down tree. If you visualize a tree turned upside down, you'll see that the root becomes the top of the tree. Beneath the root will be several main branches. Each of the main branches may host several smaller branches. Each of those sub-branches may also have a number of sub-sub-branches and so on.

A "hierarchical structure" means that all these branches and sub-branches are not equal. The higher-up branches are the parents of the next generation of (child) branches. The child branches can be parents to another set of branches below them and so on.

On a hard disk, the branches are called directories. The purpose of each directory is to provide a storage area for your files and programs. The system of directories is generally referred to as the "tree structure" or "directory structure."

Another way to look at this directory system is to imagine your hard disk as a house. An *expensive* house.

Other directories

As you enter your expensive home you will find yourself in the entryway. This is equivalent to the "root" of the hard disk (the top of your inverted tree). Once you are in the root/entryway, you see several doors leading to other rooms/branches.

If you want to watch TV, for instance, the first step would be to go to the room that contains the TV. In a computer, if you want to use your word processor, the first step is to go into the directory where your word processor is stored. Once you are in the TV room, you can turn on the TV. Similarly, once you are in the word processing directory, you're ready to activate your word processing program.

When a work session is concluded and you'd like to work in another program, you must exit the first program (i.e., turn off the TV) and go back to the root (exit the TV room and go back to the entryway). The entryway (root) is the place where you can then access the other doors (directories) leading to the other parts of the house (hard disk). You must travel through the directories to get to your program or data. After all, you can't go walking through the walls of your expensive house!

Describing the route you must follow to get from one directory to another is called a *path*. (A path statement plays an important role in the setup of your system, which we'll discuss on page 186).

You may wonder where all these directories and branches come from. Well, they come from you. You are the architect of your hard disk. You make and delete directories when the need arises.

When to create more directories Your hard disk may start out with two or three directories (e.g. a directory named DOS in which you store your DOS files, and a directory for each software program). But as time goes by, you'll want to create additional directories to accommodate new software, or to reduce overcrowding.

Too many files in one directory can seriously slow down file retrieval and degrade hard disk performance. Exactly what constitutes *too many* files depends on what book or manual you're reading. Some recommend no more than 50 files in a directory, most agree on 100. If you've got more than 200 files in one directory, it's *definitely* time to split things up into separate areas.

On the other hand, it's not wise to go overboard in the other direction and makes lots and lots of directories. Every directory, by virtue of being created, eats up some disk space and takes up some memory.

The simple rule is to make a place for everything and keep everything in its place. You'll save wear and tear not only on your hardware, but on your wetware (a/k/a your brain) as well.

· ·
What is the purpose of directories?

Pop Quiz

For the answer, go to page 288.
· ·

■ *System Prompt*

So far we've discussed DOS (the operating system), drives, and directories.

When you're *not in a program*, the computer displays a *system prompt* on the screen which should tell you two things: the computer is ready for another command (it's prompting, or asking you to do something); and it also shows you which drive and directory you are in (as in the mall map "you are here now").

You get to the system prompt either by turning on your computer, or by exiting a program.

When you first turn on your computer, the prompt will *probably* look something like this:

The reason I say that your prompt will *probably* look like the one above is that the "look" of the system prompt is something that you or your computer dealer (or your best friend who knows about computers) has set up. A fancy system prompt can have the date and time, happy faces, and a lot of other junk. However, most people have the typical "plain" system prompt — which is the one you see above.

The first item in the system prompt above is the name of the current drive (including the infamous colon). After the drive name, the directory you are in is displayed. Basically, a prompt like this tells you that you're on the C drive in the root directory (that's what the backslash means). (The greater-than symbol (>) is the end of the prompt.)

Here's another system prompt:

    C:\WP >

This says you're on the C drive in the WP directory.

    C:\WP\LETTERS >

This tells you you're still on the C drive, but now you're in a *sub*directory called "LETTERS" which is situated underneath the "WP" directory.

The system prompt looks different, depending on where you are.

Note: If your system prompt doesn't change when you go to different directories — if it always looks like this: C> then a simple adjustment to your AUTOEXEC.BAT file is in order. We'll show you how on page 186. Then *your* system prompt will behave as described above!

Pop Quiz

· ·

The system prompt tells you what two things?

For the answer, go to page 288.

· ·

■ *Files*

The computer, the operating system, and the disk, with its structure of directories, all exist to house files. What are files?

Two kinds of files

A file may be a program or it may be data.

A program file is a file that will *do* something. A data file *holds information.* It is something you created while using a program. Your word processor is an example of a program and the documents you create using it are data.

Although there are many different kinds of program and data files, the differences are not worth dwelling on right now (or ever, probably).

The bottom line is that although there are many, many kinds of files with many different purposes, they all have one thing in common: the "pattern" of their names.

Naming a file

All file names must be *at least* one character long, and at most, eight characters. If you want more than eight measly characters in your file name, you have to enter a period (.) in the file name, and then DOS generously allows you up to three more characters. That's it.

Some typical file names:

```
report.doc
c
billing.wk1
recipes
#566.rep
```

A *character,* by the way, can be a letter or a number as well as some (but not all) punctuation. For instance, underlines, hyphens, and pound signs (#) are okay, but question marks (?), asterisks (*), and spaces are forbidden.

If it seems there are a lot of little rules to remember when naming a file, you can take comfort from the fact that the computer will not allow you to save a file with an *invalid* file name. So you can't go wrong. However, understanding this file-naming business is extremely important when it comes to running XTree.

• •

Given: a file name can be up to eight characters long, optionally followed by a period and up to three more letters.

Which of the following file names are *legal,* and which are *invalid*?

1. **mary**
2. **letter#1.doc**
3. **big lake.txt**
4. **bob_let**
5. **a.ov**
6. **jimmy.olsen**

Mid-Point Pop Quiz

Answers: The invalid file names are number three (which contains an illegal space in the name), and number six (which has more than three letters after the period).

The remaining valid file names illustrate acceptable variations in the file-naming rules. Number one illustrates that a file can be shorter than eight letters long. Number two shows the longest file name possible and a legal pound sign and number.

Number four has a legal punctuation mark in it. Number five illustrates a file that has only one character before the period, then only two letters after. (After the period you can have *up to three* characters, but you don't have to use all three characters.)

• •

Each file name must be unique The last rule about file naming is that, like snowflakes, no two can be exactly alike. You can't have two files in the same *directory* with the same name. If you try to do this (either on purpose or accidentally) DOS may, without warning or asking permission, simply delete the oldest of the two files (the oldest, being the one that was there first).

Extensions Another subtlety about a file name is that the part after the period (the last three letters of the file name) is called the *extension*.

The extension works a bit like a person's last name — it can identify to which group it belongs. A look at a file's extension may reveal to the semi-casual observer what type of file it is.

Common extensions For instance, in the above example, the EXE extension tells you that you've got a program file. (Program files can also have a COM extension.) The BAK extension indicates that the next file was an automatically created word processing backup file. The file ending in BAT is a batch file — a kind of little program that you can (and will) write to simplify your chores.

There are lots of extensions in general use, but the most common are EXE, COM, BAK, and BAT. Two other commonly used extensions are DOC, which indicates that the file was created by a word processor, and TXT, which usually means that the file is an ASCII file. (An ASCII file is a file that contains only letters and numbers. If you're wondering what *else* can be in a file other than letters and numbers, wait till you get to the VIEW command in XTree and you'll find out.)

However, unless you're a programmer or something, you can use the last three characters of a file name for whatever you want. Sometimes people put their initials or the date in the last three characters.

Now that you're a file-naming expert, let's pretend you

have a hard disk, with a directory containing your word processing program and four data files. The four data files are:

daffy.doc
data.doc
donald.doc
papa.doc

These four files all have one thing in common. Can you spot it?
Right, they *all* have the same DOC extension!

Wildcards

We can use the fact that these four file names have the same extension to sort them out from other files when a command is issued. If we wanted to copy only these files, for instance, then we could tell DOS, "copy everything that ends in DOC."

Of course, DOS has its own way of phrasing such a statement. DOS uses *wildcards* for this sort of thing. Just like in poker. You have one card (or symbol) that can mean anything.

Unlike poker, however, the DOS wildcard symbol is not a one-eyed jack. In DOS the wildcard is an asterisk (*). When using the wildcard symbol, you still have to follow the rules for file names (up to eight characters long, a period, and up to three more characters). So, using a wildcard to say "anything that ends in DOC" looks like this:

*.doc

Let's try another example.
You might notice that three of our four files begin with the letter "D". We can carve those three files away from the pack by typing: D*.DOC. (The file names all start with "D", but after that first letter, we'll allow anything. After the period we only want files that end with the DOC extension.)
You try one.

What if we wanted to single out the first two files? Do they have anything in common? Sure they do. You could type: **DA*.DOC** since both the first and second files begin with "DA".

Here's the "fine print" on using the wildcard asterisk. It can be used once before the period in the file name and once after the period. Also, while you can use characters *before* you type the asterisk, you cannot type letters *after* the asterisk unless it's after the period.

■ CORRECT WILDCARD USES

chap*.doc	Indicates any file starting with "CHAP" and ending with DOC
t*.*	Indicates any file starting with T no matter what the ending or extension is
.	Indicates every file, regardless of its name

■ INCORRECT WILDCARD USES

d*so.doc	No letters after the asterisk (unless it's after the period)
d*.doc*	There are only three letters allowed in the extension (and the wildcard is considered to be a character). The wildcard would be ignored.

Question mark The question mark (?) can also be used to single out files. As you might expect, it works a bit differently than the asterisk.

The question mark takes the place of one *single* character in a file name. (The asterisk takes the place of any and *all* characters, no matter how many or few.)

Let's see how this works.

To match the pattern ????.doc, a file would have to be *up to four* characters long, a period, and end with DOC. (With *.DOC, you're asking for a file name of any length ending in DOC.)

Back to our four-name list, the second letter in three of the files was the letter "A". To indicate just those three files, ?A*.DOC would do the trick. This says that we don't care what the first letter of the file is — but the second letter must be an "A". The wildcard after the "A" indicates that we'll take anything else after the "A". Finally, the files we want must end in DOC.

By using wildcards like this, it's easy to differentiate a certain set of files from the rest of the files in a directory. Keep this in mind when naming files.

● ●

What do these mean?

```
*.txt
1*.doc
chap?.doc
*.*
```

Pop Quiz

For the answer, go to page 288.

● ●

Just when you think there's nothing more that could possibly be said about a file, we're going to trot out another concept: attribute.   *File attributes*

You may already know that when you save a file, DOS also saves the date and time the file was saved. In addition to this, DOS also secretly maintains additional information on each file. This additional information, which remains hidden to the naked eye unless you've got something like XTree, is known as the file's *attributes.* As you might guess, these attributes have nothing to do with being thrifty, reverent, and clean. These are *computer* attributes. They are "read-only," "archive," "system," and "hidden."

■ READ-ONLY. The first attribute is called "read only." This means you can look at the file (call it up), but you can't change it in *any* way. If you've ever tried to delete a file but it just wouldn't go away, it was probably because the file was "read-only."

■ ARCHIVE BIT. Next is the ever-popular "archive bit." This keeps track of whether the file has been backed up since the last time it was saved. This is used by some of the programs that back up your hard disk.

■ SYSTEM. Third is the "system" attribute. This attribute tells the computer that the file is really important to DOS. You might correctly guess this implies that you should never delete a system file.

■ HIDDEN. The fourth attribute is called "hidden." This attribute can render files invisible to the un-XTree'd eye. Why have an invisible file? Basically because if you don't know a file is there, you're less likely to delete it. Usually only "system" files are "hidden."

Special files   While we're on the subject of system files and hidden files, let's briefly mention the ones you've got on your hard disk. Remember that when the computer is powered up, its first job is to find DOS, which it locates on the hard disk. DOS comes in three files: COMMAND.COM, IBMBIO.COM, and IBMDOS.COM.

■ OPERATING SYSTEM FILES. Of these three files, you have direct access only to COMMAND.COM. Direct access means you have the power to delete it — but *do not delete* COMMAND.COM, ever. No COMMAND.COM, no working computer. Got it?

The other two files (IBMBIO.COM and IBMDOS.COM) are protected as read-only, system, and hidden files. That means you can't delete them, they are part of the system, and that you will not even see them listed when you ask DOS for a list of files (except in XTree).

■ CONFIG.SYS. After DOS finds these three files and the computer starts up, the next job on the computer's agenda is to find a file called CONFIG.SYS. This file tells the computer about how it should handle memory, whether you've got a mouse or other special devices attached, that sort of thing. CONFIG.SYS tells your operating system about *your* personal computer. Though all computers should have a CONFIG.SYS file, the contents of your CONFIG.SYS are unique to your computer.

■ **AUTOEXEC.BAT.** After DOS finishes with CONFIG.SYS, it looks for a file called AUTOEXEC.BAT. This file contains a series of commands which the computer will perform every time your computer is turned on. The contents of the AUTOEXEC.BAT file are unique to your computer. After the computer finishes doing whatever is in your AUTOEXEC.BAT file, you get a system prompt.

∙ ∙

Here are a few more questions about files:

1. If you can't delete a file, what does that tell you about the file's attributes?

2. Is it okay to delete system files?

3. Which one of the attributes would tell you whether you've backed up the file or not?

Pop Quiz

4. Do all computers have the same CONFIG.SYS and AUTOEXEC.BAT files?

For the answers, go to page 289.

∙ ∙

■ Copy

The concept of copying, or duplicating, a file is so straight-forward that you can learn it in two short paragraphs (and without a quiz!).

Unlike copying a videotape, each copy of a file doesn't "lose" anything in the copying. The twentieth copy of a copy is exactly the same as the first. That's why, instead of using terms like "original" and "duplicate," DOS prefers to use terms like "source" (original) and "destination" (duplicate) during the copying process.

You can also copy a file and change its name during the copying process. In addition to copying one or more files, you can also copy a whole disk, or a bunch of files *and* their directories.

■ The End. . . Or Is It?

Well, that's it. Those are the MS-DOS concepts you need to understand to successfully operate XTree. All of these ideas will be used (repeatedly) throughout the "Quick Reference Guide."

However, although that's all the MS-DOS you need to know to run XTree, it's not all the MS-DOS you need to know to run your computer. Some other important DOS commands are covered elsewhere in the book:

FORMAT   Whenever you open a box of floppy disks, they must be *formatted* before you can use them (see page 117).

CHKDSK   Helps keep your disk "fit" (see page 184).

BACKUP   Makes sure you've got a duplicate copy of your hard disk on a set of floppies (see page 191).

BATCH   Automates your system — saves
FILE   keystrokes (see page 55).

VER   This command tells you what version of DOS you own. Who cares? Well, you'll find out why you care in the very next section. For more detail on VER, see page 190.

XTree Basics

2

As you might guess from the section title, we're going to start getting into XTree. In this book, the name "XTree" will continue to be used to indicate all versions of except where noted. This section introduces basic XTree concepts and commands for all XTree products. The specifics of each program are covered in the "Quick Reference Guide" (Part 3) and the "Quick Update Guide" (Part 5).

■ Introducing: The Family XTree

XTree, the original hard disk maintenance program, has been updated a number of times since its original debut in 1985. Naturally, as the scope of the programs grew, so did the system requirements and the price.

System requirements:

	memory	MS-DOS	Retail
XTree	192K	2.0*	$ 39
XTreePro	256K	2.1*	$ 89
XTreePro Gold	256K	3.1*	$129
XTree Easy	256K	3.1*	$ 69
XTreeGold	256K	3.1*	$149
		*or later	

To find out how much memory you have, run CHKDSK (see page 184). It will tell you.

Compare and contrast

Every version of XTree contains the features of the previous version, plus additional ones.

The following is a rough comparison of the differ versions to give you a general idea of how they differ. The "Quick Reference Guide" to XTree, XTreePro and XTreePro Gold (Part 3) and the "Quick Update Guide" to XTreeGold, XTree Easy and XTreeNet (Part 5) afford you *detailed* comparisons of the versions. If you're interested in a particular function, cruise over to one or the other for details.

■ XTREE. Even the simplest version of XTree is a powerful program. It has the ability to visually display your hard disk's directory structure; copy, delete, rename, view, find, and print files; make, delete, and rename directories; change file attributes; see hidden files; run programs and batch files; act as a "DOS shell," and more.

■ XTREEPRO. The major features added in XTreePro were the ability to edit ASCII files, log (count) files faster and over several drives, keep track of more files (up to 16,000, compared with XTree's 2,500 maximum), view word processor files, and more.

■ XTREEPRO GOLD. XTreePro Gold was given *application menu* abilities (you can launch your programs from a menu inside XTreePro Gold); the ability to look at two directories simultaneously; hide, unhide, collapse, prune, and graft directories; associate file extensions with their programs; format disks (in the middle of a backup, even!); make deleted files unretrievable; provide mouse and EGA/VGA support; and a lot more.

■ XTREEGOLD AND XTREE EASY. The life-saving Undelete command was added, along with nifty pull-down menus and a thorough reworking of the application menu. Also the Zip archiving format was added to Gold. If you want to see exactly what is new right now, flip over to the "Quick Update Guide," Part 5, page 205.

■ XTREENET. If you need the help of XTree on your personal hard disk, you *really* need XTree's help to manage the multiple hard drives on a network! Luckily, there's XTreeNet to save the day. See Part 5 for more.

Which one's for you?

As you can see, the original simple program has evolved into an all-in-one comprehensive hard disk management system. XTree has held its position as one of the highest-rated pieces of software in the hard disk management category for good reason.

■ Global XTree Basics

When you first activate XTree, your screen is replaced by a large rectangle, containing several smaller rectangles. XTree starts *reading* (or *logging*) the *current* disk drive (i.e., if you had a system prompt that read: **C:\>**, XTree would log the C drive). As XTree scans the disk, a file count is displayed on the right-hand side of the screen. Once XTree has finished logging the disk, the visual display changes to look something like Screen 2-1.

Although this is the XTree program display, XTreePro and XTreePro Gold have very similar displays (remember, each program builds on the previous one).

The display is composed of several rectangular "windows." Each of these windows provides a special "view" of your hard disk. Underneath the windows is the current command menu.

Windows

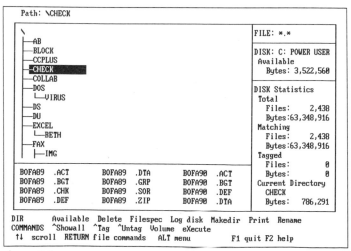

Screen 2-1

■ DISK WINDOW. On the right, the Disk and Disk Statistics windows give current "bottom line" data on your disk — how much space is left on the drive, how many files you've got, that sort of thing.

■ DIRECTORY WINDOW. The biggest window provides a visual representation of your disk's directory structure (ye olde inverted tree hierarchical structure). You can use the up and down arrow keys to travel up and down through the directory structure.

■ SMALL FILE WINDOW. The Small File Window below the Directory Window reveals some (or all) of the files contained in the above directory highlighted by the cursor. As you move up and down through the structure, the sample files in the little window change to reflect the files in the directory highlighted by the cursor up in the directory display window.

■ CURRENT COMMANDS. At the bottom of the display are the current *commands*. Commands are activated by typing the first letter (or the bold-faced letter) of the thing you want to do.

■ THE ^ SYMBOL. In the command area, you may have noticed the mysterious ^ symbol. This symbol is shorthand for "hold down the **<CTRL>** key." (Although this may be semi-obscure knowledge these days, the ^ symbol was used a great deal in the "old days.") If you see a command like **^C** on the screen, you are expected to hold down the **<CTRL>** key while you hit C. The ^ (**<CTRL>**) in front of a letter usually orders XTree to perform the *bigger* version of a command (we'll see that in action momentarily).

■ RETURN. At the bottom of the commands you'll see: "RETURN file commands." "Return" means hit the **<ENTER>** key on your keyboard. (Again, a throwback reference, this time all the way back to the "carriage *return*" key on the typewriter.)

Current directory In Screen 2-1, the cursor is in the Directory Window highlighting a directory named CHECK — the *current* directory. (If you have any doubt about what the current directory is, a glance at the top of the display will show you the *path*.) Any command issued affects the current directory. Hitting **R** (for rename) at this point would allow you to rename the CHECK directory.

On the left side of the commands is the legend "DIR COMMANDS," which reminds you that your cursor is in the Directory Window, and that the displayed commands will have an effect on the current DIRectory.

Also, in the commands at the bottom, are the words: "RETURN file commands." This means that if you want to do something with your files, rather than your directories, you must first hit **<ENTER>**. When you do hit **<ENTER>**, the cursor jumps down to the small window that contains file names.

Current file

Once your cursor is highlighting a file — rather than a directory — all commands will affect the currently high-lighted *file*. So if you hit **R** for Rename this time, you'd be renaming the file you're pointing at (Screen 2-2).

Please note that once your cursor is in the Small File Window, the message at the bottom of the screen changes from "RETURN file commands" to "RETURN expand display."

```
Path: \CHECK

 \                              FILE: *.*
 ├─AB
 ├─BLOCK                        DISK: C: POWER USER
 ├─CCPLUS                        Available
 ├─CHECK        ←                Bytes: 3,522,560
 ├─COLLAB
 ├─DOS                          DIRECTORY Stats
 │  └─VIRUS                     Total
 ├─DS                             Files:          26
 ├─DU                             Bytes:     786,291
 ├─EXCEL                        Matching
 │  └─BETH                        Files:          26
 ├─FAX                            Bytes:     786,291
 │  ├─IMG                       Tagged
                                  Files:           0
 BOFA89  .ACT   BOFA89 .DTA   BOFA90 .ACT  Bytes:           0
 BOFA89  .BGT   BOFA89 .GRP   BOFA90 .BGT  Current File
 BOFA89  .CHK   BOFA89 .SOR   BOFA90 .DEF  BOFA89   ACT
 BOFA89  .DEF   BOFA89 .ZIP   BOFA90 .DTA  Bytes:           1

 FILE      ^Attributes ^Copy ^Delete Filespec Log disk ^Move ^Print
 COMMANDS  ^Rename ^Tag ^Untag View eXecute
 ←↑↓→ scroll  RETURN expand display  ALT menu      F1 quit F2 help F3 cancel
```

Screen 2-2

```
Path: \CHECK

┌─────────────────────────────────────────────────────────┐
│ BOFA89  .ACT     CHECK3  .EXE       FILE: *.*            │
│ BOFA89  .BGT     CHECK4  .EXE                            │
│ BOFA89  .CHK     CHKRTM  .EXE       DISK: C: POWER USER  │
│ BOFA89  .DEF     ORDER   .BAT       Available            │
│ BOFA89  .DTA     PATHTEST.             Bytes: 3,522,560  │
│ BOFA89  .GRP     REMINDER.EXE                            │
│ BOFA89  .SOR     SETUP   .EXE       DIRECTORY Stats      │
│ BOFA89  .ZIP                        Total               │
│ BOFA90  .ACT                          Files:        26  │
│ BOFA90  .BGT                          Bytes:   786,291  │
│ BOFA90  .DEF                        Matching            │
│ BOFA90  .DTA                          Files:        26  │
│ BOFA90  .GRP                          Bytes:   786,291  │
│ BOFA90  .SOR                        Tagged              │
│ CHECK   .EXE                          Files:         0  │
│ CHECK   .PRO                          Bytes:         0  │
│ CHECK1R .ZIP                        Current File        │
│ CHECK2  .EXE                          BOFA89    ACT     │
│ CHECK2R .ZIP                          Bytes:         1  │
│                                                         │
│ FILE      ^Attributes  ^Copy  ^Delete  Filespec  Log disk  ^Move  ^Print │
│ COMMANDS  ^Rename  ^Tag  ^Untag  View  eXecute          │
│ ←↑↓→ scroll  RETURN dir commands    ALT menu       F1 quit F2 help F3 cancel │
└─────────────────────────────────────────────────────────┘
```

Screen 2-3

Expanded file window Hitting **<ENTER>** again at this point would cause the Directory Window to disappear (for the moment) and the file display window to *expand,* enabling you to see approximately five times more files listed! (See Screen 2-3.)

Moving between windows Each time you hit **<ENTER>** the cursor moves one step forward in the Directory Window/Small File Window/Expanded File Window loop.

So if you're in the Directory Window and you hit **<ENTER>** your cursor will end up in the Small File Window. **<ENTER>** again takes you to the Expanded File Window. No matter which window you're in, **<ENTER>** will take you to the next one. And, depending on which window you're in, a different variation of commands are offered at the bottom of the screen.

Hint: Hitting **<ESC>** or **<BACKSPACE>** will always bring you back to the Directory Window.

An example Let's say you want to delete a number of files. First, you move your cursor up or down the directory tree until you arrive at the directory containing the files to be deleted. Hit **<ENTER>** to go into the small file display window. **<ENTER>** again will activate the expanded file display.

One way to delete a file is to point at it with the cursor

```
Path: \CHECK

BOFA89  .ACT♦    CHECK3  .EXE        FILE: *.*
BOFA89  .BGT♦    CHECK4  .EXE
BOFA89  .CHK♦    CHKRTM  .EXE        DISK: C: POWER USER
BOFA89  .DEF♦    ORDER   .BAT        Available
BOFA89  .DTA♦    PATHTEST.           Bytes: 3,522,568
BOFA89  .GRP♦    REMINDER.EXE
BOFA89  .SOR     SETUP   .EXE        DIRECTORY Stats
BOFA89  .ZIP                         Total
BOFA98  .ACT                           Files:         26
BOFA98  .BGT                           Bytes:    786,291
BOFA98  .DEF                         Matching
BOFA98  .DTA                           Files:         26
BOFA98  .GRP                           Bytes:    786,291
BOFA98  .SOR                         Tagged
CHECK   .EXE                           Files:          6
CHECK   .PRO                           Bytes:     99,118
CHECK1R .ZIP                         Current File
CHECK2  .EXE                           BOFA89    GRP
CHECK2R .ZIP                           Bytes:          8

FILE       ^Attributes  ^Copy  ^Delete  Filespec  Log disk  ^Move  ^Print
COMMANDS   ^Rename  ^Tag  ^Untag  View  eXecute
←↑↓→ scroll  RETURN dir commands      ALT menu        F1 quit F2 help F3 cancel
```

Screen 2-4

and then hit **D** for Delete — and follow that procedure for each file to be deleted.

This will become quite tedious, however, when you want to delete a dozen files (or more). The best way to delete a number of files is to indicate to XTree which files to delete and then delete them with one command.

Tagging

In XTree, when you select a file, it's called *tagging*. When you tag a file (accomplished by hitting **T** for Tag while pointing to the file) a diamond appears to the right of the file name indicating its tagged status (Screen 2-4). Once all files to be deleted are tagged, hit **<CTRL>D** to delete them.

Untagging

If you accidently tag a file, hitting **U** will untag it. If you wanted to untag all files, **<CTRL>U** would do the job.

Current window - current commands

While in a *File Window*, commands happen on the file level. **T** will tag the current file and **<CTRL>T** will tag all the files in the current directory.

If you are in the *Directory Window*, however, commands take place on the directory level. So **T** would tag a directory, and **<CTRL>T** tags all the directories.

Filespec One of the most powerful tools in XTree is the *Filespec* command. This is where you get to use all that wildcard stuff we discussed earlier (page 31).

If you want to find all files on your hard disk with a BAK extension, you don't have to manually look through all your files to find them. Just change the search file specification (or "file spec") to ***.BAK**. Then, only those files meeting that criterion (i.e. ends in BAK) will be displayed in the windows. Of course, this also works with *.WK1 files, *.DOC files, or any sort of file name you care to specify.

Any directory that doesn't have any files meeting the current file specs will flash a "No Files!" message. It doesn't mean there are no files at all in that directory. It means there are no files in that directory matching the current file specifications.

■ FILESPEC WINDOW. In the upper right-hand corner of the XTree screen is the File Window. This is where the current file specs are displayed. Usually, unless you've changed it, the file specs are set to ***.*** (which means everything).

Getting help XTree has online help. Anytime you're using the program and need a hint, you're a function key (**F2** in XTree and **F1** in the others) away from a helpful screen and index. If you get in a jam, try it out.

Command shell XTree also has a feature known as a "command shell" or a "DOS Shell." Unlike your other programs, XTree is designed not only to manage your files, but to actually *start* other programs and remain in the background, ready to pop up the moment you're finished working with that other program.

The command to do this is **X** for eXecute.

When you hit **X**, the XTree display disappears. This is *almost* like being at the system prompt. In fact, everything will work as though you are at the system prompt. But the big difference between the system prompt and the command shell is that XTree is still in memory. When finished with the program you're using, you'll automatically end up back in XTree. XTree becomes your *command central.*

This book addresses the needs of the person thinking, "Yeah, I get this stuff so far, but tell me, how do I copy a directory. . . how do I delete all my BAK files, how do I — ?" Answers to these questions are what you'll find in the "Quick Reference Guide" and "Quick Update Guide." If you want to copy something, look under "Copy." You don't need to wade through the CTRL commands to get to **<CTRL>C** (unlike some manuals).

However, those of you who still daydream about lists of Control and Alt commands and function keys will be thrilled to see such a list starting on page 243.

This handbook

"IT'S XTREE PRO GOLD AND QUICKLY VIEWS FILES ON YOUR HARDDISK FOR EASY MAINTENANCE. I CALL IT 'X-PRO-VISION.' THEN AGAIN, I CALL MYSELF 'XTREE-MAN' AND RUN AROUND IN A CAPE AND BLUE TIGHTS."

Quick Reference Guide

3

For many years, XTree, XTreePro and XTreePro Gold lived in peaceful coexistence — each fitting perfectly into its own niche. The "Quick Reference Guide" covers these three programs simultaneously, side by side.

As was inevitable, however, XTree Company decided it was time to re-vamp the XTree line, rather than just keep adding new, enhanced versions in endless ranks. So they stopped making XTree and XTree Pro (though there are still plenty of copies around), gave new features to XTreePro Gold and capped it off by giving it an easier-to-pronounce name: XTreeGold. Finally, a petite version of XTreeGold has been dubbed Xtree Easy.

As with previous XTree products, the new kids on the block build from the previous programs. The "Quick Update Guide" that starts on page 205 covers, side by side, the new features found in XTreeGold and XTree Easy (XTreeNet is covered in Part 6, starting on page 235).

This side-by-side approach means we don't have to repeat the many commands all versions have in common. It also makes it easy to see what various versions offer. And finally, if you upgrade to another version, you don't have to buy another how-to book. (Such a deal!)

How does this side-by-side comparison work?

Next to the text throughout the "Quick Reference Guide" is a heading that looks like this:

XTree PRO GOLD

These instructions are common to all three programs.

These instructions are common to XTreePro and XTreePro Gold only.

These instructions work in XTreePro Gold only.

Find the program you own (this section covers **XTree**, XTree**Pro**, and XTree**Pro Gold**; Part 5 starting on page 205 covers the new XTree **Easy** and XTree**Gold**) and follow the shaded bar down the page, reading the selections appropriate to your software. In some cases, although XTreePro Gold, say, can perform an operation exactly like the original XTree, Gold may also have an improved way to handle that task, which will be explained as you continue reading.

■ Mouse

If you use a mouse, you can use it with XTreePro Gold. For the most part, clicking the mouse button on the command you wish to use will take the place of typing in the command. There are some additional things you can do with a mouse, which are noted as we go along.

■ Where to start

You may either read, browse through, or just look up a particular command in this section. A good place to start, however, is with TAG/UNTAG (page 169) and FILESPEC (page 108), since so many XTree operations are made easier by efficient use of these two features.

APPLICA-TIONS MENU

See COMMAND SHELL and EXECUTE.

If you are unfamiliar with batch files, and XTreePro Gold's special batch file variables, you may want to review the "Batch Files" section on page 55 first.

XTree PRO GOLD

■ XTREEPRO GOLD. If you wanted to, you could get into XTreePro Gold the moment you turn on your computer and *stay* in Gold without ever quitting — and *still* use all your other software.

Gold can escort you around your hard disk and start up your other programs, as well as carry out its own maintenance chores.

The secret is that when you activate your other programs with Gold, and Gold disappears from the screen, it's not *entirely* gone. While you work on your application, a kernel of Gold is, like an attentive servant, waiting silently in the background until called upon. Once you exit your application, Gold senses this, and automatically pops up again, ready to escort you to your next destination.

There are three approaches to having Gold manage your computer life. The first is via the Command Shell, the second is the Execute system, and the third is the Applications Menu.

First of all, "Application" means programs. Software. Stuff like WordPerfect, Lotus 1-2-3, Microsoft Word, Quicken, etc. and etc.

A menu of your applications would be a list of the different programs that you use, as well as routines that you find yourself repeating often. By consolidating all your programs and DOS chores into one menu, you can now carry out your commands with a highlight and an **<ENTER>**. This allows you to free up the brain cells devoted to remembering DOS commands, and use those cells for something more profitable (or fun).

Activate the Applications Menu by hitting **F9** (Screen 3-1).

Although the first time you hit **F9** your menu will be blank, there are four items in the sample menu below. You can have up to thirteen.

To activate an item in the menu, just highlight it and hit **<ENTER>**.

If you want to delete an item, just highlight it and hit **D** for Delete Item.

XTree PRO GOLD

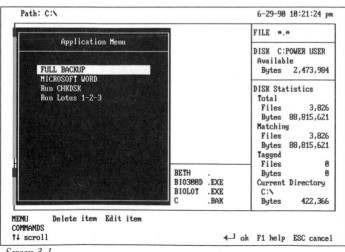

Screen 3-1

XTree PRO GOLD

```
XTreeGOLD (tm) Application Menu                    6-29-90 10:23:16 pm

 Item name: FULL BACKUP

 01>  backup c:\ A:/S
 02>
 03>
 04>
 05>
 06>
 07>
 08>
 09>
 10>
 11>
 12>
 13>
 14>
 15>
 16>
 17>

 EDIT      Copy  Delete  Edit  Insert  Move  edit Name  Undo
 COMMANDS
 ↑↓ scroll                                      F1 help  ESC menu
```

Screen 3-2

If you want to add another item, move the highlight down
to an empty space and hit **E** for Edit Item. At the bottom of
the screen you'll be asked for an Item Name. This is the
name that will appear on the menu. Type in whatever you
want and hit **<ENTER>**.

You have the opportunity to write up to seventeen lines of
instructions. Screen 3-2 shows what you would type if you
wanted to perform a full system backup (via DOS's backup
program).

For now, you can see the cursor is on line 01. If you want
to edit that line, it's a matter of hitting **E** for Edit, then
typing the command you want. When you're finished, hit
<ENTER> (Screen 3-3).

Please note the **%2**. When Gold sees that **%2**, it understands to substitute the letter of the current drive (in this
case "**C**") in place of the **%2** when the command is carried
out. You still need the colon to make the command work.
(See BATCH FILES for all the percent sign parameters.)

The Edit Commands at the bottom of the screen allow
you to copy, delete, edit, insert, and move the line the
cursor is on. (You can even undo a change!)

Once the cursor is on a blank line and you have finished
editing, hitting **<ESC>** will put you back in the
Applications Menu.

```
┌─────────────────────────────────────────────────────────────┐ XTree PRO GOLD
│ XTreeGOLD (tm) Application Menu              8-09-90 12:38:06 pm │
│                                                               │
│ Item name: Run CHKDSK                                         │
│                                                               │
│ 01> CHKDSK %2:                                                │
│ 02>                                                           │
│ 03>                                                           │
│ 04>                                                           │
│ 05>                                                           │
│ 06>                                                           │
│ 07>                                                           │
│ 08>                                                           │
│ 09>                                                           │
│ 10>                                                           │
│ 11>                                                           │
│ 12>                                                           │
│ 13>                                                           │
│ 14>                                                           │
│ 15>                                                           │
│ 16>                                                           │
│ 17>                                                           │
│                                                               │
│ EDIT      Copy Delete Edit Insert Move edit Name Undo         │
│ COMMANDS                                                       │
│ ↑↓ scroll                              F1 help  ESC menu       │
└─────────────────────────────────────────────────────────────┘
```

Screen 3-3

The Applications Menu can play a key role in hard disk management in three situations:

1. You want an ultra-customized system to perform your repetitive tasks.

2. You need to design a system simple enough for computer novices. (If you do set up a system for someone else, consider configuring Gold to prohibit others from changing what you've set up.)

3. Although Open (see EXECUTE) is a great command, the Applications Menu will allow you to do a lot more than just start up a program.

See Part 5 for new XTreeGold and XTree Easy features!

As you may recall from the "MS-DOS Concepts" section, there are four file attributes: Read-only, Archive, System, and Hidden. (If you don't remember what this means, you may want to go back to page 33 and refresh your memory.)

ATTRIBUTES

If you attempt to copy, delete, move, or rename a file that has a "read-only" attribute, XTree will refuse to carry out your command. The only way to force XTree to do what you want in this situation is to turn off the file's read-only attribute.

```
Path: \

ANSI     .RTF   4,403 ....    CONFIG  .OLD     128 ....   FILE: *.*
ANSI     .SCR   2,000 ....    CONFIG  .SYS     256 ....
ASCII    .DOC   3,584 ....    FRECOVER.BAK  78,336 ra..   DISK: C: POWER USER
ASCII    .RTF   4,403 ....    FRECOVER.DAT  78,336 ra..   Available
ASCII    .SCR   2,000 ....    FRECOVER.IDX      29 rash     Bytes: 2,686,976
AUTOEXEC.BAK     512 ....    HIMEM   .SYS  11,304 ....
AUTOEXEC.BAT     512 ....    IBMBIO  .COM  23,591 r.sh   DIRECTORY Stats
AUTOEXEC.DBK     512 ....    IBMBIO  .XUP     201 ....   Total
BETH     .        82 ....    IBMDOS  .COM  30,632 r.sh     Files:        34
BIO300D  .EXE  36,363 ....    IBMDOS  .XUP     255 ....     Bytes:   420,121
BIOLOT   .EXE  48,919 ....    OLDAUTO .BAT     512 ....   Matching
C        .BAK     128 ....    PIX     .BAT      19 ....     Files:        34
C        .BAT     128 ....    VTECH   .CFG       8 ....     Bytes:   420,121
CAP      .BAT      20 ....    VTECH   .EXE  32,174 ....   Tagged
CHECKUP  .LOG  34,733 .a..    WED     .CHK      13 .a..     Files:         0
COMMAND  .COM  25,332 ....                                 Bytes:         0
COMMAND  .XUP     312 ....                                Current File
CONFIG   .BAK     256 ....                                 ANSI     RTF
CONFIG   .DBK     128 ....                                 Bytes:     4,403

FILE        ^Attributes  ^Copy  ^Delete  Filespec  Log disk  ^Move  ^Print
COMMANDS    ^Rename  ^Tag  ^Untag  View  eXecute
←↑↓→ scroll  RETURN dir commands       ALT menu          F1 quit F2 help F3 cancel
```

Screen 3-4

However, read-only files are usually set that way for a reason. Before you turn this attribute off, please be sure it's safe to do so.

XTree PRO GOLD

You may want to change your file display to reveal the attributes, but it's not required (the command is **<ALT>F** — see FILE DISPLAY for more details). For clarity, however, Screen 3-4 shows the Expanded File Window with the file attributes divulged.

```
Path: \

ANSI     .RTF       CONFIG  .OLD         FILE: *.*
ANSI     .SCR       CONFIG  .SYS
ASCII    .DOC       FRECOVER.BAK         DISK: C: POWER USER
ASCII    .RTF       FRECOVER.DAT         Available
ASCII    .SCR       FRECOVER.IDX           Bytes: 2,695,168
AUTOEXEC.BAK        HIMEM   .SYS
AUTOEXEC.BAT        IBMBIO  .COM         DIRECTORY Stats
AUTOEXEC.DBK        IBMBIO  .XUP         Total
BETH     .          IBMDOS  .COM           Files:        34
BIO300D  .EXE       IBMDOS  .XUP           Bytes:   420,121
BIOLOT   .EXE       OLDAUTO .BAT         Matching
C        .BAK       PIX     .BAT           Files:        34
C        .BAT       VTECH   .CFG           Bytes:   420,121
CAP      .BAT       VTECH   .EXE         Tagged
CHECKUP  .LOG       WED     .CHK           Files:         0
COMMAND  .COM                              Bytes:         0
COMMAND  .XUP                            Current File
CONFIG   .BAK                              CHECKUP  LOG
CONFIG   .DBK                              Bytes:    34,733

ATTRIBUTES for file: CHECKUP.LOG   .a..   6-27-90  10:44 am
                   :
enter attribute changes (+/- R A S H)               F1 quit F2 help F3 cancel
```

Screen 3-5

```
 Path: \                                              XTree PRO GOLD
┌──────────────────────────────────────────────────────────────┐
│ ANSI    .RTF    CONFIG  .OLD      FILE: *.*                     │
│ ANSI    .SCR    CONFIG  .SYS                                    │
│ ASCII   .DOC    FRECOVER.BAK      DISK: C: POWER USER           │
│ ASCII   .RTF    FRECOVER.DAT      Available                     │
│ ASCII   .SCR    FRECOVER.IDX        Bytes: 2,695,168            │
│ AUTOEXEC.BAK    HIMEM   .SYS                                    │
│ AUTOEXEC.BAT    IBMBIO  .COM      DIRECTORY Stats               │
│ AUTOEXEC.DBK    IBMBIO  .XUP      Total                         │
│ BETH    .       IBMDOS  .COM        Files:           34         │
│ BIO300D .EXE    IBMDOS  .XUP        Bytes:      420,121         │
│ BIOLOT  .EXE    OLDAUTO .BAT      Matching                      │
│ C       .BAK    PIX     .BAT        Files:           34         │
│ C       .BAT    VTECH   .CFG        Bytes:      420,121         │
│ CAP     .BAT    VTECH   .EXE      Tagged                        │
│ CHECKUP .LOG    WED     .CHK        Files:            0         │
│ COMMAND .COM                        Bytes:            0         │
│ COMMAND .XUP                      Current File                  │
│ CONFIG  .BAK                      CHECKUP  LOG                   │
│ CONFIG  .DBK                        Bytes:       34,733         │
│                                                                │
│ ATTRIBUTES for file: CHECKUP.LOG  .a..   6-27-90  10:44 am      │
│                    : -A                                         │
│ enter attribute changes (+/- R A S H)      F1 quit F2 help F3 cancel │
└──────────────────────────────────────────────────────────────┘
```

Screen 3-6

Next to the file name and size are either four dots, or one or more of the initials "R," "A," "S," or "H" (signifying Read-only, Archive, System, and Hidden, of course).

To change the attributes of a file, highlight the file and hit **A** for attributes (Screen 3-5).

Then enter either minus (−) to turn off an attribute or plus (+) to turn the attribute on and enter the letter of the attribute to be turned off or on. In Screen 3-6, we're going to remove the Archive bit by typing **−A <ENTER>**.

You can also tag a number of files, and then use **<CTRL>A** to change the attributes of all tagged files.

See EXECUTE and APPLICATION MENU.

BATCH FILES

A *batch file* is a file that contains a series of commands — the sort of commands that you normally type at your keyboard at the system prompt. Once the commands are gathered together in one file, merely typing the name of that file will cause the commands to be implemented as though they were typed by you. The idea is that you save time and keystrokes by reducing all your commands down to one file and processing them as a group (or a batch). (If you're familiar with macros, a batch file is like a DOS macro.)

Here's how it works:

Let's say you use WordPerfect and every time you turn on the computer you type:

CD \WP <ENTER>   to get to the directory where your program is stored.

WP <ENTER>   to start WordPerfect.

You could put those two commands into a batch file and name the file W.BAT. Then, when you type **W <ENTER>**, the two commands in the W.BAT file will be executed and you'll find yourself automatically in WordPerfect. Batch files are, in essence, simple programs.

All batch files must have the BAT extension (i.e. W.BAT). You can use XTree and XTreePro to launch batch files. XTreePro Gold also uses batch files in conjunction with the Applications Menu and the Open command to enable you to automate repetitive tasks and to customize your computer system. Beyond the use of "normal" batch files, Gold also uses special batch file parameters. Before we get into the "special batch file parameters" issue, let's start at the beginning. Making a batch file.

Remember, even though Gold has some fancy batch file tricks, you can create and use batch files whether or not you're using Gold or any of the XTree products. Creating and using batch files is part of DOS's domain.

■ Making a batch file

There are dozens of ways to create batch files. One way is via XTreePro or XTreePro Gold's text editor, 1Word. However, we're going to start out by creating a simple batch file without *any* text editor. (See EDIT for details on using 1Word.)

Let's say you must frequently format floppy disks. You decide to reduce the number of keystrokes required to accomplish this task by creating a batch file. Since you're creating a shorthand way to format disks in A, you decide that an easy-to-remember name for this batch file is "FA.BAT" ("Format the disk in A"). Whenever you need to format a floppy disk in the A drive, all you'll have to do is type **FA <ENTER>**.

The first step in creating a batch file is to get to the DOS prompt. (Which you can do by quitting the program you're in, if you're in XTree; just hit **X** to get to the Command Shell.)

Once you see the DOS prompt, type **COPY CON FA.BAT** and hit **<ENTER>**.

This starts the batch file creation process, and names the batch file FA.BAT. When you next create another batch file, substitute *your* batch file name in the place of FA.BAT.

Now it's time to type in the command we want FA.BAT to do for us: type **FORMAT A:** and hit **<ENTER>**.

That's all we need FA.BAT to do. However, if in the future you want to create a more complex batch file, continue typing the necessary commands, hitting **<ENTER>** at the end of each line. **Note:** Using this method, you cannot edit a previous line. If you realize you have made a mistake, you can hit **<CTRL>C** to void out the batch file and start again.

When you are finished typing in the commands, make sure you are on an empty line. Then, to finish the file, hit function key **F6** (which puts a **^Z** on the screen), and hit **<ENTER>**. The computer will then say "1 File(s) copied." Screen 3-7 shows how it looks.

From now on, whenever you type **FA <ENTER>**, you'll see the computer type the **format a:<ENTER>** for you, and DOS will ask you to "Insert new diskette for Drive A and strike ENTER when ready" just as though you had typed **format a:<ENTER>** yourself.

```
C:\XTREE >copy con fa.bat
format a:
^Z
        1 File(s) copied

C:\XTREE >
```

Screen 3-7

XTree PRO GOLD

Batch files can be created to move you around directories, start up programs, and accomplish anything else you can do from a DOS prompt.

You can even do some tricky things that *can't* be done from a DOS prompt.

For instance, most word processing programs allow you to specify the name of the file you want to edit when you launch the program. Typing **wp daffy.doc <ENTER>**, for instance, would start WordPerfect and automatically retrieve the DAFFY.DOC file for you.

Even though you're working on DAFFY.DOC today, *tomorrow* you might want WHATSUP.DOC. Making a batch file whose sole purpose is to call up DAFFY.DOC (unless you work on DAFFY.DOC exclusively) would have a very limited application.

In DOS, there's a way to make a batch file that says, in effect, start WordPerfect and get a file to be named later. The "file to be named later" is called a *variable* — because the name of the file will vary. Naturally, there's an arcane symbol that signifies a variable, the percent sign (%).

A batch file that goes to the LETTERS subdirectory (under WordPerfect's WP directory), starts WordPerfect, and retrieves a "file to be named later" would look like this:

```
cd \wp\letters
wp %1
```

Once this batch file is executed, the file to be named later will be placed in the %1 spot.

The way that you specify the file to be named later is by typing its name after the batch file name.

In this case, assuming our batch file is still named W.BAT, we'd type **w daffy.doc <ENTER>** and DOS would stick DAFFY.DOC in the %1 spot and the computer would act as though the batch file had actually read:

```
cd \wp\letters
wp daffy.doc
```

Or, if we typed **w bills.doc <ENTER>** it would place BILLS.DOC in the %1 spot.

By the way, if you don't have a preference about which file you want to work on, you can still type plain old **w** **<ENTER>** and WordPerfect will kick into action, ignoring the %1.

You can have more than one % (variable) in a file. The next one would be %2, the next after that %3, and so forth. You can actually have *lots* of variables and labels, If-Then and Goto statements, and — well, let's just say there are *books* the size of Yuletide logs that cover the programming of batch files. Obviously, therefore, there's a lot more to say about batch files than what you'll find here. This is just a bare-bones course in batch files to get you by. (For more, check out the books recommended in "Where To Go From Here" in Appendix C.)

■ XTREEPRO GOLD. XTreePro Gold took DOS's variables and extended the concept for use in Gold. They decided (rightfully) that it would be great to be able to highlight a file in Gold and be able to use it as a variable in a batch file.

Gold, of course, came up with their own version of what a variable means. (XTreePro Gold's special variables work *only* in Gold. Don't try these in DOS. In DOS, use the definition of a variable as described previously.)

Gold's batch command variables are used exclusively by the Applications Menu and the Open command. After you've learned about Gold's variables below, go to the APPLICATIONS MENU or EXECUTE sections to see how batch files get put to work.

In Gold, the variables are:

variable	action	example
%1	the file's path & name	**C:\WP\LETTERS\DAFFY.DOC**
%2	the file's drive ID	**C**
%3	the file's path	**\WP\LETTERS**
%4	the file's name	**DAFFY**
%5	the file's extension	**DOC**

XTree PRO GOLD

Let's start with a simple example.

```
C:\WP\WP.EXE %1
```

Imagine you've highlighted a file called REPORT.DOC and have invoked the above batch file. The batch file starts WordPerfect (because the batch file specifies where WordPerfect is and the name of the program) and the current file and its full path name would also be used. (You don't have to do the "CD" command because the full path of the file is handed down with the %1 variable.)

Another example:

```
chkdsk %2:
```

This batch file will run CHKDSK on the current drive. Again, to put this to practical use, see the EXECUTE and APPLICATIONS MENU sections.

CANCEL

Ooops! You've changed your mind and don't want to carry out a particular command after all. To countermand any command, just hit the *cancel* command which appears in the lower right-hand corner of your XTree screen whenever you initiate any action that might need to be canceled. You can cancel a command at any time.

```
Path: \CHECK

 BOFA89   .ACT     CHECK3  .EXE          FILE: *.*
 BOFA89   .BGT     CHECK4  .EXE
 BOFA89   .CHK     CHKRTM  .EXE          DISK: C: POWER USER
 BOFA89   .DEF     ORDER   .BAT          Available
 BOFA89   .DTA     PATHTEST.               Bytes: 3,276,800
 BOFA89   .GRP     REMINDER.EXE
 BOFA89   .SOR     SETUP   .EXE          DIRECTORY Stats
 BOFA89   .ZIP                           Total
 BOFA90   .ACT                             Files:        26
 BOFA90   .BGT                             Bytes:   786,291
 BOFA90   .DEF                           Matching
 BOFA90   .DTA                             Files:        26
 BOFA90   .GRP                             Bytes:   786,291
 BOFA90   .SOR                           Tagged
 CHECK    .EXE                             Files:         0
 CHECK    .PRO                             Bytes:         0
 CHECK1R  .ZIP                           Current File
 CHECK2   .EXE                             BOFA89    ACT
 CHECK2R  .ZIP                             Bytes:         1

DELETE file: BOFA89.ACT

delete this file (Y/N) ?                  F1 quit F2 help F3 cancel
```

Screen 3-8

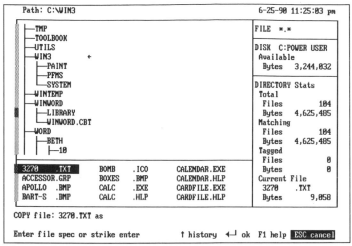

```
 Path: C:\WIN3                              6-25-90 11:25:03 pm

  ├─TMP                               FILE *.*
  ├─TOOLBOOK
  ├─UTILS                            DISK  C:POWER USER
  ├─WIN3        ←                    Available
  │  ├─PAINT                          Bytes   3,244,032
  │  ├─PFMS
  │  └─SYSTEM                        DIRECTORY Stats
  ├─WINTEMP                           Total
  ├─WINWORD                            Files         104
  │  ├─LIBRARY                         Bytes   4,625,485
  │  └─WINWORD.CBT                    Matching
  ├─WORD                               Files         104
  │  ├─BETH                            Bytes   4,625,485
  │  │  ├─10                          Tagged
  │                                    Files           0
  3270     .TXT    BOMB    .ICO    CALENDAR.EXE   Bytes           0
  ACCESSOR.GRP    BOXES   .BMP    CALENDAR.HLP   Current File
  APOLLO   .BMP    CALC    .EXE    CARDFILE.EXE   3270     .TXT
  BART-S   .BMP    CALC    .HLP    CARDFILE.HLP   Bytes       9,058

 COPY file: 3270.TXT as

 Enter file spec or strike enter      ↑ history  ←┘ ok  F1 help  ESC cancel
```

Screen 3-9

Note: Quit is not the same as cancel. Quit is used to exit the XTree program itself.

XTree PRO GOLD

■ *F3*

In Screen 3-8, you are about to delete a file. Hitting **F3** cancels this activity. (Also, in this case, you could have also responded **"N"** to the prompt, "delete this file?", instead of hitting **F3** to cancel. Both options would have the same effect.)

■ *<ESC>*

In Screen 3-9, we are about to copy a file. **<ESC>** will cancel this command.

Even after the files start "copying," **<ESC>** can stop the command from being carried out any further.

Alternatively, if you have a mouse, you can click on the "ESC cancel" command at the bottom of the screen.

See EXECUTE and APPLICATIONS MENU.

COMMAND SHELL

The purpose of a "command shell" is to let you work with DOS directly, without actually quitting XTree.

When you enter the DOS Shell, it look as if XTree has disappeared. Actually, it's waiting in background memory until you're finished with your commands.

To activate the DOS Shell, merely press **X** for eXecute. Depending on where your cursor is when you hit **X** one of two things will happen.

If you're pointing at a program's name when you hit **X**, that program's name will be typed for you at XTree's system prompt. (More about this in EXECUTE.) Once a program's name appears at XTree's prompt, hitting **<ENTER>** will activate that program. If you want to do something else, however, just backspace over the program's name and type in any command you have in mind.

If you hit **X** while in the Directory Window, you'll find yourself at XTree's system prompt where you can carry out any DOS command or start any program.

XTree PRO GOLD

■ XTREE. Hitting **X** at the Directory Window will put you in the command shell (Screen 3-10).

When it says "Enter a DOS command," it doesn't mean you can only perform DOS commands per se (like FORMAT or DIR). It means you can enter in *any* command you might normally type at a system prompt (like starting Microsoft Word, or Lotus 1-2-3).

■ Exit the Command Shell

When you want to return to XTree, hit **<ENTER>** without a command. You'll be back in XTree.

```
Current Path: C:\DOS
Enter a DOS command, or press RETURN on an empty line to return to XTREE.
>
```

Screen 3-10

■ XTREEPRO. Hitting **x** at the Directory Window will
put you in Pro's Command Shell — which is a bit more
informative (Screen 3-11).
   At this point, you may enter any command you might
normally enter at your system prompt.

■ *History*

Pro will remember the last fifteen command shell
commands you used. By hitting the up or down arrow key,
you'll see all the previously executed commands (See Screen
3-12).
   Use the up and down arrow keys to highlight a command.
As the cursor travels up and down the command history,
the commands are automatically placed at the prompt
where you can either edit them and hit **<ENTER>** or just hit
<ENTER>.

■ *Exit the Command Shell*

When you're finished with your chores, hitting ESC will
return you to Pro.

■ *Re-Logging*

In Pro and Gold when you create or delete a file while in
the command shell, you must re-log your drive (hit **L** for
log) before the changes will appear in the files window.

```
┌────────────────────────────────────────────────────────────┐
│ Thu Aug  9, 1990 │ 1:57:17 pm │ 222,400 Free Memory │ 2,318,336 Disk Space │
│ C:\XTPRO>                                                    │
│                            ── Press ESC to return to XTreePro ─┘
```

Screen 3-11

XTree PRO GOLD

```
┌─────────────────────────────────────────────────────────────┐
│  Thu Aug  9, 1990  │ 1:55:07 pm │ 222,400 Free Memory │ XTreePro  Disk Space │
│  C:\XTPRO>dir \dos\*.txt                                      │
│                            ─── Press ESC to return to XTreePro ─┘
│
│
│    dir b:
│    dir /w
│    cd \lotus
│    cd\xtpro
│    dir \dos\*.tx
│
└─────────────────────────────────────────────────────────────┘
```

Screen 3-12

■ Memory

If, when you try to carry out a command from the DOS shell, you get an "insufficient memory" error message, try hitting **<ALT>X** instead of just **X**. This makes Pro reduce itself to the smallest size.

■ XTREEPRO GOLD. Naturally, Gold puts its own twist on things.

■ History

Hitting **X** at the Directory Window will put you in Gold's system prompt and you may enter any command that you normally enter at a system prompt.

Gold's history command is a significant step up the evolutionary ladder from Pro's history command.

First of all, Gold has a "History Prompt" at the bottom of its screen to remind you to use it. Most importantly, however, Gold remembers the last thirteen commands even if they were issued several days ago. If you hit the up or down arrow key, the "command history" window pops up (Screen 3-13).

If you want to perform one of the commands you previously used, just highlight that command and hit **<ENTER>**. At this point you may either correct or edit the command.

XTree PRO GOLD

```
┌──────────────────────────────────────────────────────────────┐
│ Thu Aug  9, 1998 │ 12:44:88 pm │ 177,768 Free Memory │ 2,363,392 Disk Space │
├──────────────────────────────────────────────────────────────┤
│ C:\XTPRO>                                                       │
├──────────────────────────────────────────────────────────────┤
│                                                                │
│                                                                │
│      XTG_CFG                                                   │
│      dir                                                       │
│      dir\u                                                     │
│      cd\                                                       │
│      cd word                                                   │
│      cd\check                                                  │
│      CHECK                                                     │
│      ▓XTG▓                                                     │
│                                                                │
│                          ↑ history  ↵ ok  ESC cancel          │
│                                                                │
└──────────────────────────────────────────────────────────────┘
```

Screen 3-13

Then hit **<ENTER>** again to execute the command.

Another use for the command history is to edit a typo. If you get "bad command or file name" after entering a command, hit the up arrow for your history, and highlight the "bad" command and hit **<ENTER>**. This will put the "bad" command in Gold's system prompt. Then, correct your command and, when ready, hit **<ENTER>** to execute it. This way you don't have to type the whole thing over again.

■ Mouse

Another way to eXecute a file is to double-click the file name with the left mouse button. It starts the program right up without a pause.

■ Memory

If you get an "insufficient memory" error message when you try to execute a program, try hitting **<ALT>X** instead of **X**. This makes Gold reduce itself to the smallest size.

CONFIGURA-TION

"Configuration" refers to the way things are set up. XTree, like most software programs, can be altered to behave in a certain fashion to accommodate your desires. You may think of this as "personalization," rather than "configuration." This is probably also an aspect of XTree that you'll want to explore *after* you've been using the program for a little while and have an idea about how things can suit you better.

Each of the three programs has items that can be changed. For instance, if you have a color monitor and you don't like how XTree looks, you can change the colors to something more pleasing.

The three configuration programs are pretty straightforward. You'll learn how to start them up, and an example of what it's like when you get in there.

You can activate the configuration programs from inside all versions of XTree. The only disadvantage of doing it this way, however, is that the changes you make to the configuration won't take effect until you exit the program and start again.

XTree PRO GOLD

■ XTREE. There are two aspects of XTree that can be altered with the configuration program. One is to change the kind of computer and monitor you have, and the second is to change the colors.

To make an adjustment, go to the directory where XTree is stored, highlight **XTREEINS.EXE** and hit **X**, then **<ENTER>** to execute (start) the program (Screen 3-14). (If you want to do this from DOS, go to the directory where XTree is stored and type **xtreeins <ENTER>**.)

If you choose A or B, you'll be shown another screen with an explanation of what to do. If you make a mistake, you can always go back to the way it was by *not saving your changes* when given the opportunity to do so. Then, start again.

■ XTREEPRO. There are quite a few things that can be changed about XTreePro, and the best thing to do is go take a peek at all of your options.

Go to the directory where XTree is stored, highlight **XTPROCFG.EXE** and hit **X**, then **<ENTER>** to execute

```
                XTREE (tm) Installation Program V2.0

     A - Install XTREE according to your computer and monitor type
     B - Change the display attributes or colors used by XTREE
     C - Exit this install program


 Enter Option ( A,B,C ):
```

Screen 3-14

(start) the program. (If you want to do this from DOS, go
to the directory where XTreePro is stored and type
xtprocfg <ENTER>.)

You'll see a main menu (Screen 3-15), from which you can
modify XTreePro configuration items, Display color
selection, Restore default configuration (translation: put
things back the way they were), Save configuration and exit,
or Quit without saving changes.

```
                  XTreePro Configuration Items

 XTreePro Path                          C:\XTPRO
 File/Directory Limit                   18,000
 Disk Logging Method                    QUICK
 Display Type                           RGB/MONOCHROME
 Display is "flicker free"              YES
 Audible Error Indicator                ON
 Directory Display Highlight Bar        SCROLLING
 Keep Filespec                          NO
 File Display Format                    THREE COLUMNS
 Filename Separator                     " "
 Small File Window Access               SELECTABLE
 System and Hidden File Access          YES
 Sort Criteria                          NAME
 Sort Order                             ASCENDING
 Printer Redirection                    PRINTER
 Print Form Length                      55

 Return to Main Menu

   Set the maximum number of files and directories to hold in memory.

 ←↑↓→ Select Item    ENTER Change Item
```

Screen 3-15

XTree PRO GOLD

You can always quit without saving your changes if you feel you have made some less-than-elegant choices.

Most of the main menu choices are self-explanatory. We're going to look at Modifying Configuration Items. Highlight that choice and press **<ENTER>**.

As you move the highlight up and down the list, the box at the bottom of the screen will inform you about the currently highlighted item. If you want to change an item, highlight it and hit **<ENTER>**. At this point you may be prompted to fill in a blank with your new preference, or the item will toggle to a new choice automatically.

Here are two examples of how this works.

If you aren't wild about the way Pro sorts files, you could highlight "Sort Order," hit **<ENTER>**, and the ASCENDING would change into DESCENDING. Another **<ENTER>** and it's back to ASCENDING. Those are the only two acceptable responses and hitting **<ENTER>** toggles you back and forth between them.

Let's say, we want to change the File/Directory Limit. (Pro assumes you'll be counting the maximum number of files. If you don't have that many, you can reduce the amount of memory Pro uses by reducing the "limit." More about this in the MEMORY section.) Anyway, you highlight "File Directory Limit" and hit **<ENTER>**. Then you'll be prompted to type in a new limit and hit **<ENTER>**.

Once you have finished exploring the configuration items, highlight "Return To Main Menu" at the bottom of the screen and hit **<ENTER>**. At this point you may either save your modifications, or you may exit without saving them. Highlight your choice and hit **<ENTER>**.

(Remember, if you started the configuration program from the command shell, the changes won't take effect until after you quit and re-enter Pro.)

XTree PRO GOLD

■ XTREEPRO GOLD. There is a virtual cornucopia of options available via Gold's configuration program. (If you're a control freak, you'll love this!)

To start the configuration program, the easiest thing to do is to hit **<ALT>F10**. However, if you wish to activate it through DOS, go to the directory where XTreePro Gold is stored and type **xtg_cfg <ENTER>**.

You'll get a main menu from which you can Modify configuration items, Display color selection, Read permanent settings from disk (put things back the way you had them), Restore factory default settings (put things back the way they were when you got the program out of the box), Save configuration and quit, and Quit configuration program.

If you select the first item (Modify Configuration Items), you'll be able to page through four screens of configuration items (see Screen 3-16 for one) by highlighting the words New Page and hitting **<ENTER>**. (Highlighting and hitting **<ENTER>** on Main Menu, will take you back to the beginning.)

While you are viewing the configuration items, you can move the highlight up and down the list while the box at the bottom of the screen tells you about the currently highlighted item. Once an item is highlighted, hitting **<ENTER>** will either change the current choice to another choice, or you'll be prompted to fill in a blank.

An example of some of the items you can change:

Item six, "Initial directory," allows you to select between the root or the current directory as your initial directory. What that means is that when you invoke Gold, depending on how you set "initial directory," your cursor will be highlighting either the root directory or whatever directory you

```
┌─────────────────────────────────────────────────────────────────────┐
│ XTreePro Gold - Configuration Items                      Page 4       │
│                                                                       │
│ Miscellaneous                                                         │
│    1 Program path:                              C:\X                   │
│    2 Editor program:                            C:\WORD\WORD.EXE       │
│    3 Disk logging method                        QUICK                 │
│    4 Audible error indicator                    ON                    │
│    5 Archive file attribute on copied files     COPIED                │
│    6 Initial directory                          CURRENT DOS           │
│    7 Directory window highlight bar             SCROLLING             │
│    8 Mouse scroll bar display                   SCROLL BAR            │
│    9 Skip Edit command prompt                   YES                   │
│    A Skip Quit command prompt                   YES                   │
│    B Show actual path for Substituted drives    YES                   │
│    C Pause after application program execution  NO                    │
│    D Date format                                MM-DD-YY              │
│    E Time format                                1:00:00 pm            │
│    F Numeric format                             1,234,567             │
│ Main menu                                                             │
│                                                                       │
│ Enter the full path and file name of your preferred text editor program.│
│                                                                       │
│ ↑↓ Select item    ENTER Change item         ESC Return to main menu   │
└─────────────────────────────────────────────────────────────────────┘
```

Screen 3-16

XTree PRO GOLD

happened to be in ("current directory") when you started Gold.

Item A, "Skip Quit command," turns off that "Quit XTreePro Gold and return to DOS?" invective. Also, if you don't like to be beeped at, turn off item four, "Audible error indicator."

■ EGA/VGA

An item of special interest to EGA and VGA owners is on page 1. If you want to see more files and more of your directory tree at one time, you can set the screen to 43 lines (EGA) or 51 lines (VGA). (Note, however, using this extended display may cause some systems to slow down.)

(You don't have to be in the configuration section to *temporarily* change the display for the duration of the session. Gold will allow you to toggle between normal and extended display with **<ALT>F9**.)

Let your fingers do the walking through the configuration pages. You may find something that will make life a little easier (or, at least, more attractive).

COPY

Copy allows you to duplicate something, resulting in two of the original item.

Sometimes, however, what you *really* want to do is move something to a new location — so you end up with one copy in a new place. For that type of action, see the MOVE command. Please note, however, that you cannot "move" something to another *disk* (you have to use Copy for that). You can only move something to another directory.

The one important rule for copying is that you can't have two files with the same name in the same place. If you want to have two versions of the same file in the same place, one of them has to have a name change.

Having said all that — let's jump into the wacky world of the Copy command.

XTree PRO GOLD

■ Copy a file to another drive (including a floppy drive)

To copy a file, highlight the file and hit **C** for Copy. A screen appears, at the bottom of which is a question: XTree

XTree PRO GOLD

wants to know what to copy the file "as" (Screen 3-17). Basically, this question (which you'll see every time you want to copy something) means "do you want to rename the file when you copy it?" If you don't want to change the name, hit **<ENTER>** and the file name will remain the same. (If you do want to give the copy a new name, type it in. You need to do this if you want to keep different versions of the same file.)

Once that is settled, the next question is "*where* do you want to put the copy?" In this case, let's copy it to the floppy disk (Screen 3-18).

After we type in **A:** and hit **<ENTER>** the file will be copied to the A drive.

Now, let's say there's already another file there with the same name. If a file with the same name already exists on A, you'll be asked if you want to replace it.

■ XTREE. XTree handles the question by simply asking you if you want to replace the file, as in Screen 3-19.

■ XTREEPRO and GOLD. Pro and Gold also ask if you wish to replace the file, but they show you the stats on the two files for comparison of date, time, size, and attributes (Screen 3-20). Most likely, the newer or bigger file will be

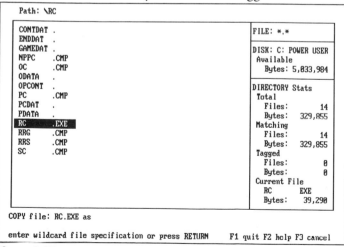

```
 Path: \RC

 CONTDAT .                              FILE: *.*
 EMDDAT  .
 GAMEDAT .                              DISK: C: POWER USER
 NPPC    .CMP                           Available
 OC      .CMP                             Bytes: 5,833,984
 ODATA   .
 OPCONT  .                              DIRECTORY Stats
 PC      .CMP                           Total
 PCDAT   .                                Files:         14
 PDATA   .                                Bytes:    329,855
 RC      .EXE                           Matching
 RRG     .CMP                             Files:         14
 RRS     .CMP                             Bytes:    329,855
 SC      .CMP                           Tagged
                                          Files:          0
                                          Bytes:          0
                                        Current File
                                          RC      EXE
                                          Bytes:     39,290

 COPY file: RC.EXE as

 enter wildcard file specification or press RETURN    F1 quit F2 help F3 cancel
```

Screen 3-17

XTree PRO GOLD

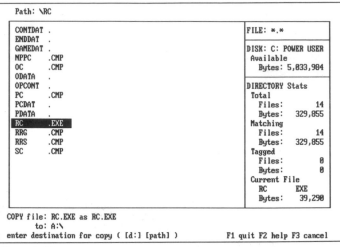

Screen 3-18

the one you want to keep, although not always.
In any case, hitting **Y** will continue the copying process and hitting **N** will stop it.

■ Copy a file to another directory

The process of copying a file to another directory is virtually identical to copying a file to a floppy. The only difference is the destination.

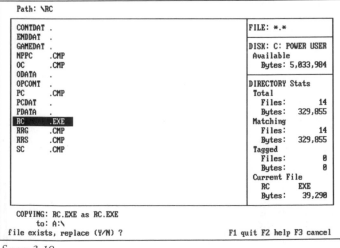

Screen 3-19

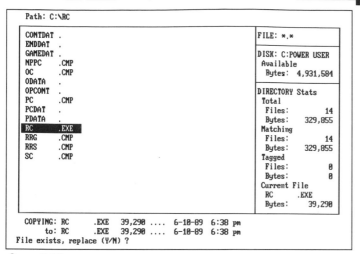

Screen 3-20

Start out by highlighting the file to be copied. Press **C** for Copy.

Press **<ENTER>** to keep the same file name.

The last step is to enter a destination.

■ XTREE. At this point, you can type in the destination *path* (Screen 3-21). In this case, we've decided to send it to the \DOS\VIRUS directory. It's a good idea, in XTree, to

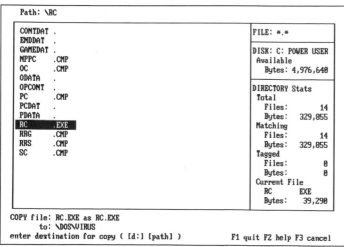

Screen 3-21

XTree PRO GOLD

know where you want to send your file *before* you start the copy command. Once you've typed in your destination, hit **<ENTER>**, and the file will be copied.

■ XTREEPRO and GOLD. XTreePro and XTreePro Gold make it easier for you by adding the **F2** Select Path option (at the bottom of the screen). This is a très handy item. After you've highlighted the file to be copied, hit **C** for Copy, hit **<ENTER>** to let the copy keep the same file name, and you are ready to specify where the file is going to (Screen 3-22).

Hit **F2** and the "Destination Window" pops up over what you're doing (Screen 3-23). Now you can highlight your directory destination.

You can also log onto another disk drive and travel its tree as well. When you finally select your destination, hit **<ENTER>** and the file will be copied.

■ XTREEPRO GOLD. In Gold you can also use the History command (Screen 3-24).

After you've highlighted the file to be copied, hit **C** for Copy, and then **<ENTER>** to let the copy keep the same file name. Now you're ready to specify where the file is going to.

You can now also hit the up (or down) arrow key to reveal

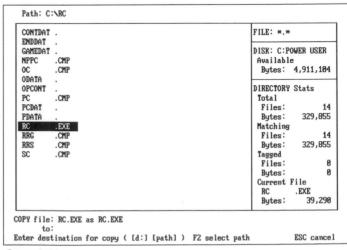

```
Path: C:\RC

CONTDAT  .                              FILE: *.*
ENDDAT   .
GAMEDAT  .                              DISK: C:POWER USER
MPPC     .CMP                           Available
OC       .CMP                           Bytes:  4,911,104
ODATA    .
OPCONT   .                              DIRECTORY Stats
PC       .CMP                           Total
PCDAT    .                                Files:          14
PDATA    .                                Bytes:     329,855
RC       .EXE                           Matching
RRG      .CMP                             Files:          14
RRS      .CMP                             Bytes:     329,855
SC       .CMP                           Tagged
                                          Files:           0
                                          Bytes:           0
                                        Current File
                                          RC       .EXE
                                          Bytes:      39,290

COPY file: RC.EXE as RC.EXE
       to:
Enter destination for copy ( [d:] [path] )  F2 select path        ESC cancel
```

Screen 3-22

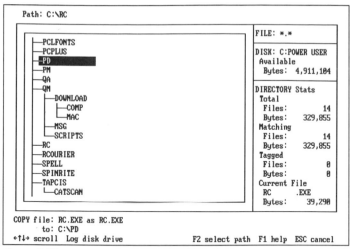

Screen 3-23

the last thirteen destinations (or names) you've used. Then you can conveniently highlight one of your previous destinations, hit **<ENTER>** to put the destination in the command line, then **<ENTER>** to start copying.

■ Copy more than one file

To copy more than one file, it's a matter of tagging the files to be copied, press **<CTRL>C** to copy all tagged files, and

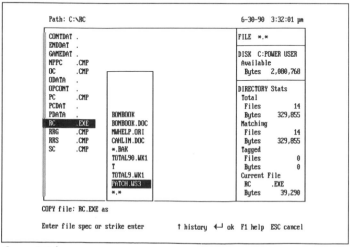

Screen 3-24

following the procedures outlined above.

Note: If you still haven't looked at TAG/UNTAG and FILESPEC yet, now's a good time. It's easy to tag a whole disk, directory, or portions of a directory, etc. for copying (or deleting, or whatever). It's all spelled out in these two sections.

However, we can still get a little taste for how tagging and Filespec work right now. Let's say we want to copy all the files that end in DOC to a floppy disk.

The best way to start this procedure would be to go to an Expanded File Display of the directory containing the files to be copied. (Translation: highlight the directory you want to copy from and then hit **<ENTER>** twice.)

Next, hit **F** for Filespec (Screen 3-25).

Filespec lets you exercise what you learned about wildcards to single out particular files. (If you don't remember learning this, slide on over to the "MS-DOS Concepts" section and read up on wildcards on page 31.)

Anyway, once you hit **F**, you must type a file specification. In this case we want all files that end in DOC, so we type ***.DOC <ENTER>**.

Now the File Window displays only those files with the DOC extension (Screen 3-26). The upper right-hand corner of the screen reminds you of the current file specifications.

```
Path: \KEYS

2KEYS    .DTX    DIALPNT .DTX    SKLASJET.DTX    FILE: *.*
89       .DTX    DOSEDIT .COM    SKSETUP .COM
ASCII    .DTX    DOSEDIT .DOC    SKWINDOW.EXE    DISK: C: POWER USER
BARMENU .DTX     DVORAK  .DOC    SMARTKEY.EXE     Available
CLICK    .COM    DVORAK17.COM    STUFF   .DTX      Bytes: 4,919,296
COMMANDS.DTX     DVORAK20.COM    SUNBOW  .DTX
COMMCMD1.DTX     LOTUS   .DTX    TEST    .DTX    DIRECTORY Stats
COMMCMD2.DTX     MENU    .DTX    TREK    .DTX     Total
COMMDEFN.DTX     MENUDEMO.DTX    TUNE    .DTX      Files:          49
COMMFILE.DTX     PCKEY17 .COM    WORDPERF.DTX      Bytes:     330,365
COMMMODI.DTX     PCKEY20 .COM    WORDSTAR.DTX     Matching
COMMOPT .DTX     README  .1ST                      Files:          49
COMMSYS .DTX     README  .COM                      Bytes:     330,365
CRYPTOR .COM     SAMPLE  .DTX                     Tagged
D        .COM    SKBATCH .COM                      Files:           0
DATASCRN.DTX     SKBLANK .COM                      Bytes:           0
DBASE    .DTX    SKBLANK .DOC                     Current File
DIALER   .DTX    SKEPSON .DTX                      2KEYS    DTX
DIALPAUS.DTX     SKIBMPRO.DTX                      Bytes:       1,152

FILE specification:

enter a file spec or press RETURN for *.*        F1 quit F2 help F3 cancel
```

Screen 3-25

XTree PRO GOLD

```
Path: \KEYS

┌────────────────────────────┬──────────────────────────┐
│ DOSEDIT .DOC               │ FILE: *.DOC              │
│ DVORAK  .DOC               │                          │
│ SKBLANK .DOC               │ DISK: C: POWER USER      │
│                            │ Available                │
│                            │ Bytes: 4,919,296         │
│                            │                          │
│                            │ DIRECTORY Stats          │
│                            │ Total                    │
│                            │   Files:        49       │
│                            │   Bytes:   330,365       │
│                            │ Matching                 │
│                            │   Files:         3       │
│                            │   Bytes:    14,464       │
│                            │ Tagged                   │
│                            │   Files:         0       │
│                            │   Bytes:         0       │
│                            │ Current File             │
│                            │ DOSEDIT  DOC             │
│                            │   Bytes:     5,760       │
├────────────────────────────┴──────────────────────────┤
│ FILE      ^Attributes ^Copy ^Delete  Filespec  Log disk  ^Move  ^Print │
│ COMMANDS  ^Rename  ^Tag  ^Untag  View  eXecute         │
│ ←↑↓→ scroll  RETURN dir commands    ALT menu       F1 quit F2 help F3 cancel │
└────────────────────────────────────────────────────────┘
```

Screen 3-26

Now that we've narrowed down the files to those ending in DOC, **<CTRL>T** will tag them. Next, **<CTRL>C** will Copy all of the tagged files. An **<ENTER>** is next as shown in Screen 3-27 (so the files can keep their original names).

All that's left is to supply an exotic destination for the DOC files. For this example, let's send them to the A drive by hitting **A: <ENTER>**. You'll be asked about automatically replacing files with the same name. A **Y** reply will send the files on their way!

```
Path: \KEYS

┌────────────────────────────┬──────────────────────────┐
│ DOSEDIT .DOC♦              │ FILE: *.DOC              │
│ DVORAK  .DOC♦              │                          │
│ SKBLANK .DOC♦              │ DISK: C: POWER USER      │
│                            │ Available                │
│                            │ Bytes: 4,919,296         │
│                            │                          │
│                            │ DIRECTORY Stats          │
│                            │ Total                    │
│                            │   Files:        49       │
│                            │   Bytes:   330,365       │
│                            │ Matching                 │
│                            │   Files:         3       │
│                            │   Bytes:    14,464       │
│                            │ Tagged                   │
│                            │   Files:         3       │
│                            │   Bytes:    14,464       │
│                            │ Current File             │
│                            │ DOSEDIT  DOC             │
│                            │   Bytes:     5,760       │
├────────────────────────────┴──────────────────────────┤
│ COPY ALL TAGGED FILES as *.*                           │
│        to: A:\                                          │
│ enter destination for copy ( [d:] [path] )    F1 quit F2 help F3 cancel │
└────────────────────────────────────────────────────────┘
```

Screen 3-27

XTree PRO GOLD

(By the way, if you don't want to "automatically replace existing files" with the same name, a **N** response will prompt XTree to ask you, a file at a time, every time it locates a file with the same name as the one being copied. This way, you can make a case-by-case decision.)

Note: Whenever you finish an operation like this, be sure to put the filespec back to ***.*** or you'll freak yourself out later on when it seems as though some of your files are missing.

■ Copy files and directory structure

To copy not only the files, but the directory structure information as well, first tag all the files in all the directories you want to copy. (See TAG/UNTAG if you don't know how to tag.)

Then, while in a File Window, hit **<ALT>C** for Copy.

At the bottom of the screen you'll be given the opportunity to rename your files as you copy them — just hit **<ENTER>** to decline that option.

Then, you'll have to decide on a destination drive (Screen 3-28). In this case, let's say the A drive is your destination. Type **A**, and the colon and backslash will be put in for you. Then you can hit **<ENTER>**.

Finally, you'll be asked if you want to "replace existing files." In other words: If there are already files on the floppy

```
Path: C:\WORD\BETH\SCRIPTS

┌──────────────────────┐        ┌────────────────────────────┐
│ HORTNOTE.DOC♦         │        │ FILE: *.*                  │
│ HORTON  .DOC♦         │        │                            │
│ LIVEAC  .STY♦         │        │ DISK: C:POWER USER         │
│ LIVEOUT .STY♦         │        │ Available                  │
│ LIVOUTSS.STY♦         │        │   Bytes:  4,497,408        │
│ MENQUIZ .DOC♦         │        │                            │
│ OUTDFT  .STY♦         │        │ DIRECTORY Stats            │
│ SCRIPTOR.STY♦         │        │ Total                      │
│ SMOU    .DOC♦         │        │   Files:          10       │
│ SMOUBEAT.DOC♦         │        │   Bytes:      31,232       │
│                       │        │ Matching                   │
│                       │        │   Files:          10       │
│                       │        │   Bytes:      31,232       │
│                       │        │ Tagged                     │
│                       │        │   Files:          10       │
│                       │        │   Bytes:      31,232       │
│                       │        │ Current File               │
│                       │        │   HORTNOTE.DOC             │
│                       │        │   Bytes:       1,920       │
└──────────────────────┘        └────────────────────────────┘

DUPLICATE PATHS ON ANOTHER DISK AND COPY ALL TAGGED FILES as *.*
     to: A:\
Enter destination disk for alt copy                    ESC cancel
```

Screen 3-28

XTree PRO GOLD

disk with the same name, do you *really* want to replace them with the files you are copying now? Generally, you do. So, you hit **Y <ENTER>**. At this point the copying commences and the files *and their directories* are put on the floppy drive.

■ Copy a directory to another directory (Graft)

XTreePro Gold allows you to *Graft* a directory. This means you can take a directory (and its contents) and attach it to another directory. This is not, actually, copying a directory. It is, in fact, *moving* a directory. Once a directory has been grafted, it no longer exists in its original location.

However, since you're here — here's how to do it.

To graft a directory, just highlight the directory to be moved and type **<ALT>G** for Graft.

You'll then get a screen like that in Screen 3-29.

At the bottom of the screen you're asked *where* you want to move your directory to, and you're given the Destination Window so you can highlight the directory you want to move to.

In this case, we're moving the directory CHECK90 so that it will appear under the directory CHKBOOK. When you're ready, hit **<ENTER>**.

As a precaution, you'll be asked one more time if you're sure you want to do this. Just hit **Y** if you are, and Gold will carry out the command.

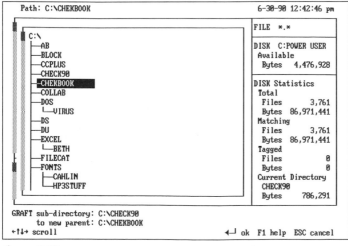

Screen 3-29

XTree PRO GOLD

After you graft a directory, hit **L** to re-log the drive so the grafted directory will appear in order on the tree. (And see Part 5 for an added feature in XTreeGold and XTree Easy.)

Note: If you receive a "Can't Update Parent Directory" error message, you have an older version of Gold that doesn't get along with your version of DOS. An upgrade is available to fix this. (See page 285.)

DATE & TIME STAMP

When you save a file, DOS records the date and time the file was saved. Assuming you've got a clock inside your computer, and it works, the date and time will be accurate. If you don't have a clock, DOS will assign *some* date and *some* time to the file when it's saved. (That's why you may find that you have some files dated *before* personal computers were invented.) Anyway, this is called the "date and time stamp."

If your computer doesn't have a clock, you can still get your computer to keep time for you, *as long as the computer remains turned on.* To do this, type **date <ENTER>** at the system prompt and type the correct date and press **<ENTER>**. Now type **time <ENTER>** and type the correct time and press **<ENTER>**. (Remember, most computers are on a 24-hour clock. One o'clock is 13:00 to the computer.)

If you wish to alter the DOS-assigned date and time info, however, you can do so with Gold's Newdate command. One use for this feature would be for correcting the date and time on files transferred from another computer. Or, since XTree will display files sorted by Date and Time, this could allow you another way of grouping files together for some sort of action.

XTree PRO GOLD

To change the date and time stamp on a file, just highlight the file (or tag a group of files) then type **N**.

At the bottom of the screen you'll see the highlighted file name, its attributes, and the current date and time stamp.

You'll be asked to enter the new date and time (Screen 3-30). Gold will suggest using *the current* date and time.

If the current date and time is what you want, just hit **<ENTER>**. If you want to use another date and time, you can change the date and time offered.

Backspacing erases the current date and time. The arrow keys allow you to move *over* the time and date without

```
Path: C:\CHECK                              6-27-90 11:54:48 am

 BOFA89  .ACT      CHECK3  .EXE      FILE  *.*
 BOFA89  .BGT      CHECK4  .EXE
 BOFA89  .CHK      CHKRTM  .EXE      DISK  C:POWER USER
 BOFA89  .DEF      ORDER   .BAT      Available
 BOFA89  .DTA      PATHTEST.          Bytes    2,437,120
 BOFA89  .GRP      REMINDER.EXE
 BOFA89  .SOR      SETUP   .EXE      DIRECTORY Stats
 BOFA89  .ZIP                        Total
 BOFA90  .ACT                         Files              26
 BOFA90  .BGT                         Bytes         786,291
 BOFA90  .DEF                        Matching
 BOFA90  .DTA                         Files              26
 BOFA90  .GRP                         Bytes         786,291
 BOFA90  .SOR                        Tagged
 CHECK   .EXE                         Files               0
 CHECK   .PRO                         Bytes               0
 CHECK1R .ZIP                        Current File
 CHECK2  .EXE                        BOFA89  .ACT
 CHECK2R .ZIP                         Bytes               1

STAMP file: BOFA89  .ACT      1 ....  4-19-90  3:40:20 pm
          to: 6-27-90 11:54:30 am
Enter date and time                 ↑ history  ↵ ok  F1 help  ESC cancel
```

Screen 3-30

deleting anything so you may make discrete changes.

If you want to see a file's date and time *before* you hit **N** to change it, hit **<ALT>F <ALT>F** to change the file display. If you want to sort the display by date and time, it's **<ALT>S <ALT>D** (see Screen 3-31). (See FILE DISPLAY, and SORT CRITERIA.)

Gold also displays the current date and time in the upper right-hand corner of the screen at all times.

```
Path: C:\CHECK                              8-09-90 12:49:35 pm

 BOFA89  .CHK        52 .... 10-04-89  8:24:08 am   FILE  *.*
 BOFA89  .BGT     2,162 .... 12-31-89 12:53:54 pm
 BOFA89  .SOR     1,334 .... 12-31-89  1:37:18 pm   DISK  C:POWER USER
 BOFA89  .ZIP    18,206 .... 12-31-89  2:59:34 pm   Available
 ORDER   .BAT       514 ....  1-08-90  4:00:42 am    Bytes    2,363,392
 BOFA90  .DEF        43 ....  1-09-90  8:26:42 am
 PATHTEST.            1 ....  1-09-90  8:49:38 am   DIRECTORY Stats
 BOFA90  .GRP       506 ....  1-09-90  8:50:02 am   Total
 CHECK   .PRO     1,216 ....  1-09-90  8:56:00 am    Files              26
 BOFA89  .DEF        43 ....  1-14-90 12:16:46 pm    Bytes         813,291
 BOFA89  .GRP         0 ....  1-14-90 12:16:48 pm   Matching
 CHECK   .EXE    21,313 ....  4-02-90  4:03:00 am    Files              26
 CHECK2  .EXE   129,953 ....  4-02-90  4:03:00 am    Bytes         813,291
 CHECK3  .EXE    10,769 ....  4-02-90  4:03:00 am   Tagged
 CHECK4  .EXE    48,721 ....  4-02-90  4:03:00 am    Files               0
 CHKRTM  .EXE    70,680 ....  4-02-90  4:03:00 am    Bytes               0
 REMINDER.EXE     6,001 ....  4-02-90  4:03:00 am   Current File
 SETUP   .EXE    31,057 ....  4-02-90  4:03:00 am   BOFA89  .CHK
 CHECK2R .ZIP    78,334 ....  4-10-90  5:06:04 pm    Bytes              52

FILE        Attributes  Copy  Delete  Edit  Filespec  Invert  Log disk  Move
COMMANDS    New date  Open  Print  Rename  Tag  Untag  View  eXecute  Quit
◀ | tree   F7 autoview  F8 split    F9 menu  F10 commands    F1 help  ESC cancel
```

Screen 3-31

DELETE

Deleting obsolete files from your hard disk is essential to maintaining a healthy drive. Extra files slow down performance, shorten hard disk life, and makes it more difficult for you to find what you're looking for. The trick is to make hard disk housekeeping a part of your normal routine.

XTree PRO GOLD

▪ Delete a file

Simply go to a File Window and highlight the file you want to delete and type **D** for delete. XTree will confirm that you didn't hit **D** by mistake by asking if you really want to delete the file (Screen 3-32).

When XTree receives your **Y** acknowledgment, the file will be deleted (or **N** will cancel the process).

▪ Delete a file from a floppy drive

First, log on to the floppy drive (hit **L** for Log, then **A** **<ENTER>** for the A drive).

Next, find and highlight the file to be deleted and hit **D** for delete. Of course you'll be asked to confirm your decision to delete and when you do, the file will be deleted. (You can then log back onto the hard disk.)

▪ Delete more than one file

First, tag the files to be deleted (if you're not sure how to do that, see FILESPEC and TAG/UNTAG). Once the files to

```
Path: \QM\DOWNLOAD

 251-WARN.DOC      F10      .ARC    MW5ART  .ZIP    FILE: *.*
 387     .ZIP      FFM10    .ZIP    NAMER   .ZIP
 ADD-MACH.ZIP      FM       .EXE    NEWDOS  .ZIP    DISK: C: POWER USER
 ALTZ    .ZIP      FONTS    .ZIP    NOJTY   .ZIP    Available
 ART-XMAS.ZIP      GRAB51   .ZIP    NOPMBU  .TXT      Bytes: 4,837,376
 CHEDRR  .ZIP      GRIDMAKR.ZIP     NOTOLLS .ZIP
 CHEKKERS.ZIP      HISCORES.        NPAD    .ZIP    DIRECTORY Stats
 CHKUP   .EXE      HP3-MS   .ZIP    OCR-A   .ZIP    Total
 DBOOT1  .ZIP      L3HPGL   .ZIP    PILOT90 .ZIP      Files:        77
 DE10    .ZIP      LHC15    .EXE    PKZ110  .EXE      Bytes: 2,972,016
 DESKDLL .EXE      LJTODJ   .ZIP    POST61  .ARC    Matching
 DIALOGUE.GLY      LZESHL   .ZIP    POSTBINS.ZIP      Files:        77
 DISKBUFF.ZIP      MAKEBA   .ZIP    PRN2FILE.ZIP      Bytes: 2,972,016
 DLR     .EXE      MOREMAC  .ZIP    PSDR32  .ARC    Tagged
 DMVTEST .ZIP      MOUSE624.ZIP     PUMA100 .ZIP      Files:         0
 DT      .EXE      MOVIE1   .EXE    QUICTY  .ARC      Bytes:         0
 E-ICON  .ARC      MSAPP21  .ZIP    README  .DOC    Current File
 EDIAL12 .ZIP      MSMOUSE7.ZIP     RECONFIG.ZIP      251-WARN DOC
 ENVMACRO.ZIP      MSWITCH  .ZIP    RECYCL  .HP       Bytes:    21,571


 DELETE file: 251-WARN.DOC

 delete this file (Y/N) ?                      F1 quit F2 help F3 cancel
```

Screen 3-32

be deleted are tagged, **<CTRL>D** will delete all *tagged* files.   XTree PRO GOLD
In this example (Screen 3-33), we're about to delete all the
files in the directory.

When deleting more than one file, XTree asks if you want
to confirm the deletion of each file separately. You have two
options: 1) Press **N** to give XTree permission to delete all
the files, or 2) Press **Y** to have XTree stop at each file and
ask for confirmation.

■ Delete a directory

(Although you can follow this procedure to delete a
directory using XTreePro Gold, Gold's got an easier way to
do it — see Prune.)

First of all, you cannot delete a directory in either XTree or
XTreePro if there are any files in it or subdirectories
attached to it. Therefore, if you want to delete a directory,
your first task is to make sure that directory contains no
files or subdirectories.

To delete all the files in a directory, enter a File Window
and type **<CTRL>T** to tag all files. Then **<CTRL>D** will
delete all tagged files.

Once that's accomplished, go back to the Directory
Window, put your cursor on the directory to be deleted,
and hit **D** to delete it (Screen 3-34).

```
Path: C:\RC

┌──────────────────┐      ┌──────────────────────────┐
│ CONTDAT .   ♦    │      │ FILE: *.*                │
│ ENDDAT  .   ♦    │      │                          │
│ GAMEDAT .   ♦    │      │ DISK: C:POWER USER       │
│ MPPC    .CMP♦    │      │ Available                │
│ OC      .CMP♦    │      │ Bytes:   4,763,648       │
│ ODATA   .   ♦    │      │                          │
│ OPCONT  .   ♦    │      │ DIRECTORY Stats          │
│ PC      .CMP♦    │      │ Total                    │
│ PCDAT   .   ♦    │      │   Files:          14     │
│ PDATA   .   ♦    │      │   Bytes:     329,855     │
│ RC      .EXE♦    │      │ Matching                 │
│ RRG     .CMP♦    │      │   Files:          14     │
│ RRS     .CMP♦    │      │   Bytes:     329,855     │
│ SC      .CMP♦    │      │ Tagged                   │
│                  │      │   Files:          14     │
│                  │      │   Bytes:     329,855     │
│                  │      │ Current File             │
│                  │      │ CONTDAT .                │
│                  │      │   Bytes:      38,097     │

DELETE all tagged files

Confirm delete for each file (Y/N) ?
```

Screen 3-33

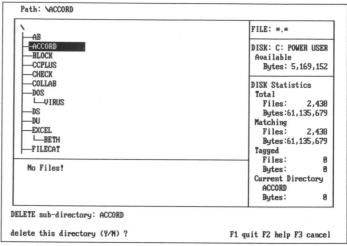

```
 Path: \ACCORD

  \                                    FILE: *.*
   ─AB
   ─ACCORD                              DISK: C: POWER USER
   ─BLOCK                               Available
   ─CCPLUS                               Bytes: 5,169,152
   ─CHECK
   ─COLLAB                              DISK Statistics
   ─DOS                                 Total
     └─VIRUS                             Files:      2,438
   ─DS                                   Bytes:61,135,679
   ─DU                                  Matching
   ─EXCEL                                Files:      2,438
     └─BETH                              Bytes:61,135,679
   ─FILECAT                             Tagged
                                         Files:         0
      No Files!                          Bytes:         0
                                        Current Directory
                                         ACCORD
                                         Bytes:         0

   DELETE sub-directory: ACCORD

   delete this directory (Y/N) ?              F1 quit F2 help F3 cancel
```

Screen 3-34

Finally, of course, you are asked if you really want to delete this directory. Enter either a **Y** for yes (or **N** for no if you've changed your mind) to wind up the operation.

■ Prune a directory

Gold allows you to delete a directory, any subdirectories underneath, and any files in those directories or subdirectories with one powerful command: Prune.

To do this, simply highlight the directory to be pruned and hit **<ALT>P** for Prune (Screen 3-35).

Since a misplaced Prune command could have dire consequences, you are asked to verify your command by typing the word **prune** and pressing **<ENTER>**.

■ Wash the hard disk

There are special programs on the market that can "unerase" deleted files and directories. The fact that deleted material can be retrieved is great news if you've accidently deleted something, and terrible news if you thought deleting a file *guaranteed* that no one would ever see it (just ask Ollie North).

If you've got confidential material on your drive that you *really* want to delete, Gold, can make all deleted files unrecoverable via the Wash Disk command.

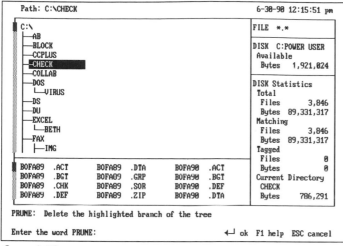

Screen 3-35

To wash your disk, go to the Directory Window, and type
<ALT>W for wash (Screen 3-36).

In the lower left-hand corner you can see Gold telling you
it's going to wash drive C. You need to confirm with an
<ENTER>. Then, while you have a cup of coffee (decaf, of
course), all deleted files and directories on the hard disk will
be rendered truly deleted.

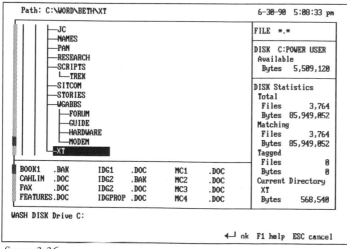

Screen 3-36

DIRECTORY

The following commands have to do with managing your directories. (See page 24 in the "MS-DOS Concepts" section for more details about directory strategies.)

XTree PRO GOLD

■ Make a directory

While in the Directory Window, position your cursor on the directory *above* where you want your new directory to be, and type **M** to Make a directory. (Put your cursor on the root (\) if you want to make a directory under the root. Or put your cursor on WP, for example, if you want to make a subdirectory under WP.)

In Screen 3-37, we're going to make a directory *below* the CHECK directory. At the bottom of the screen XTree is asking what we want to call the new directory.

If we want to call it 1990, just type in **1990** and press **<ENTER>**. And voila! (See Screen 3-38.)

There's a new directory under CHECK called 1990. That's all there is to it.

■ Rename a directory

Let's say you just realized that you needed a directory called 1991, not 1990. Highlight the 1990 directory and hit **R** to Rename. As you might expect, you are prompted at the bottom of the screen (Screen 3-39) to come up with a new

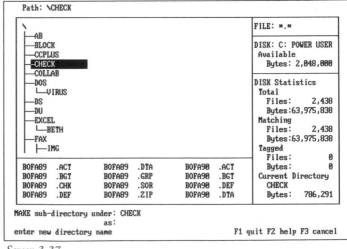

Screen 3-37

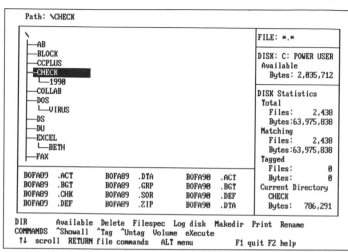

Screen 3-38

directory name — which, in this case, is **1991**.

Once you hit **<ENTER>**, you'll see that the 1990 directory has been renamed 1991 (Screen 3-40).

■ Delete a directory

(Although you can follow this procedure to delete a directory using XTreePro Gold, Gold's got an easier way to do it — see Prune.)

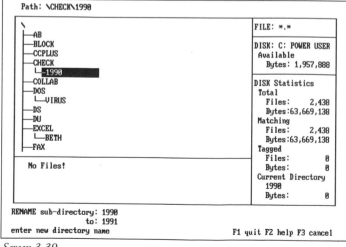

Screen 3-39

XTree PRO GOLD

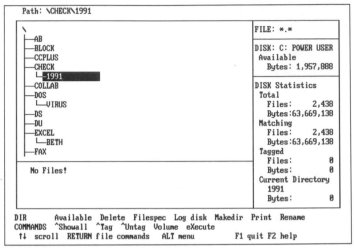

Screen 3-40

First of all, you cannot delete a directory in either XTree or XTreePro if there are any files in it or subdirectories attached to it. Therefore, if you want to delete a directory, your first task is to make sure that directory contains no files or subdirectories.

To delete all the files in a directory, enter a File Window and type **<CTRL>T** to tag all files. Then **<CTRL>D** will delete all tagged files.

Once that's accomplished, go back to the Directory Window, put your cursor on the directory to be deleted, and hit **D** to delete it. Of course, you are asked if you really want to delete this directory (Screen 3-41).

Enter either a **Y** for yes (or **N** for no if you've changed your mind) to wind up the operation.

■ Copy directory (and files) to a floppy

To copy the directory structure information along with files, first tag all the files in all the directories you want to copy. (See the TAG/UNTAG entry near the end of this chapter if you don't know how to tag.)

Then, while in a File Window, hit **<ALT>C** for Copy. (Screen 3-42).

At the bottom of the screen you'll be given the opportunity to rename your files as you copy them — just hit **<ENTER>** to decline that option.

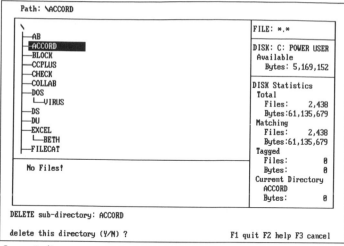

```
Path: \ACCORD                                            XTree PRO GOLD

\
 ├─AB                              │FILE: *.*
 ├─ACCORD                         │DISK: C: POWER USER
 ├─BLOCK                          │Available
 ├─CCPLUS                         │  Bytes: 5,169,152
 ├─CHECK
 ├─COLLAB                         │DISK Statistics
 ├─DOS                            │Total
 │  └─VIRUS                       │  Files:      2,438
 ├─DS                             │  Bytes:61,135,679
 ├─DU                             │Matching
 ├─EXCEL                          │  Files:      2,438
 │  └─BETH                        │  Bytes:61,135,679
 ├─FILECAT                        │Tagged
                                  │  Files:          0
 No Files!                        │  Bytes:          0
                                  │Current Directory
                                  │  ACCORD
                                  │  Bytes:          0

 DELETE sub-directory: ACCORD

 delete this directory (Y/N) ?              F1 quit F2 help F3 cancel
```

Screen 3-41

Now decide on a destination drive. In this case, let's say you want to copy to the A drive. Type **A,** and the colon and backslash will be put in for you. Then hit **<ENTER>**.

Finally, you'll be asked if you want to "replace existing files." In other words: If there are already files on the floppy disk with the same name, do you really want to replace them with the files you are copying now? Generally, you do. So, you hit **Y <ENTER>**. At this point the copying commences and the files *and their directories* are put on the floppy drive.

```
Path: C:\WORD\BETH\SCRIPTS

 HORTNOTE.DOC♦
 HORTON  .DOC♦                    │FILE: *.*
 LIVEAC  .STY♦
 LIVEOUT .STY♦                    │DISK: C:POWER USER
 LIVOUTSS.STY♦                    │Available
 MENQUIZ .DOC♦                    │  Bytes:  4,497,408
 OUTDFT  .STY♦
 SCRIPTOR.STY♦                    │DIRECTORY Stats
 SMOU    .DOC♦                    │Total
 SMOUBEAT.DOC♦                    │  Files:         10
                                  │  Bytes:     31,232
                                  │Matching
                                  │  Files:         10
                                  │  Bytes:     31,232
                                  │Tagged
                                  │  Files:         10
                                  │  Bytes:     31,232
                                  │Current File
                                  │  HORTNOTE.DOC
                                  │  Bytes:      1,920

 DUPLICATE PATHS ON ANOTHER DISK AND COPY ALL TAGGED FILES as *.*
    to: A:\
 Enter destination disk for alt copy                    ESC cancel
```

Screen 3-42

(By the way, if you don't want to "automatically replace existing files," a **N** response will prompt XTree to ask you, a file at a time, every time it locates a file with the same name as the one being copied. This way, you can make a case-by-case decision.)

■ Prune a directory

Gold allows you to delete a directory, any sub-directories underneath, *and* any files in those directories or subdirectories with one powerful command: Prune.

To do this, simply highlight the directory to be pruned and hit **<ALT>P** for Prune.

Since a misplaced Prune command could have dire consequences, you are asked to verify your command by typing the word **prune** and pressing **<ENTER>** (Screen 3-43).

■ Move a directory (Graft)

Ever want to pick up a directory (files and all) and attach it to another directory? That's what Graft is for.

To graft a directory, just highlight the directory to be moved and type **<ALT>G** for Graft (Screen 3-44).

At the bottom of the screen you're asked *where* you want to move your directory to and you're given the Destination Window so you can highlight the directory you want to move to.

In this case, we're moving the directory CHECK90 so that it will appear under the directory CHEKBOOK. When you're ready, hit **<ENTER>**.

As a precaution, you'll be asked one more time if you're sure you want to do this. Just hit **Y** if you are and Gold will carry out the command.

After you graft a directory, you will have to re-log the drive (hit **L** for log) for the grafted directory to appear in alphabetical order on the tree.

Note: If you receive a "Can't Update Parent Directory" error message, you have an older version of Gold that doesn't get along with your version of DOS. An upgrade is available to fix this see page 285.

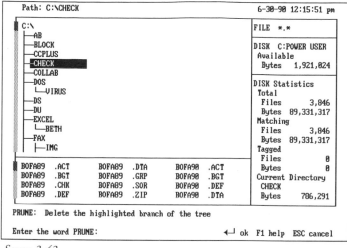

Screen 3-43

Collapse the directory display

If you have a big hard disk with a long and involved directory tree, you may find yourself wishing for a less complete view of your directory structure.

By collapsing the directory, we can select portions of the structure to disappear from view until you either quit the program or restore the view to normal. (If you're familiar with outline programs, then you've got an idea of how it works.)

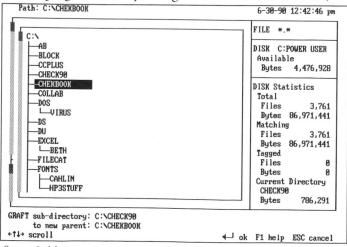

Screen 3-44

XTree PRO GOLD

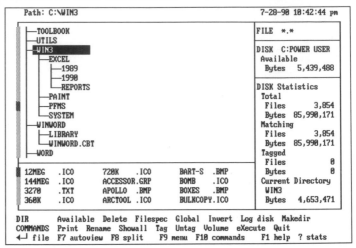

```
Path: C:\WIN3                                    7-28-90 10:42:44 pm

 ┌─TOOLBOOK                              FILE *.*
 ├─UTILS
 ├─WIN3                                  DISK  C:POWER USER
 │  ├─EXCEL                              Available
 │  │  ├─1989                             Bytes    5,439,488
 │  │  ├─1990
 │  │  └─REPORTS                         DISK Statistics
 │  ├─PAINT                              Total
 │  ├─PFMS                                Files          3,854
 │  └─SYSTEM                              Bytes     85,990,171
 ├─WINWORD                              Matching
 │  ├─LIBRARY                             Files          3,854
 │  └─WINWORD.CBT                         Bytes     85,990,171
 └─WORD                                 Tagged
                                         Files              0
 12MEG    .ICO    720K     .ICO   BART-S  .BMP   Bytes              0
 144MEG   .ICO    ACCESSOR .GRP   BOMB    .ICO  Current Directory
 3270     .TXT    APOLLO   .BMP   BOXES   .BMP   WIN3
 360K     .ICO    ARCTOOL  .ICO   BULKCOPY.ICO   Bytes      4,653,471

DIR       Available  Delete  Filespec  Global  Invert  Log disk  Makedir
COMMANDS  Print  Rename  Showall  Tag  Untag  Volume  eXecute  Quit
 ↵ file  F7 autoview  F8 split   F9 menu  F10 commands   F1 help  ? stats
```

Screen 3-45

The benefit of collapsing a directory is that when you travel up and down your directory tree, you don't have to travel through a bunch of directories you're not planning to work with anyway.

Collapsing a directory makes no changes to your hard disk. We're just talking about collapsing your *view* of the hard disk. There are two directory-collapsing commands, **F5** and **F6**.

Let's start with the following example: Screen 3-45 shows a directory called WIN3, with seven subdirectories.

■ Using F5

With your cursor on WIN3, pressing **F5** will collapse directories two levels (and below) the cursor.

In Screen 3-46, 1989, 1990, and REPORTS have disappeared from view. (Note the little plus (+) sign next to the EXCEL directory — telling you that there's more under EXCEL.)

If you put your cursor in the root directory and press **F5**, all the second level directories on the whole hard disk will be displayed (Screen 3-47).

Pressing **F5** toggles the view back to normal.

■ Using F6

With your cursor on WIN3, pressing **F6** will collapse *everything* under the WIN3 subdirectory (Screen 3-48).

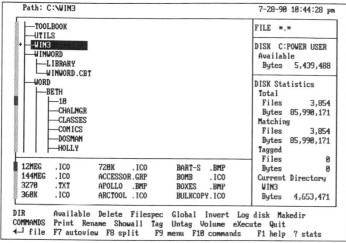

Screen 3-46

Now WIN3 is the only directory we can see. A + sign appears next to the WIN3 directory. Pressing **F6** again will return the view back to normal.

■ Hide/Unhide a directory

Gold allows you to "hide" a directory (and its files) from view.

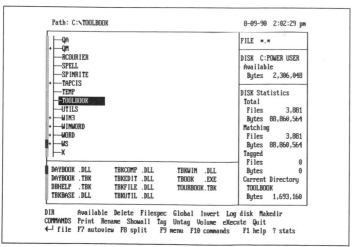

Screen 3-47

XTree PRO GOLD

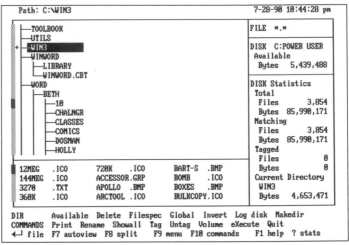

Screen 3-48

Hidden directories remain hidden *not only* while you are using Gold, but even after you've quit Gold and are using *other* programs. Even DOS's DIR command won't give away a directory's hiding place.

Why hide a directory? Is this someone's idea of a sick joke? Maybe. However, hiding a directory is one way to provide a measure of control over who accesses that directory.

If someone knows the hidden directory's name, they can still go there and use its programs. Hiding a directory does not prevent unauthorized access. It just limits access to those who know the correct directory name(s).

Let's say you've put your personal checkbook on your office computer. (Naturally you're spending time on your personal checkbook only during your lunch hour or after work.) However, you don't want the Big Boss (or even your secretary) to have access to your personal finances. So you decide to hide the directory.

The first step is to highlight the directory to be hidden, then hit **<ALT>H**. You'll be presented with something like Screen 3-49.

At the bottom of the screen you are asked to confirm this action with a **Y**, cancel with **N**. Naturally, we'll enter a **Y**.

At this point the directory name will still be visible onscreen, though in lowercase (like hidden files).

```
 Path: C:\CHECK                          7-12-90  3:53:36 pm      XTree PRO GOLD

 C:\                                    FILE *.*
 ├─AB
 ├─ACCORD                               DISK  C:POWER USER
 ├─BLOCK                                Available
 ├─CCPLUS                                 Bytes   3,940,352
 ├─CHECK
 ├─COLLAB                               DISK Statistics
 ├─DOS                                  Total
 │ └─VIRUS                                Files       3,874
 ├─DS                                     Bytes  87,284,771
 ├─DU                                   Matching
 ├─EXCEL                                  Files       3,874
 │ └─BETH                                 Bytes  87,284,771
 ├─FILECAT                              Tagged
                                          Files           0
 BOFA89 .ACT   BOFA89 .DTA   BOFA90 .ACT  Bytes          0
 BOFA89 .BGT   BOFA89 .GRP   BOFA90 .BGT  Current Directory
 BOFA89 .CHK   BOFA89 .SOR   BOFA90 .DEF  CHECK
 BOFA89 .DEF   BOFA89 .ZIP   BOFA90 .DTA  Bytes     796,851


 HIDE/UNHIDE sub-directory: CHECK

 Hide this directory?               Yes  No  F1 help  ESC cancel
```

Screen 3-49

If you want the hidden directory to disappear even from Gold's Directory Window, you'll have to go into Gold's configuration program and change "System/Hidden file and directory access" to NO. You'll find this feature on Page 3 of the configuration program.

Hint: For details on using Gold's configuration program, see CONFIGURATION. One important note, however, is that in order to make this particular change, you must follow the instructions to exit Gold and run **XTG_CFG** from DOS. You will not have access to "System/Hidden file and directory access" if you use **<ALT>F10** to enter the configuration program. This is part of the "security" system.

Later, if *you* forget the names of the directories you've hidden, just go back into the configuration and change "System/Hidden file and directory access" back to YES — and all will be revealed.

DIRECTORY WINDOW

XTree PRO GOLD

See Part 2, XTREE BASICS (starting on page 39).

The Directory Window is where the directory tree is displayed. It's what you see when you first enter the program. When the cursor highlight is in the tree, you're in XTree's Directory Window.

At any time you may get to the Directory Window by pressing **<ESC>** or **<BACKSPACE>**. (You may have to cancel the current command, first.)

Or if you are in one of the two File Windows (the Small or the Expanded), just cycle through the three windows by pressing **<ENTER>** a few times.

XTreePro and XTreePro Gold have a built-in *text editor* called 1Word.

EDIT

Although 1Word comes with its own manual, and is capable of a lot of things, don't race to delete WordPerfect or Microsoft Word from your hard disk quite yet.

XTree PRO GOLD

First of all, 1Word won't underline or boldface characters, much less have anything to do with fonts or graphics. Secondly, you can't use 1Word to edit a file any longer than thirty pages (more or less).

Then why bother with 1Word at all? Well, batch files (and ASCII files) are simple files that are not allowed to use fonts or underlines or import graphics anyway. Batch files and ASCII files contain *only* simple, un-enhanced, letters and numbers. A *text editor*, like 1Word, keeps batch files simple and clean.

Full-fledged word processing programs (WordPerfect, Microsoft Word, etc.) normally create files with a lot more than just letters and numbers in them — they've got hidden codes and symbols and a truck-load of gobbledygook that you can't see.

When you need a quick, simple way to edit a four-line batch file, 1Word appears in a flash and is very handy.

We're going to *assume* that you can live without learning a jillion 1Word commands, so this section will cover only a few elementary commands. (If you're familiar with WordStar 3.3, then you'll be astonished to learn that by a bizarre coincidence, both program's commands are virtually identical!)

However, if you do want to learn more about 1Word, take a look at the six pages of help screens available inside the program — or (ahem) read the manual.

Important reminder: you should not use 1Word to edit files created by your word processor nor use your word processor to edit files created by 1Word. Either way you could trash your file.

■ Edit an existing file

Let's start out with something really fun: editing our AUTOEXEC.BAT file. In the "Hard Disk Management In

XTree PRO GOLD

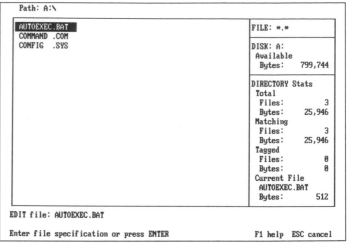

Screen 3-50

a Nutshell" chapter (Part 4), elements of your computer system setup are discussed. A key part of your system setup are your AUTOEXEC.BAT and CONFIG.SYS files. Samples on page 186 of these two files are offered as "standard" setups. Let's see how yours compare.

Warning: Before changing your AUTOEXEC.BAT file, make a backup copy *first!* The importance of doing so cannot be overly stressed.

Okay, assuming you're all backed up, move up your directory tree to the root (\) directory and hit **<ENTER> <ENTER>**. Then, highlight the AUTOEXEC.BAT file (Screen 3-50).

Hit **E** to edit.

Once the proper file name is on the screen, hit **<ENTER>** and you'll enter 1Word (Screen 3-51).

■ 1WORD COMMANDS

BACKSPACE	Deletes the character to the left
<DEL>	Deletes highlighted character
<CTRL>Y	Deletes a whole line
<ESC>	While editing pops up "Quit Commands" (Save & Exit)

XTree PRO GOLD

```
┌─────────────────────────────────Esc cancel─┐
│ A:\AUTOEXEC.BAT                  Size    41  5:32:47 │
│ Ins Hard        Num AskFrwd   Line  3 Col 1 Byte  41  6-38-98 │
├─────────────────────────────────────────────┤
│ prompt $p $g                                          │
│ PATH \:\DOS:\WORD:\Xtree                              │
│                                                       │
│                                                       │
│                                                       │
│          *                                            │
│                                                       │
│                                                       │
│                                                       │
│                                                       │
│                                                       │
└───────────────────────────────────────────────────────┘
```

Screen 3-51

<ESC>	From Main Menu returns you to "edit mode"
<ESC> <ESC>	Main Menu
F1	Help

Use arrow keys to move cursor.

■ Editing

In our sample, we can see that this AUTOEXEC.BAT file meets the proper standards. If yours does not, go ahead and edit it as needed. However, let's say that your AUTOEXEC.BAT doesn't have Gold in the path statement.

Use your arrow keys to move to the end of the existing path statement, and type **;c:\xtgold**, as shown in Screen 3-52. (This assumes, of course, that you've got a C drive and that Gold is in a directory named xtgold.)

When you're finished editing, hit **<ESC>** *once* and the Quit Commands Window will pop up. You can either quit and save or quit without saving(Screen 3-53).

Highlight whichever option you prefer and press **<ENTER>**.

The next thing you may want to examine is your CONFIG.SYS file, to make sure it's okay, too. Again, though, back up *before* changing it in any way. Also, no

XTree PRO GOLD

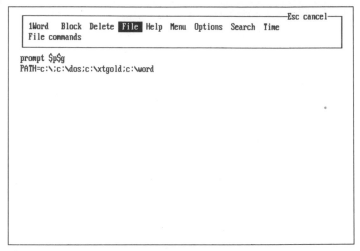

Screen 3-52

changes in either file will take affect on your computer
unless you turn it off and on again.

Your CONFIG.SYS file is also stored in the root (\)
directory. Simply follow the procedure for editing the
AUTOEXEC.BAT file.

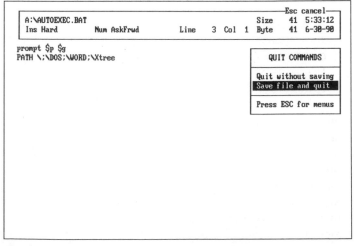

Screen 3-53

■ Create a new file

In this example, we highlighted a file to edit and pressed **E**. Pro or Gold put the name of the file on the command line and we just hit **<ENTER>** to accept it.

To create a new file, however, put your cursor on the directory you want the file to appear in and type **E** for edit. Give the new file a name by typing it and pressing **<ENTER>**.

Then type in the commands you want. When you're finished editing, hit **<ESC>** once, highlight "Save and Exit" and hit **<ENTER>**.

Hint: If you want to save a file under a different name, hit **<CTRL>K-A** and modify the name shown.

■ Swap 1Word with your word processor

Using Gold's configuration program, you can designate *any* word processing program to be the one launched with the Edit command (it doesn't have to be 1Word).

You can go into Gold's configuration program (see CONFIGURATION) by hitting **<ALT>F10**.

Once inside the configuration program:

1. Press **1** to "Modify configuration items."
2. Press **<ENTER>** three times to skip to page 4.
3. Press **2** to select "Editor program."
4. At the bottom of the screen, type in the full path name and program name of your word processor, (i.e. **C:\WORD5\WORD.EXE** or **C:\WP\WP.EXE**);
5. Press **<ESC>** to return to the main menu.
6. Choose **S** and **Y** to save your changes and exit.

Before you decide to make the swap, however, remember that most full-featured word processor programs put non-ASCII characters in files that will prevent your batch file from working as expected. If you want to use your word processor to edit or create batch files, you must learn how to save a file in "text" or "ASCII" mode.

In any case, you can always go back into the configuration program and swap 1Word back in!

```
Path: \CHECK

BOFA89  .ACT     CHECK3  .EXE      FILE: *.*
BOFA89  .BGT     CHECK4  .EXE
BOFA89  .CHK     CHKRTM  .EXE      DISK: C: POWER USER
BOFA89  .DEF     ORDER   .BAT      Available
BOFA89  .DTA     PATHTEST.         Bytes: 2,158,592
BOFA89  .GRP     REMINDER.EXE
BOFA89  .SOR     SETUP   .EXE      DIRECTORY Stats
BOFA89  .ZIP                       Total
BOFA90  .ACT                         Files:          26
BOFA90  .BGT                         Bytes:     786,291
BOFA90  .DEF                       Matching
BOFA90  .DTA                         Files:          26
BOFA90  .GRP                         Bytes:     786,291
BOFA90  .SOR                       Tagged
CHECK   .EXE                         Files:           0
CHECK   .PRO                         Bytes:           0
CHECK1R .ZIP                       Current File
CHECK2  .EXE                         CHECK    EXE
CHECK2R .ZIP                         Bytes:      21,313

FILE       ^Attributes  ^Copy  ^Delete  Filespec  Log disk  ^Move  ^Print
COMMANDS   ^Rename  ^Tag  ^Untag  View  eXecute
+↑↓+ scroll  RETURN dir commands       ALT menu          F1 quit F2 help F3 cancel
```

Screen 3-54

EXECUTE

See COMMAND SHELL and APPLICATIONS MENU.

The word "execute" means to carry out or perform. In the case of computers, execute means carry out a command. You can execute programs and batch files and DOS commands.

XTree's Execute command gives you the ability to execute programs, batch files, and DOS commands from *inside* XTree.

Even when you activate other programs from inside XTree and XTree disappears from the screen, XTree's not *entirely* gone. While you work on your application, a "kernel" of XTree is, like an attentive servant, waiting silently in the background until it's called upon. Once you exit your application, XTree automatically pops up again, ready to escort you to your next destination.

Using XTree as a "DOS Shell" in this way means that you can use XTree as your command center.

Each version of XTree provides higher levels of finesse for customizing your system and for launching your programs. (However, the more finesse — the more work required to set it up.)

```
Current Path: C:\CHECK
Enter a DOS command, or press RETURN on an empty line to return to XTREE.
>CHECK
```

Screen 3-55

Executing programs is very simple. Just highlight the program's name, type **X**, and press **<ENTER>**.

In this case , we're highlighting **CHECK.EXE**, as shown in Screen 3-54. (You'd find WORD.EXE for Microsoft Word, or WP.EXE for WordPerfect, and so on.)

Then hit **X** for eXecute.

What happens next varies slightly with the three versions of the program.

Continuing with XTree, it put the program's name on the screen and all you need to do is press **<ENTER>**.

Whenever you finish a command you'll get something like Screen 3-55. You can either execute another command or, when you're ready to return to XTree, press **<ENTER>** without a command.

In Pro, you still highlight the file to be executed, and press **X**. However, you get a much more informational screen. At this point, press **<ENTER>** to start the program at the command line.

Whenever you finish a command you'll get something like Screen 3-56. You can either execute another command or, when you're ready to return to Pro, press **<ESC>**.

XTree PRO GOLD

XTree PRO GOLD

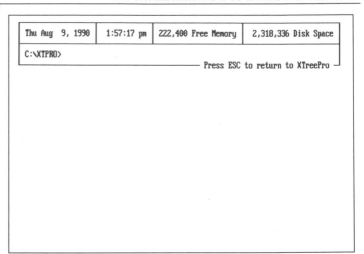

Screen 3-56

■ Memory

If you get an "insufficient memory" error message when
using eXecute, use **<ALT>X** instead of plain **X**. **<ALT>X**
releases more memory for the other program to use.

Gold works a lot like Pro (Screen 3-57). As before, highlight
the file to be executed, press **X** and then **<ENTER>** to carry
out the command.

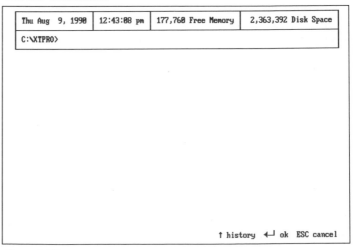

Screen 3-57

Whenever you finish a command you'll get the above screen again. You can either execute another command or, when you're ready to return to Gold, press **<ESC>**.

XTree PRO GOLD

■ Memory

If you get an "insufficient memory" error message when using eXecute, use **<ALT>X** instead of plain **X**. **<ALT>X** releases more memory for the other program to use.

■ Open (and associate)

Although "Open and associate" may *sound* like some sort of New Wave singles scene, it isn't. It is a convenient feature that puts file name extensions to use in a unique way.

Most programs give their data files a common extension. For instance, Microsoft Word files all end in DOC, Lotus 1-2-3 files end in WK1, and so forth. In Gold you can link (or "associate") an extension with its program. In other words, you can tell Gold that all files ending with DOC are Microsoft Word files.

Then, while in Gold, you can highlight a Word file (like REPORT.DOC) and then type **O** (for open). Gold will then know to automatically launch Word and load REPORT.

■ Create an association

Extensions and programs become associated via a batch file that you write. (If you're not familiar with creating batch files, there's a whole section devoted to them — and Gold's "variables" — starting on page 55.)

The key to the association is the way in which the batch file is named. You must use the file extension as the first part of the file name, then add **.BAT**. For Microsoft Word, the associated batch file would be called: **DOC.BAT**. The Lotus file would be called **WK1.BAT**.

The associated batch file must contain the name and location of the program you want to launch, followed by **%1**. %1 means "the currently highlighted file." (Gold has a number of variables you can use, all listed in the BATCH FILES section.)

DOC.BAT would, therefore, contain this single command line:

```
C:\WORD5\WORD.EXE %1
```

XTree PRO GOLD

Highlighting a **DOC** file and hitting **O** will activate the **DOC.BAT** file. **DOC.BAT** will find and execute the Word program with the currently highlighted **DOC** file in place of the **%1**.

Another example of an associate batch file might be one named **XLS.BAT** that contained this line:

```
C:\EXCEL\EXCEL.EXE %1
```

(Yes, you can start Excel from within Gold!)

■ Mouse

If you have a mouse, you can place your mouse cursor on the file name to be opened and double-click the left mouse button.

■ Troubleshooting

If a file refuses to Open, either you've run out of memory (see below) or the associate batch file can't be found. Make sure the associate batch file is in the same directory area as Gold. (Also, it wouldn't hurt to double-check the commands in the batch file!)

■ Memory

If memory is tight on your system (or you get an "insufficient memory" error message), you might want to use **<ALT>O** instead of plain **O** because then as much memory as possible will be released to the program you're trying to use.

FILE DISPLAY

XTree PRO GOLD

When viewing files in the File Windows, normally only the names are shown. If you wish to see more information — their attributes, size, date and time saved — you need to invoke the file display command.

Screen 3-58 is an example of a normal file display. File names are listed in a three-column format. You are looking at the largest number of file names, with the least amount (i.e. none) of information on each file.

Hitting **<ALT>F** will give you something like Screen 3-59.

Now you've got a two-column listing of files and their attributes.

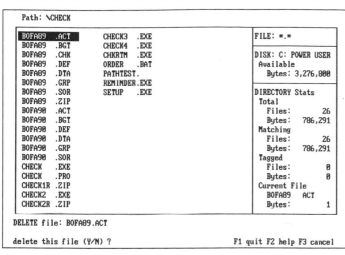

XTree PRO GOLD

Screen 3-58

Hitting **<ALT>F** one more time produces something like Screen 3-60.

Now, although only one column of files is displayed, there is a wealth of information now seen on each of those files (size, attributes, and date and time saved).

Another **<ALT>F** will restore the file display back to the original three-column motif.

```
Path: \CHECK

BOFA89  .ACT        1 ....   CHECK3  .EXE   10,769 ....  FILE: *.*
BOFA89  .BGT    2,162 ....   CHECK4  .EXE   48,721 ....
BOFA89  .CHK       52 ....   CHKRTM  .EXE   70,680 ....  DISK: C: POWER USER
BOFA89  .DEF       43 ....   ORDER   .BAT      514 ....  Available
BOFA89  .DTA   96,860 ....   PATHTEST.           1 ....  Bytes: 2,560,000
BOFA89  .GRP        0 ....   REMINDER.EXE    6,001 ....
BOFA89  .SOR    1,334 ....   SETUP   .EXE   31,057 ....  DIRECTORY Stats
BOFA89  .ZIP   18,206+.a..                                Total
BOFA90  .ACT    2,101 ....                                  Files:         26
BOFA90  .BGT    1,973 ....                                  Bytes:    813,291
BOFA90  .DEF       43 ....                                Matching
BOFA90  .DTA  106,420 ....                                  Files:         26
BOFA90  .GRP      586 ....                                  Bytes:    813,291
BOFA90  .SOR      678 ....                                Tagged
CHECK   .EXE   21,313 ....                                  Files:          3
CHECK   .PRO    1,216 ....                                  Bytes:    280,893
CHECK1R .ZIP  184,353+.a..                                Current File
CHECK2  .EXE  129,953 ....                                  BOFA89    ACT
CHECK2R .ZIP   78,334+.a..                                  Bytes:          1

ALT FILE   Copy  File display  Sort criteria  Tag  Untag  eXecute
COMMANDS
                                                    F1 quit
```

Screen 3-59

XTree PRO GOLD

```
Path: \CHECK

BOFA89  .ACT        1    ....   4-19-90   3:40 pm    FILE: *.*
BOFA89  .BGT    2,162    ....  12-31-89  12:53 pm
BOFA89  .CHK       52    ....  10-04-89   8:24 am    DISK: C: POWER USER
BOFA89  .DEF       43    ....   1-14-90  12:16 pm    Available
BOFA89  .DTA   96,860    ....   4-19-90   3:40 pm     Bytes: 2,560,000
BOFA89  .GRP        0    ....   1-14-90  12:16 pm
BOFA89  .SOR    1,334    ....  12-31-89   1:37 pm    DIRECTORY Stats
BOFA89  .ZIP   18,206+   .a..  12-31-89   2:59 pm    Total
BOFA90  .ACT    2,101    ....   8-06-90  11:22 am     Files:          26
BOFA90  .BGT    1,973    ....   7-01-90   5:20 pm     Bytes:     813,291
BOFA90  .DEF       43    ....   1-09-90   8:26 am    Matching
BOFA90  .DTA  106,420    ....   8-06-90  11:22 am     Files:          26
BOFA90  .GRP      586    ....   1-09-90   8:50 am     Bytes:     813,291
BOFA90  .SOR      678    ....   8-06-90  11:22 am    Tagged
CHECK   .EXE   21,313    ....   4-02-90   4:03 am     Files:           3
CHECK   .PRO    1,216    ....   1-09-90   8:56 am     Bytes:     200,893
CHECK1R .ZIP  184,353+   .a..   4-10-90   5:11 pm    Current File
CHECK2  .EXE  129,953    ....   4-02-90   4:03 am     BOFA89   ACT
CHECK2R .ZIP   78,334+   .a..   4-10-90   5:06 pm     Bytes:           1


ALT FILE   Copy  File display  Sort criteria  Tag  Untag  eXecute
COMMANDS
                                                       F1 quit
```

Screen 3-60

Hint: If you find yourself constantly changing the file display to one of these other settings, you can change the configuration of Pro or Gold so that a one- or two-column setting is the norm. (See CONFIGURATION to learn how to get into the configuration programs.)

FILE WINDOW

XTree PRO GOLD

See the "XTree Basics" section.

Whenever your highlight is resting on a file name, you are in a File Window.

File windows come in two sizes: Small and Expanded. The Small File Window is what you see underneath the Directory Window. The Expanded File Window, logically, is a larger version of the Small File Window. To get to the Small File Window, hit **<ENTER>** from the Directory Window. If you hit **<ENTER>** from the Small File Window, you'll end up in the Expanded File Window (Screen 3-61).

FILESPEC

The Filespec command uses what you learned about wildcards to single out a group of files. (If you don't remember wildcards, jump back to the "MS-DOS Concepts" section and read up on "Wildcards" on page 31 before proceeding.)

Once you set a file specification with the filespec

```
 Path: C:\                                    7-02-90 12:13:29 pm
┌──────────────────────────────────────────────────────────────────┐
│ ANSI    .RTF     CONFIG  .OLD          FILE *.*                     │
│ ANSI    .SCR     CONFIG  .SYS                                       │
│ ASCII   .DOC     FRECOVER.BAK          DISK C:POWER USER            │
│ ASCII   .RTF     FRECOVER.DAT          Available                    │
│ ASCII   .SCR     frecover.idx          Bytes   5,033,984            │
│ AUTOEXEC.BAK     HIMEM   .SYS                                       │
│ AUTOEXEC.BAT     ibmbio  .com          DIRECTORY Stats              │
│ AUTOEXEC.DBK     IBMBIO  .XUP          Total                        │
│ BETH    .        ibmdos  .com          Files            34          │
│ BIO300D .EXE     IBMDOS  .XUP       .  Bytes       425,726          │
│ BIOLOT  .EXE     MON     .CHK          Matching                     │
│ C       .BAK     OLDAUTO .BAT          Files            34          │
│ C       .BAT     PIX     .BAT          Bytes       425,726          │
│ CAP     .BAT     VTECH   .CFG          Tagged                       │
│ CHECKUP .LOG     VTECH   .EXE          Files             0          │
│ COMMAND .COM                           Bytes             0          │
│ COMMAND .XUP                           Current File                 │
│ CONFIG  .BAK                           ANSI      .RTF               │
│ CONFIG  .DBK                           Bytes         4,403          │
├──────────────────────────────────────────────────────────────────┤
│ FILE      Attributes  Copy  Delete  Edit  Filespec  Invert  Log disk  Move │
│ COMMANDS  New date  Open  Print  Rename  Tag  Untag  View  eXecute  Quit   │
│ ◄┘ tree  F7 autoview  F8 split    F9 menu  F10 commands    F1 help  ESC cancel │
└──────────────────────────────────────────────────────────────────┘
```

Screen 3-61

command, only those files on your hard disk *matching* the
file specification will be visible in the File Windows. In
addition, any file commands you perform affect *only* the
files currently displayed.

Hint: Any directory that doesn't have any files meeting the
current filespecs will flash a "No Files!" message. It doesn't
mean there are no files at all in that directory. It just means
there are no files in that directory matching the current file
specifications. A Filespec of ***.*** will display all files.

Even though XTree allows only the most simple use of
filespec, it's still a powerful tool. When you are either in the
Directory Window or a File Window, hit **F** for filespec, and
you'll be asked to enter a filespec.

We typed in ***.zip** as the file specification (Screen 3-62).
That means we are looking for any file with the ZIP
extension. When you hit **<ENTER>**, two things happen
immediately: only files ending in ZIP are displayed in the
File Window and the box in the upper right hand corner
now confirms that the filespec is ***.zip** (Screen 3-63).

When you are entering a filespec, you can use any legal
combinations of ***** and **?** to help single out the files you
want to see.

XTree PRO GOLD

XTree PRO GOLD

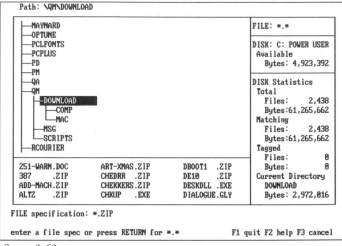

```
Path: \QM\DOWNLOAD

 ┌─MAYNARD                                    FILE: *.*
 ├─OPTUNE
 ├─PCLFONTS                                   DISK: C: POWER USER
 ├─PCPLUS                                     Available
 ├─PD                                            Bytes: 4,923,392
 ├─PM
 ├─QA                                         DISK Statistics
 └─QM                                         Total
     ├─DOWNLOAD                                   Files:    2,438
     │  ├─COMP                                    Bytes:61,265,662
     │  └─MAC                                 Matching
     ├─MSG                                        Files:    2,438
     └─SCRIPTS                                    Bytes:61,265,662
 ├─RCOURIER                                   Tagged
                                                 Files:        0
 251-WARN.DOC    ART-XMAS.ZIP    DBOOT1  .ZIP    Bytes:        0
 387     .ZIP    CHEDRR  .ZIP    DE10    .ZIP Current Directory
 ADD-MACH.ZIP    CHEKKERS.ZIP    DESKDLL .EXE    DOWNLOAD
 ALTZ    .ZIP    CHKUP   .EXE    DIALOGUE.GLY    Bytes: 2,972,016

 FILE specification: *.ZIP

 enter a file spec or press RETURN for *.*        F1 quit F2 help F3 cancel
```

Screen 3-62

Hint: if you are looking for one particular file, type in its name, then go into Showall mode by typing **s**. You'll see the file's name and path displayed.

XTreePro added some flexibility to the filespec command (Screen 3-64).

```
Path: \QM\DOWNLOAD

 387     .ZIP    LZESHL  .ZIP    REMOVE  .ZIP FILE: *.ZIP
 ADD-MACH.ZIP    MAKEBA  .ZIP    SAYINV  .ZIP
 ALTZ    .ZIP    MOREMAC .ZIP    SCRIPT  .ZIP DISK: C: POWER USER
 ART-XMAS.ZIP    MOUSE624.ZIP    SERMON  .ZIP Available
 CHEDRR  .ZIP    MSAPP21 .ZIP    SETENV  .ZIP    Bytes: 4,923,392
 CHEKKERS.ZIP    MSMOUSE7.ZIP    SETPTH14.ZIP
 DBOOT1  .ZIP    MSWITCH .ZIP    SHELLP  .ZIP DIRECTORY Stats
 DE10    .ZIP    MW5ART  .ZIP    ST251ART.ZIP Total
 DISKBUFF.ZIP    NAMER   .ZIP    STUFFKEY.ZIP    Files:       77
 DMVTEST .ZIP    NEWDOS  .ZIP    SUBMIT  .ZIP    Bytes: 2,972,016
 EDIAL12 .ZIP    NOJTY   .ZIP    TECHREF .ZIP Matching
 ENVMACRO.ZIP    NOTOLLS .ZIP    TURBOEMS.ZIP    Files:       51
 FFM10   .ZIP    NPAD    .ZIP    UXARC   .ZIP    Bytes: 1,909,212
 FONTS   .ZIP    OCR-A   .ZIP                 Tagged
 GRAB51  .ZIP    PILOT98 .ZIP                    Files:        0
 GRIDMAKR.ZIP    POSTBINS.ZIP                    Bytes:        0
 HP3-MS  .ZIP    PRN2FILE.ZIP                 Current File
 L3HPGL  .ZIP    PUMA100 .ZIP                    387     ZIP
 LJTODJ  .ZIP    RECONFIG.ZIP                    Bytes:   24,472

 FILE     ^Attributes ^Copy ^Delete Filespec Log disk ^Move ^Print
 COMMANDS ^Rename ^Tag ^Untag View eXecute
 ←↑↓→ scroll  RETURN dir commands    ALT menu       F1 quit F2 help F3 cancel
```

Screen 3-63

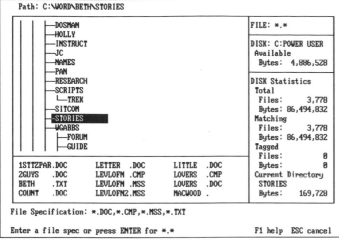

Screen 3-64

You can enter up to four *different* filespecs (separated by commas). Any file meeting at least one of the specifications will be listed.

A lengthy file specification will not fit in the tiny filespec window. A little arrow tells you there's more (Screen 3-65).

A keystroke-saving feature in Pro is that when you begin the filespec command, you can press the up arrow key to

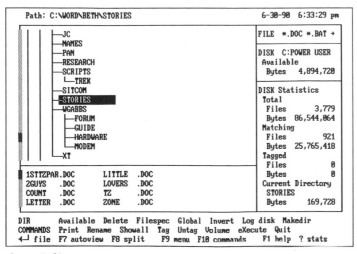

Screen 3-65

XTree PRO GOLD

```
Path: C:\QM\MSG

ART      .BAK       X1      .BAK        FILE: *.BAK
AUTOEXEC.BAK       X2      .BAK
BLU      .BAK       XINTRO  .BAK        DISK: C:POWER USER
BOOK1    .BAK       XOUT    .BAK        Available
C        .BAK       XTQ&A   .BAK        Bytes:  4,886,528
CONFIG   .BAK
DOC      .BAK                           SHOWALL Statistics
FRECOVER.BAK                            Total
FREEDOM  .BAK                            Files:      3,779
HERO     .BAK                            Bytes: 86,495,367
IDG2     .BAK                           Matching
NORMAL   .BAK                            Files:         24
OUTLINE  .BAK                            Bytes:    448,663
PART1    .BAK                           Tagged
PGOUT    .BAK                            Files:          0
PROTEST .BAK                             Bytes:          0
SCROLL   .BAK                           Current File
THOTZ    .BAK                            ART     .BAK
X        .BAK                            Bytes:      1,212

FILE      Attributes  Copy  Delete  Edit  Filespec  Log disk  Move  Print
COMMANDS  Rename  Tag  Untag  View  eXecute  Quit
←↑↓→ scroll  ENTER tree commands   ALT menu  CTRL menu      F1 help  ESC cancel
```

Screen 3-66

pop the most recent file specification into the screen.

Another way filespec can be used is in conjunction with the Showall command. Showall displays all the files on the drive (Screen 3-66). If you entered a filespec of ***.BAK** and used the Showall command (**S**), you'd be able to see all BAK files stored on your hard disk.

Just when you think it couldn't get more fun, Gold comes in with more interesting features.

Gold allows up to sixteen different specifications. That means you could hit **F** for filespec and type in: ***.DOC *.BAK *.TXT A*.*** (either a space or a comma between filespecs is required), then press **<ENTER>** and those files meeting at least one of the filespecs will be displayed.

It gets better. Gold also allows "Exclusionary specifications." That means you can say "I want everything *except...*," and exclude certain file types from being displayed. To do this, hit **F** for filespec and type a minus sign (-) in front of the filespec to be excluded. For instance, **-*.DOC** would mean all files *except* those ending in DOC. (Important note: If you use this in a list of specifications, make sure the exclusionary specification is listed *first*.)

As you might expect, hitting the up arrow while in filespec will activate your Filespec History. You can highlight and **<ENTER>** previously used filespecs.

```
┌──────────────────────────────────────────────────────────┐   XTree PRO GOLD
│ Path: C:\WORD\BETH\STORIES            6-30-90  6:32:30 pm │
│┌─────────────────────────────────────────────────────────┐
││        ├─JC              │FILE  *.*                       │
││        ├─NAMES           │                                │
││        ├─PAN             │DISK  C:POWER USER              │
││        ├─RESEARCH        │ Available                      │
││        ├─SCRIPT          └─────────────────────────────── │
││        └─TRE                                              │
││        ├─SITCOM    *.bat                                  │
││        ├─STORIE    *.bak                                  │
││        └─WGABBS    mw5art.zip                             │
││          ├─FOR     *.exe *.txt                            │
││          ├─GUI     *.exe *.txt *.zip *.doc                │
││          ├─HAR     -*.arc                                 │
││          ├─MOD     -*.arc -*.zip                          │
││        └─XT        ?                                      │
││                    *.exe                                  │
││ 1STTZPAR.DOC       spin*.*                                │
││ 2GUYS   .DOC       *.dow                                  │
││ BETH    .TXT       *.prd                                  │
││ COUNT   .DOC       *.*                                    │
│└──────────────────────────────────────────────────────────│
│ File specification:                                        │
│                                                            │
│ Enter file specification      ↑ history  ↵ ok  F1 help  ESC cancel │
└──────────────────────────────────────────────────────────┘
```

Screen 3-67

Screen 3-67 shows the filespec history command. The last thirteen filespecs used are on display, waiting to be highlighted and used.

■ Global

Since Gold allows you to log multiple drives simultaneously (say, drive A and drive C and drive D), you can enter a filespec, and then type **G** for Global to display the files on all logged drives that match the filespec. You can do some intense searching and comparing.

■ Invert

Also, you can invert an existing filespec by typing **I** to Invert. Then, all the files that *don't* match the filespec will be displayed.

In Screen 3-68, ***.DOC** was entered as the filespec. Typing **I** activates the invert command. A choice between inverting filespecs or tags is offered. Choose **F** for File Specifications to reveal the files that do *not* end in DOC. (**Note:** the screen goes into a reverse video as a visual clue that you're in invert mode.) To return to normal mode, just repeat the process (choose **I–F** again).

```
Path: C:\WORD\BETH\XT                          6-30-90  7:38:45 pm

 13260957.                            FILE  *.DOC
 BOOK1    .BAK
 IDG2     .BAK                        DISK  C:POWER USER
 MC4      .TXT                        Available
 NORMAL   .BAK                          Bytes    4,882,432
 NORMAL   .GLY
 OUTLINE  .BAK                        DIRECTORY Stats
 OUTLINE  .STY                        Total
 PART1    .BAK                          Files           42
 TEST     .BAT                          Bytes      958,703
 THOTZ    .BAK                        Matching
 X        .BAK                          Files           19
 X        .STY                          Bytes      698,095
 X1       .BAK                        Tagged
 X2       .BAK                          Files            0
 XINTRO   .BAK                          Bytes            0
 XOUT     .BAK                        Current File
 XTQ&A    .BAK                        13260957.
 XTREE    .CMP                          Bytes      360,979

 FILE       Attributes  Copy  Delete  Edit  Filespec  Invert  Log disk  Move
 COMMANDS   New date  Open  Print  Rename  Tag  Untag  View  eXecute  Quit
 ←┘ tree  F7 autoview  F8 split    F9 menu  F10 commands    F1 help  ESC cancel
```

Screen 3-68

FIND

Locating something on a hard disk can make finding the proverbial "needle in a haystack" seem simple by comparison. Nothing is more frustrating than being under a deadline and not being able to remember which one of REPORT1 though REPORT24 was the one that had that legal phrasing everyone liked. But of course, XTree has ways to find words, files, and anything else you may want to track down.

XTree PRO GOLD

■ Find a directory

To find a particular directory, move the cursor up or down the Tree. The directories are listed in alphabetical order. The Home key will take you to the top of the list, and End to the bottom. **<Pg Up>** and **<Pg Dn>** will take you up and down a screenful at a time.

■ Find a file — on the currently logged disk

Use the filespec command (type **F**) and type the name of the file you want to find. Type **S** for Showall and all the files on the disk matching your filespec will be displayed. (The file's location, or "path," will be displayed at the top of the screen.) This is a very simple way to find duplicate files.

■ Find a file — on floppies

Here's the scenario: you need to find a file that is on one of several floppy disks. XTree can help track it down for you.

The 5th Wave   By Rich Tennant   XTree PRO GOLD

"OOO-KAY, LET'S SEE, IF WE CAN ALL REMAIN CALM AND STOP ACTING CRAZY,
I'M SURE I'LL EVENTUALLY REMEMBER WHAT NAME I FILED THE ANTIDOTE UNDER."

Enter the file name via the filespec command, then hit **F5**
(XTree's undocumented "Keep Filespec" key). You need to
"keep filespec" because XTree normally returns to ***.***
when you log another drive. Put your first floppy in the A
drive and log it (hit **L**). If the file is on that floppy, you'll see
it displayed on the screen (and the Matching File Statistics
will change from zero). If the file isn't on that floppy, take it
out, put the next one in and log it.

Finding a file on a stack of floppies is a little more arcane
for XTreePro. First of all you must start with **XTPRO /K+
<ENTER>**. The **/K+** option will tell Pro to keep the filespecs
even though you log a new drive. Once you've start Pro
with the **/K+** option, enter the filespec you are looking for.
Then put the first floppy drive into the A drive and log it.
When the Matching File Statistics is no longer zero, you've
found your file.

XTree PRO GOLD

```
Path: C:\WORD\BETH                                    8-09-90  1:40:11 pm

#1REC89D.ZIP♦    00000268.MAI♦   11       .TXT♦   FILE  *.*
$$$$$$$$.F5 ♦    00000317.MAI♦   12       .TXT♦
$DEFAULT.F1 ♦    000003A2.MAI♦   123      .CMP♦   DISK  C:POWER USER
$DEFAULT.F10♦    000003DB.MAI♦   123      .CNF♦   Available
$DEFAULT.F2 ♦    00000484.MAI♦   123      .EXE♦     Bytes  2,088,960
$DEFAULT.F3 ♦    00000485.MAI♦   123      .HLP♦
$DEFAULT.F4 ♦    0000098E.MAI♦   123      .SET♦   SHOWALL Statistics
$DEFAULT.F5 ♦    000009A6.ATT♦   123SETUP.DOC♦    Total
$DEFAULT.F6 ♦    000009A7.MAI♦   12MEG    .ICO♦     Files       3,886
$DEFAULT.F7 ♦    00000B83.ATT♦   12_19ID  .DOC♦     Bytes  89,067,358
$DEFAULT.F8 ♦    1        .BAT♦  12_22PRM.DOC♦    Matching
$DEFAULT.F9 ♦    1        .DOC♦  144MEG   .ICO♦     Files       3,886
$UPDATE .IFS♦    1        .TXT♦  1990     .ARC♦     Bytes  89,067,358
(C)ALDUS.'88♦    10       .BAT♦  1STTZPAR.DOC♦    Tagged
(C)ALDUS.'90♦    10       .TXT♦  1WORD1   .PIX♦     Files       3,886
(C)BITS .'89♦    10MAN    .CMP♦  1WORD2   .PIX♦     Bytes  89,067,358
00000043.KEY♦    10MAN    .DOC♦  1WORD3   .PIX♦    Current File
000001A5.MAI♦    10MAN    .STV♦  1WORD4   .PIX♦     #1REC89D.ZIP
00000213.MAI♦    10_10    .DOC♦  2        .BAT♦     Bytes     106,479

Search all tagged files for text: computer

Enter a search string                    ↑ history  ↵ ok  F1 help  ESC cancel
```

Screen 3-69

XTreePro Gold automatically keeps a filespec until you changed it. Get your pile of floppies and keep logging them until the Matching File Statistics change from zero.

■ Find text

When looking for text, the first step is to tag all the suspect files.

```
File: C:\WORD\BETH\INSTRUCT\HOWTOARC.DOC              WRAP  (masked )


======================================================
CONFESSIONS OF AN ARC FILE
======================================================


CONCEPT:

Computer files, like clothes, can be packed together in a suitcase.
 Why you would want to do that with clothes is obvious:  it keeps things
together and protected from loss and besides, it's much more convenient
than if everything was loose.  In computers the reasons are similar.
 If, for instance, you had three premises you wanted to send to an editor
you could upload them one at a time to the bulletin board OR you could
put them in a suitcase (an ARC file) and upload just the one suitcase
file (the ARC file).  Then when the editor got the ARC file (the suitcase
file) he/she could UNPACK the suitcase and extract the three files for
reading.

VIEW      ASCII  Dump  Formatted  Gather  Hex  Mask  Wordwrap
COMMANDS  F2 F3 F4 F5 F6 goto bookmark  F9 search  F10 search again
↑↓ scroll  ALT SHFT menus                             F1 help  ESC cancel
```

Screen 3-70

For instance you may know that one of a series of files has the text you're looking for. You need to tag those files.

XTree PRO GOLD

Or you may decide you don't have a clue where the text is and want to tag all the files on the hard disk. (Hit **S** to go into Showall. Type **<CTRL>T** to tag all files on the hard disk.)

After the suspect files are tagged, type **<CTRL>S** for Search, to search all tagged files. Gold asks you what text you want to find (Screen 3-69).

Type in the word (or words) you're looking for and then press **<ENTER>**.

Gold will search through each tagged file and untag any that do *not* contain your search phrase.

When Gold is finished, hit **<ESC>** followed by **<CTRL>S**, and only the remaining tagged files (i.e. those containing your search text) will be displayed.

If you hit **V** for View, the highlighted file will be displayed, with the search phrase highlighted, as in Screen 3-70. (See VIEW for more about this command.)

■ Find text over several logged drives

This is the same as finding text on one hard disk, except you must go into Global mode, rather than Showall mode.

Whenever you open a box of floppy disks, they must be *formatted* before you can use them. (Formatting allows DOS to lay down a magnetic system for recording and retrieving information — an "electronic honeycomb.")

FORMAT A DISK

■ Is the disk formatted already?

An unformatted disk looks exactly like a formatted one. However, a formatted disk may already have files stored on it. If you re-format an already-formatted disk, you'll erase anything that might be stored on it. (If you re-format a blank disk, that's fine.) You can see why it's a good idea, if you're not sure, to verify that a floppy disk isn't already formatted before you start to format it.

You can determine whether the disk is or isn't formatted with XTree's Log command.

To do this, put the suspect floppy in the drive and hit **L** for log disk. When XTree asks you for the drive to log on to, type **A** (or **B** as the case may be).

After you hit **A**, there will be a pause and one of two things will happen:

1. You'll get an error message, which you can interpret to mean that the disk is *not* formatted and you should cancel the log command, or —
2. The disk will log normally, indicating that the disk is *already* formatted.

■ High-density and low-density

Both 5^1/4- and 3^1/2-inch floppy drives come in either low-density (also known as double-density) or high-density flavors. ("Density" means, basically, how much information can be stored on the disk.)

Note: If you don't know whether you have a high-density drive or a low-density drive, one way to find out is to put an *unformatted* floppy disk in the drive and hit **L** to log the disk and *watch the drive light* as XTree tries to access it. If the drive light changes colors (red to green or amber to green), it's a high-density drive. If it stays red, it's low-density.

■ Rule of thumb

A low-density drive can format only low-density disks. A high-density drive can, theoretically, format both high- and low-density disks. A word of caution: some computers cannot format low-density disks in high-density drives very well (the disk will work fine in your computer, but not anywhere else). It doesn't hurt anything to try, just don't copy an important file to a disk and then erase it off your hard drive without making sure other computers can use the disk. The newer the computer, the better the chances it will work.

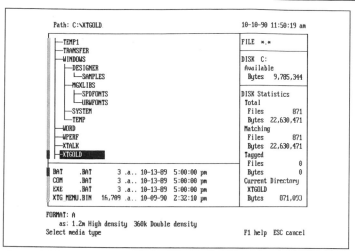

Screen 3-71

Since neither XTree nor Pro has the capacity to format a disk built in, you have to do it the old-fashioned way, via DOS. You can hit **X** (to execute a command), which would give you the command shell prompt (see COMMAND SHELL).

Once at a system prompt, type **format a: <ENTER>** (or **format b: <ENTER>** if you want to format a floppy in drive B). These commands assume that you've got a low-density disk in a low-density drive and a high-density disk in a high-density drive. (It takes a different DOS command to format a low-density disk in a high-density drive.)

After you've entered the format command, you'll be told to put a disk in the drive (whether there's one already in the drive or not) and hit a key (or **<ENTER>**). After you do, the formatting process commences. You'll thrill to the visual feedback of heads and cylinders being counted.

When the formatting is concluded, you'll be given the chance to format another disk. If you want to do so, respond with **Y <ENTER>**, if not, type **N <ENTER>**.

For XTreePro Gold users, however, there's a wonderfully convenient way to format disks.

To start the process, just hit **<ALT>F2** . (If you've got more than one floppy drive, Gold will want to know which one you want to format.)

XTree PRO GOLD

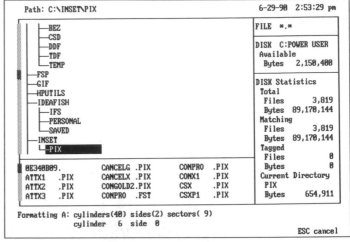

```
Path: C:\INSET\PIX                              6-29-90  2:53:29 pm

     ├─BEZ                              FILE  *.*
     ├─CSD
     ├─DDF                             DISK  C:POWER USER
     ├─TDF                             Available
     └─TEMP                            Bytes    2,150,400
    ├─FSP
    GIF                               DISK Statistics
    ┤HPUTILS                          Total
    ├─IDEAFISH                          Files        3,819
     ├─IFS                             Bytes   89,170,144
     ├─PERSONAL                       Matching
     └─SAVED                            Files        3,819
    ├─INSET                            Bytes   89,170,144
    └─PIX                             Tagged
                                        Files            0
 0E340B09.         CANCELG .PIX    CONPRO  .PIX    Bytes            0
 ATTX1   .PIX      CANCELX .PIX    CONX1   .PIX   Current Directory
 ATTX2   .PIX      CONGOLD2.PIX    CSX     .PIX    PIX
 ATTX3   .PIX      CONPRO  .FST    CSXP1   .PIX    Bytes      654,911

Formatting A: cylinders(40) sides(2) sectors( 9)
             cylinder   6  side  0
                                                          ESC cancel
```

Screen 3-72

Once you've selected your drive, you'll be presented with another option (Screen 3-71).

What kind of media do you have? *Media* is a fancy way of referring to your floppy disk. Gold wants to know whether your floppy disk is high density or low density (also known as double density). After responding appropriately, Gold will start formatting.

You'll see the heads and cylinders being counted, as in Screen 3-72 (so you know that things are moving forward).

When finished, you'll have to decide whether you want to format another disk. Hit **<ENTER>** to cycle the process, or **<ESC>** to cancel any further disk formatting.

FUNCTION KEYS

Function keys (those keys on your keyboard labeled "F-something") are used by most programs to keep important commands down to the fewest number of keystrokes. Other times function keys are used to synthesize otherwise keystroke-intensive operations.

Since XTree is basically a simple program, the need for shortcuts isn't exactly pressing (if you'll pardon the pun). In other words, XTree doesn't make much use of function keys.

Of the function key commands that it does use, you'll find that some times they work and some times they don't. It's not that XTree's "buggy," it's just that some of XTree's function keys have a "function" *only* under certain circumstances.

For instance, if you're traveling up and down your directory tree, the Cancel command doesn't appear at the bottom of the screen. Why? Simply because there's no operation to cancel (you can't "cancel" the tree unless you quit the program, or go to an Expanded File Window).

If, on the other hand, you're about to copy a bunch of files, the Cancel command appears as a choice at the bottom of the screen, reminding you that the operation can be canceled.

As you get yourself in and out of different situations with XTree, applicable function keys will appear and disappear at the bottom of the screen. So pay attention to the command menu — it's your friend.

Which, if you think about it, is kind of cool.

A few function key commands (like the "Alt Lock" and "Ctrl Lock" keys) are never listed as an option at the bottom of the screen. You just have to know they're there. There are even a couple of function keys that aren't listed in the manual.

So here is a list of function key commands for XTree, XTreePro, and XTreePro Gold.

Since many of these function keys work *in conjunction* with other commands, you see a reference to that other command next to the function key. Looking up the other command will give you all the detail you need on the function key in its *context*.

A few keys work independently of any other function and an explanation of how they work is provided in the list on the following page.

These function key listings are repeated, plus those for XTree Easy, XTreeGold, and XTreeNet, at the end of Part 5, which starts on page 205.

XTree PRO GOLD

■ XTREE

F1	Quit XTree (see QUIT).
F2	Help (see HELP).
F3	Cancel (see CANCEL).
F4	Makes the Directory and File Commands disappear from the bottom of the screen. Fun! Try it (see DIRECTORY).
F5	Keep Filespec. Normally, if you log another drive, the filespec defaults back to *.*. If you set a filespec, then hit **F5**, then log another drive, the filespec will not default back to *.*. This is useful when hunting through several disks for a file (see FILESPEC and FIND).
F10	**ALT** lock. An alternative to holding down the **ALT** key. Hitting and releasing **F10** leaves you in the ALT menu. You may peruse the ALT menu without the physical exertion of holding down the **ALT** key.

■ XTREEPRO

F1	Help (*see* HELP).
F2	Destination Directory Window. When in COPY or MOVE mode, pressing **F2** pops up the Destination Window, allowing you to merely *point* to where you want to copy or move your files to (see COPY and MOVE).
F9	**CTRL** lock. An alternative to holding down the **CTRL** key. Hitting and releasing **F9** leaves you in the CTRL menu. You may peruse the CTRL menu without the physical exertion of holding down the ALT key.
F10	**ALT** lock. An alternative to holding down the **ALT** key. Hitting and releasing **F10** leaves you in the ALT menu. You may peruse the ALT menu without the physical exertion of holding down the **ALT** key.

■ XTREEPRO GOLD

XTree PRO GOLD

F1	Help (see HELP).
F2	Destination Directory Window. When in COPY MOVE or GRAFT mode, pressing **F2** pops up the Destination Window, allowing you to merely *point* to where you want to copy or move your files to (see COPY and MOVE).
F2	Screen Update. When in CTRL/Showall, hitting **F2** redisplays the screen, eliminating those items which have been untagged since CTRL/Showall was invoked (see SHOWALL).
<ALT>F2	Formats a floppy disk (see FORMAT).
F3	When entering text, displays last response.
<ALT>F3	Re-logs the current directory (see LOG).
F4	Menu toggle. Cycles through the standard CTRL and ALT menus. Hit **F4** once and the CTRL menu will be displayed. Hit it again, and the ALT menu will be displayed. Hit it again and you'll cycle back to the standard Menu.
F5	Collapses or expands directories two levels below the current directory (see DIRECTORY).
<ALT>F5	Opens an arc file (see "XTree In Action").
<CTRL>F5	Archives tagged files (see "XTree In Action").
F6	Collapses or expands directories below the current directory (see DIRECTORY).
<CTRL>F6	Merges tags between two file windows (see SPLIT/UNSPLIT).
F7	Autoview. Can see the contents of a file (*see* VIEW).
F8	Splits/unsplits the display into two directories (see SPLIT/UNSPLIT).
<ALT>F8	Untags all tagged files that have been operated on (see TAG/UNTAG).
<CTRL>F8	Same as **<ALT>F8**.

XTree PRO GOLD

```
Path: B:\                                        7-12-90 11:02:46 am

COMM     .DRV    COMMMODI.DTX    CONFIG  .DBK    FILE *.*
COMMAND  .COM    COMMMODI.DTX    CONFIG  .DOC
COMMAND  .COM    COMMOPT .DTX    CONFIG  .DUM    DISK  C:POWER USER
COMMAND  .COM    COMMOPT .DTX    CONFIG  .EG     Available
COMMAND  .XUP    COMMSYS .DTX    CONFIG  .IMP    Bytes   3,731,456
COMMANDS.DTX     COMMSYS .DTX    CONFIG  .NOW
COMMANDS.DTX     COMMUNI .DOC    CONFIG  .OLD    GLOBAL Statistics
COMMCMD1.DTX     COMPANY_.CAL    CONFIG  .OLD    Total
COMMCMD1.DTX     COMPLOT .DOC    CONFIG  .STD    Files        3,886
COMMCMD2.DTX     COMPUTER.INF    CONFIG  .SYS    Bytes   87,960,715
COMMCMD2.DTX     COMTOEXE.DOC    CONFIG  .SYS    Matching
COMMDEFN.DTX     COMTOEXE.EXE    CONFIG  .SYS    Files        3,886
COMMDEFN.DTX     CONFID  .DES    CONFIG  .SYS    Bytes   87,960,715
COMMENT  .DOC    CONFID  .PCX    CONFIG  .SYS    Tagged
COMMENT  .TXT    CONFIG  .       CONFIG  .UNI    Files            0
COMMENTS.SSF     CONFIG  .       CONFIG  .WIN    Bytes            0
COMMFILE.DTX     CONFIG  .828    CONFIGTS.EXE    Current File
COMMFILE.DTX     CONFIG  .BAK    CONGOLD2.PIX    CONFIG  .SYS
COMMITTE.DOC     CONFIG  .CAH    CONGRESS.TXT    Bytes           34

FILE     Attributes Copy Delete  Edit Filespec Invert Log disk New date
COMMANDS Open  Print Rename Tag Untag View eXecute Quit
←┘ tree F7 autoview F8 split   F9 menu F10 commands   F1 help  ESC cancel
```

Screen 3-73

F9   Pops up the Application Menu (see APPLICATION MENU).
<ALT>F9 Toggles between the 25-line and 51-line modes for EGA and VGA systems (see CONFIGURATION).
F10   Pops up the Quick Reference Help Window (see HELP).
<ALT>F10 Starts the configuration program (see CONFIGURATION).

GLOBAL

See FILE DISPLAY and SORT CRITERIA.

Global lets you display and operate on files from more than one disk drive (actually, up to twenty-six). Think of Global as a Showall for several drives. In Global mode, all the files on the currently logged disks are displayed in alphabetical order. (If you prefer the files to be sorted and displayed by size or date, you can change the sort criteria to accommodate your desires. Just type **<ALT>S**. (See SORT CRITERIA for details.)

Since Global needs at least two drives to be logged to work, let's log another drive (like drive A) in addition to the currently logged drive. To log drive A, type **L** and a drive letter. Now this second drive and the previously logged one are both in memory.

XTree PRO GOLD

Once you've logged two or more drives, go to the directory Window and type **G** for Global, and *bingo!* All the files from all the logged drives are displayed in alphabetical order.

In Screen 3-73, although the current drive is C, the file highlighted (CONFIG.SYS) is actually in the root of the B drive.

You can hit **G** to invoke Global from any of the logged drives. You can also can enter a filespec before or after you hit **G** (like *.WK1 to see all the WK1 files on all the logged drives to check for duplicates).

Once you're in Global mode, you can perform any normal sort of function you want (delete, copy, etc.).

Another variation of the Global command is invoked with **<CTRL>G** which displays only those *tagged* files on all drives. This allows you to tag some files on each of the drives, *then* hit **<CTRL>G** to see those files "side by side." Now you can compare the size or date and time, or copy, or delete, or whatever.

See DIRECTORY.

GRAFT

Graft lets you move one directory (and its files and subdi-rectories) to a new location on the directory tree.

HELP

Each version of XTree offers some form of online help. This means that while you are using XTree, you can hit a function key and up will pop some help with what you're doing. When you've finished using Help, you'll be put back exactly where you were (though, hopefully, wiser) before you invoked Help.

XTree PRO GOLD

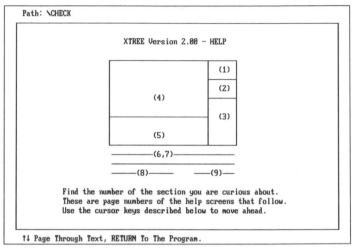

Screen 3-74

■ XTREE. **F2** is the Help key in XTree. When you hit
F2 you see something like Screen 3-74.

This is sort of a table of contents for XTree's help. Pressing
the up or down arrow key will page you through the Help
text. If you have a question about the command line, you
can tell from the "table of contents" screen that you'll find
that information on pages 6 through 9. Just press the down
arrow key until you get to page 6, and start reading. Once
you're finished with Help, press **<ENTER>** to return to the
program — exactly where you were before you hit **F2**.

■ XTREEPRO. **F1** is the Help key in XTreePro. When
you hit **F1** you'll see something like Screen 3-75.

From this screen, you can choose from a dizzying array of
topics. In the example above, the cursor is on "Next Page"
so hitting **<ENTER>**, would get you to the next screenful of
alphabetical information.

Alternatively, the up arrow would highlight "Window
Control Keys." Or you could highlight any other subject
you're interested in learning more about.

Once you've highlighted your selection, hitting **<ENTER>**
will transport you to a screen of information on *that* particular topic.

Another approach is to cursor on over to "Index" (or save

```
┌──────────────────────────────────────────────────────────┐   XTree PRO GOLD
│                    Window Displays                         │
│                                                            │
│  There are eight screen section on the XTreePro display which provide you
│  with information about your disks, directories and files. │
│                                                            │
│         ┌──────────────────┬─────────────────┐            │
│         │                  │  * FILES:        │            │
│         │ * Directory Window│─────────────────│            │
│         │                  │  * DISK:         │            │
│         │                  │─────────────────│            │
│         │                  │  * Statistics    │            │
│         │ * File Window    │                  │            │
│         └──────────────────┴─────────────────┘            │
│                                                            │
│       * Directory Commands   OR  * File Commands           │
│                                                            │
│       * Window Control Keys      * Function Keys           │
│                                                            │
│  Using Help: Use the TAB or ARROW keys to move the highlight bar to the
│  section about which you want more information and press ENTER.  Select
│  Next Page for a step-by-step tutorial.  Or, select Index to choose from a
│  table of help sections or for more information about how to use Help.
│                                                            │
│  ▐Next Page▌  Last Page   Directory Commands   File Commands   Index
│  ┌─────────────────────────────────────────────────────┐
│  ←↑↓→ - move cursor        ENTER - select        ESC - to XTreePro
└──────────────────────────────────────────────────────────┘
```

Screen 3-75

keystrokes by just typing **I**) and hit **<ENTER>** to get the
Index (Screen 3-76).

Just like before, cursor over to the topic you want help
with, and hit **<ENTER>**. (In this case, pressing the first letter
won't work.)

Another nice feature about Help is that if you happen to
be in the middle of an operation (copying a file, say) when
you hit **F2**, Pro will assume you have a question about

```
┌──────────────────────────────────────────────────────────┐
│                                                            │
│         Index - Table of XTreePro Help Sections            │
│                                                            │
│                                                            │
│           ▐* Directory and File Windows▌                   │
│            * Information Windows                            │
│            * Destination Directory Window                  │
│            * Function Keys                                  │
│            * Editing Keys                                   │
│            * Directory Commands                            │
│            * File Commands                                 │
│            * Command Shell                                 │
│            * Command Line Switches                         │
│                                                            │
│            * Tutorial                                      │
│            * How To Use XTreePro Help                      │
│            * Technical Support Information                 │
│                                                            │
│                                                            │
│  ┌─────────────────────────────────────────────────────┐
│  ↑↓ - move cursor          ENTER - select        ESC - to XTreePro
└──────────────────────────────────────────────────────────┘
```

Screen 3-76

XTree PRO GOLD

```
                              Main Display

There are eight screen sections on the main XTree Gold display which provide
you with information about your disks, directories and files.


        ┌──────────────────────────┬─────────────────────┐
        │   Directory Window       │  FILES:             │
        │                          ├─────────────────────┤
        │                          │  DISK:              │
        │                          ├─────────────────────┤
        │                          │  Statistics         │
        │   File Window            │                     │
        └──────────────────────────┴─────────────────────┘

        Directory Commands     OR     File Commands

        Window Control Keys           Function Keys

Using Help: Use the TAB or ARROW keys to move the highlight bar to the
section about which you want more information and press ENTER. Select
Next Page for a step-by-step tutorial. Or, select Index to choose from a
table of help sections or for more information about how to use Help.

 ▌Next Page▐   Last Page    Directory Commands    File Commands    Index

 ←↑↓→ - move cursor          ENTER - select          ESC - exit Help
```

Screen 3-77

copying (because that's what you were doing) and jump you straight to the section on copying. This is called context-sensitive help — which is time-saving.

■ XTREEPRO GOLD. **F1** is the Help key in XTreePro Gold (same as Pro). When you hit **F1** you'll see something like Screen 3-77.

From this screen, you can choose from a dizzying array of topics. In the example above, the cursor is on "Next Page," so hitting **<ENTER>**, would get you to the next screenful of alphabetical information.

Alternatively, the up arrow would highlight "Window Control Keys." Or you could highlight any other subject you're interested in learning more about. Once you've highlighted your selection, hitting **<ENTER>** will transport you to a screen of information on *that* particular topic.

Another approach is to cursor on over to "Index" (or save keystrokes by just typing **I**) and hit **<ENTER>** to get the Index (Screen 3-78).

Just like before, cursor over to the topic you want help with, and hit **<ENTER>**. (In this case, pressing the first letter won't work.)

Another nice feature about Help is that if you happen to be in the middle of an operation (copying a file, say) when

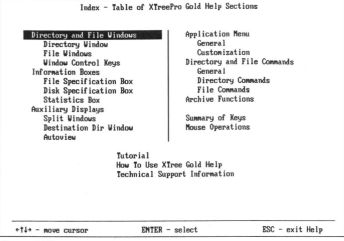

Screen 3-78

you hit **F1**, Gold will assume you have a question about copying (because that's what you were doing) and jump you straight to the section on copying. This is called context-sensitive help — which is time-saving.

■ *Quick reference*

Gold has the added feature (and pleasure) of the Quick Reference screen. Hitting **F10** while in the Directory

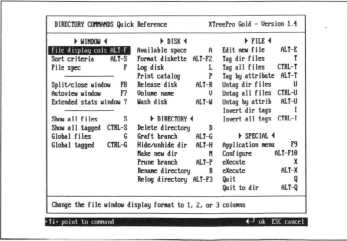

Screen 3-79

XTree PRO GOLD

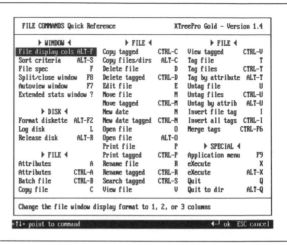

Screen 3-80

Window will net you the helpful Screen 3-79.

Hitting **F10** while in one of the File windows will get you Screen 3-80.

In either screen, a quick explanation of whatever command is highlighted will be displayed at the bottom of the screen. In the above example, for instance, **<ALT>F** will "Change the File Window display format..." **<ESC>** will get you back to where you were in Gold before you hit **F10**.

HIDE/ UNHIDE

See DIRECTORY, FILE, and SECURITY.

HISTORY

Whenever you type an answer to a Gold prompt, your response is saved in what's called a "history file." Gold maintains separate histories for the command shell, filespec, and many other different operations. You'll see the word "history" at the bottom of the screen as a reminder to use this *great* resource.

XTree PRO GOLD

Let's see how this works.

If you hit **F** for filespec (just as an example) and Gold asks for the "File Specification" you want, whatever you type in

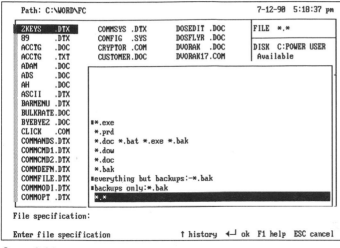

Screen 3-81

is not only used by Gold at that time, but is also saved for future reference.

The next time you hit **F** for filespec and you're asked for a "File Specification," you have the option of hitting the up (or down) arrow key to reveal your past responses.

In Screen 3-81, there are nine history entries in the history screen (you can have up to thirteen). If you wanted to use *.exe, you could continue cursoring up until you got to that entry, then hit **<ENTER>**.

Gold automatically types *.exe for you at the "file specification" command line and the history screen disappears.

At this point you can either hit **<ENTER>** to have Gold carry out the command, or you can edit the command line entry. (e.g. If what you *really* wanted was **s*.exe**, you could just cursor over to the beginning of the line and add the "**s**").

When the command is perfect, hit **<ENTER>** and Gold will carry out your command.

Hint: If the highlight is at the top and you want the bottom entry, hitting the up arrow is a quick way to get to that entry. The cursor keys "wrap" from the top to the bottom and vice versa.

The advantage of using history is that it eliminates typos and brain-strain from trying to remember what that command was you used *last* time.

XTree PRO GOLD   And, the contents of your History file is saved from day to day. Your History file stays no matter how many times you start and quit Gold. A command used a week ago could very well still be saved in the History file. Remember, only the last thirteen responses are saved. The oldest responses make way for new responses after the limit is reached.

Which segues nicely into the topic of:

■ Permanent history

You can *save* your favorite responses — the ones you use all the time — so they'll never get the heave-ho. Gold calls these saved responses *permanent entries.*

You can make any entry permanent by highlighting the entry and hitting **<INSERT>**. When you do this, a little square appears to the left of the item.

In Screen 3-81, the item at the top of the list (***.exe**) is a permanent entry.

You can make your permanent entries temporary again by highlighting them and hitting **<INSERT>** again.

■ Labels

You can also *name* your history entries with *labels*. In the above example, there are two entries with labels, "everything but backups" and "backups only." This way you can use English (remember *that?*) with your entries. (You can also set things up to be simpler for others to use.)

To make a label, your cursor must be in the command line. You can type anything you want as long as it's followed by a colon (:). After the colon must come the actual response. For example:

         documents only:*.doc

Once you hit **<ENTER>** your command line entry will go to the History file for use later on (be sure to make it permanent).

Hint: Although we've used filespec as the example here, history files are maintained on most Gold commands (including the command shell, copy, edit, date, print, and execute to name just a few).

See TAG/UNTAG.

INVERT

Invert is the Gold command that allows you to reverse current filespecs or tags.

More and more people have two computers: a desktop and a laptop. Doubtless this is a practice all computer manufacturers encourage.

LAPTOP CONFIGURA- TION

However, a lot of laptops have less storage and less memory than their desktop sisters (or brothers).

Of course you'll want to have XTree on your "to-go" computer, but with space at a premium, you may feel as though you have to leave XTree at home.

But maybe not!

You may have noticed that the XTrees are composed of a number of modules. You can actually run the program without all the modules. So if you need to conserve disk space, here's what you can leave at home, and how you can run XTree in memory-lean mode. (See Laptop Configuration in Part 5, page 217 for the same info on XTreeGold and XTree Easy.)

■ Disk space

XTree PRO GOLD

XTREE
REQUIRED:

XTREE.EXE	(43K)

OPTIONAL:

XTREEINS.EXE	(43K) The configuration program. Once you have configured your program, you no longer need it.
XTREEINS.DAT	(21K) This is an information file for XTREEINS.EXE Once you've configured your system, you no longer need it.
READ.ME	(13K) This is a file that contains stuff that didn't make it to the manual. After you've read it or printed it out, you may delete it.

XTree PRO GOLD

XTREEPRO

REQUIRED:

XTPRO.COM   (48K)

OPTIONAL:

README.DOC   (11K)   This is a file that contains stuff that didn't make it to the manual. After you've read it or printed it out, you may delete it.

XTPROCFG.EXE   (22K)   The configuration program. Once you've configured your program, you no longer need it.

XTPRO.X01   (25K)   If you want to use 1Word, you'll need this file. Otherwise, you can do without it.

XTPRO.X02   (4K)   This, and the following files, compose Pro's Help system. If you can do without Help, you can do without these files.

XTPRO.X10   (15K)   Part of the Help system.
XTPRO.X20   (15K)   Part of the Help system.
XTPRO.X30   (13K)   Part of the Help system.
XTPRO.X40   (14K)   Part of the Help system.
XTPRO.X50   (14K)   Part of the Help system.
XTPRO.PIF   (.3K)   Allows Pro to work with Microsoft Windows version 2.XX.

Naturally, Gold comes with the most files. You only really need three.

XTREEPRO GOLD

REQUIRED:

XTG.EXE   (70K)
XTGOLD.COM   (1K)
XTGOLD.CFG

OPTIONAL:

XTG_CFG.EXE   (38K)   The configuration program. Once you have configured your program, you no longer need it.

XTG_HELP.XTP   (6K)   Part of the Help system. IF

you don't need Help, you can   XTree PRO GOLD
live without this.

XTG_HELP.X10	(15K)	Part of the Help system.
XTG_HELP.X20	(14K)	Part of the Help system.
XTG_HELP.X30	(14K)	Part of the Help system.
XTG_HELP.X40	(14K)	Part of the Help system.
XTG_HELP.X50	(14K)	Part of the Help system.
XTG_HELP.X60	(14K)	Part of the Help system.
XTG_HELP.X70	(14K)	Part of the Help system.
XTG_HELP.X80	(14K)	Part of the Help system.
XTG_HELP.X90	(8K)	Part of the Help system.

The following files control various features and functions. If
you don't need the feature or
function, you can delete the
file:

XTG_ARC1.XTP	(33K)	Archive Manager com pression module.
XTG_ARC2.XTP	(43K)	Archive Manager open module.
XTG_EDIT.XTP	(25K)	Internal text editor.
XTG_FIND.XTP	(7K)	Search file module (CTRL/S).
XTG_FORM.XTP	(11K)	Format diskette module (ALT/F2).
XTG_HEXX.XTP	(15K)	View Hex editor module.
XTG_MENU.BIN	(17K)	Application Menu module (F9).
XTG_MENU.XTP	(19K)	Application Menu module (F9).
XTG_MOVE.XTP	(5K)	Graft module (ALT/G).
XTG_QREF.XTP	(11K)	Quick Reference module (F10).
XTG_VIEW.XTP	(28K)	View file module.
XTG_WASH.XTP	(7K)	Wash disk module (ALT/W).
XTG_WBAT.XTP	(8K)	Write batch file module (CTRL/B).

The following files help the View system work. Select the

XTree PRO GOLD

modules for the types of files you will be viewing. Delete the ones you don't need.

XTG_VWKS.XTP	(64K)	View 1-2-3 file module.
XTG_VDBF.XTP	(53K)	View dBase file module.
XTG_VDET.XTP	(9K)	Word processor auto file type detect.
XTG_V_TO.XTP	(31K)	Word processor conversion utility (for all formats).
XTG_V_MW.XTP	(31K)	View Microsoft Word file module.
XTG_V_MM.XTP	(27K)	View Multimate file module.
XTG_V_LM.XTP	(56K)	View Lotus Manuscript file module.
XTG_VWP4.XTP	(23K)	View WordPerfect 4 file module.
XTG_VWP5.XTP	(27K)	View WordPerfect 5 file module.
XTG_V_DC.XTP	(30K)	View DCA file module.
XTG_V_WS.XTP	(35K)	View WordStar file module.

The following files are needed if you want to use the Open and associate (see EXECUTE) command to start BAT, COM, and EXE files. (However, they are so small in size that they will not impact one way or the other on your system.)

BAT.BAT	Association batch file for .BAT files.
COM.BAT	Association batch file for .COM files.
EXE.BAT	Association batch file for .EXE files.

Additional miscellaneous files:

README.DOC	(19K)	Addendum to the manual.
XTGOLD.HST		History file. (A new one is created as you use the program.)
XTGOLD.PIF		Required to run Gold under Windows (very small file). Call XTree Tech Support for the latest info on PIF files for Windows 3.0.

■ Memory

■ XTREEPRO. You can reduce the amount of memory needed to run Pro by reducing the File/Directory limit (*see* CONFIGURATION). Also, if you execute a program from within Pro, be sure to use the **<ALT>X** version of the command so that Pro will release the maximum amount of memory to the program you're executing.

■ XTREEPRO GOLD. Gold promises to get itself down to what's called a "7K Wedge." But you have to follow three rules to make that happen.

1. Make sure the program is configured properly. Specifically, on page 3 of the configuration program, set the "memory utilization" option to "All Memory."
2. When you invoke Gold, do so by typing **xtgold** **<ENTER>** (rather than **xtg** **<ENTER>**) which will allow Gold to collapse to its smallest size.
3. Instead of using **X** (or **O**) to execute a program, use **<ALT>X** (or **<ALT>O**) or use the Application Menu (**F9**). This will allow Gold to release the maximum amount of memory to the program you're executing.

Happy camping!

When you call up XTree, the first thing it does is log the current disk. That is, it counts the number of files and directories and displays them on the screen. (The larger the disk and the number of files, the longer it takes to log.) XTree must log a disk before it can act upon it in any way.

LOG

What other disks might you want to log? Well, a floppy disk perhaps, or your other hard disks (D or E, if you have them). All drives must be logged *before* XTree can act upon either the files or the directories they contain.

The original XTree can log only one disk at a time.

Pro and Gold, however, can take a "snapshot" of each new disk logged and add it to its album. This way you can cycle through all (up to twenty-six) the logged disks instantly.

(If you own XTreeGold, see also Log in Part 5 for some useful enhancements, especially for those with big drives.)

However, keep in mind that every time you log a drive and ask Pro or Gold to remember that information — it eats up computer memory. You may run out of memory before you run out of drives.

Some of the logging commands below will keep previously logged disks in memory, and some release (or discard) previously logged disks in favor of new ones.

XTree PRO GOLD

Hitting **L** for Log (while in the Directory or File Windows) prompts XTree to ask you which disk you want to log. You type in the drive letter, tap **<ENTER>** and *boom*, you're logged on to that drive. Want to come back to C? Hit **L C <ENTER>**. XTree will re-log the disk every time you switch to it with the Log command.

In Pro and Gold, you can switch to *previously* logged disks without using the **L** command. You can go between all your logged drives (without re-logging them) with the **+** or **-** key. (Since you're not re-logging the drives, viewing disks with the **+** or **-** may not be entirely accurate especially if you've deleted or copied files in the command shell since the last log.)

<ALT>L logs a new disk and releases the currently logged disks from memory. If you have three disks logged, this will remove all three from memory and log the new one. Once a disk is released from memory, you cannot go back to it with the **+** or **-** until you log it again.

You can also log a disk when you are about to copy a file. Using the Destination Window **(F2)** you may log a new disk (or switch to an already logged disk) and travel up and down its tree to select a suitable destination for your file-to-be-copied.

■ XTREEPRO GOLD. Gold also has the **<CTRL>L** command which is exactly like the **+** or the **-**.

In Gold, **<ALT>F3** allows you to re-log the current directory. So if you've made some changes in a directory, you don't have to re-log the whole drive, just the one directory. (Though it's not always listed, **<ALT>F3** is available from all windows.)

■ *Instant log*

Instant log allows you to bypass the logging process alto-
gether. It requires some planning ahead, though. To use the
"instant log," you have to quit the program using **<ALT>Z**.
This takes a snapshot of your current tagged files, window
status, everything. When you get into Gold again, the
program will use the "snapshot" instead of logging.

Naturally, if you delete some files before returning to
Gold, the instant log will not be accurate. (It reflects the
condition of your drive *when you quit*.)

MEMORY

One thing people run out of on a computer quicker than
anything (besides patience) is memory. If you're trying to
use XTree as your "command central," you may run into
insufficient memory error messages.

First of all, make sure your computer's CONFIG.SYS is
properly set up (see Part 4, "Hard Disk Management in a
Nutshell").

■ XTREEPRO. You can reduce the amount of memory
needed to run Pro by reducing the File/Directory limit (see
CONFIGURATION).

Also, when you execute a program from within Pro, be
sure to use the **<ALT>X** version of the command so that Pro
will release the maximum amount of memory to the
program you're executing.

■ XTREEPRO GOLD. Gold promises to get itself down
to what is called a "7K Wedge." But, you have to follow
three rules to make that happen.

1. Make sure the program is configured properly.
    Specifically, on page 3 of the configuration program is
    the "memory utilization" option to "All Memory."
2. When invoking Gold, do so by typing **xtgold**
    <ENTER> (rather than **xtg <ENTER>**) which allows
    Gold to collapse to its smallest size.
3. Instead of using **X** (or **O**) to execute a program, use
    <ALT>X (or **<ALT>O**) or use the Application Menu
    (**F9**). This will allow Gold to release the maximum
    amount of memory to the program you're executing.

MOUSE COMMAND

XTree PRO GOLD

Although the original XTree made its debut when most mice were still lab animals (computer research lab "animals," of course), XTreePro Gold seamlessly integrates mouse technology for "mousers" who prefer to consolidate commands down to a Morse code-like series of clicks and double-clicks. (If you've got a three-button mouse, Gold will ignore the middle button.)

Note: Gold does not come with a "mouse driver." (A mouse driver is software that tells your computer that you have connected a mouse.) Before you can use a mouse with Gold, you must have it properly installed with the mouse driver software that came with your mouse. (The bottom line is that if you can use your mouse in other programs, you'll be able to use it in Gold.)

This section is not going to contain any illustrations because showing how to delete a file with a *mouse* looks pretty much like deleting a file with the keyboard. In short, mouse commands don't do anything more than keyboard commands. It's a matter of convenience or preference.

■ Command line

To use the mouse to execute the commands at the bottom of the screen, you just point to a command and click (either the left or right button).

If you click a command that's associated with a history file, the history will automatically be displayed. If you want to use a history entry, just double-click the appropriate item.

If you don't want to use a history item, you must enter a response the old-fashioned way — via the keyboard. However, once your entry is correct, click "**ok**."

To cancel a command: click on **<ESC>**.

If you want to go to the ALT Menu, click on the word "**ALT**." If you want to log a disk, click on the word "**log**." To see the "File Commands," just click on the words. In short, you can activate just about any command by clicking on it.

■ Directory window

Scrolling through the directory tree involves using the left-hand border of Gold's screen. The border is called the *scroll bar* and works like scroll bars in any software that uses a mouse. To travel up or down the directory tree with the scroll bar, position the mouse cursor on the scroll bar, hold down the left button, and slide the mouse up or down. You can scroll in "chunks" (like **<Pg Up>** and **<Pg Dn>**) by moving the mouse cursor up or down the scroll bar and *then* clicking.

Once you arrive at a directory you wish to work with, you have several mouse options.

Place the mouse cursor on a *directory name* and:
Click Left to make it the current directory.
Click Right to tag/untag all files in the directory.
Double-Click Left to jump to the Expanded File Window.

XTree PRO GOLD

■ File window

Scrolling through the File Window is just like scrolling through the Directory Window. Just belly up to the scroll bar.

Once you arrive at a file that you wish to work with, you have several options.

Place the mouse cursor on a *file name* and:
Click Left to make a file the current file.
Click Right to tag/untag the file (holding down the right mouse button and sliding the mouse up or down will continue to tag/untag files).
Double-Click Left opens a file (see OPEN AND ASSOCIATE).
Double-Click Right puts the file in View (see VIEW).

Move is used to transport a file from one directory to another on the same disk. You cannot use Move to put a file on another disk. (That's why Move is not available from the Global Window.) Move only works within one disk. (Sorry, gang, that's just the way DOS works.)

To move a file to another disk, copy it first and then delete the original.

To move a file, first highlight it. Then hit **M** for Move. If the destination directory already has a file with the same name, you'll be asked if you wish to delete the file that was there first.

You can also tag a bunch of files and type **<CTRL>M** to move all tagged files. (Again, you'll be asked if you want to

MOVE

XTree PRO GOLD

XTree PRO GOLD

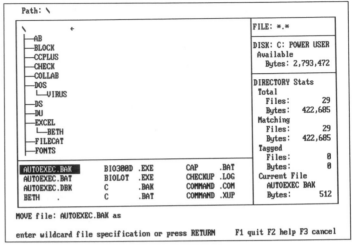

Screen 3-82

replace files in the destination directory with the files you're moving.)

XTreePro Gold also lets you move a whole directory.

To move a single file, highlight the file and hit **M** for Move. XTree then wants to know what to move the file as (Screen 3-82).

This question (which you'll see every time you want to move something) means "Do you want to rename the file

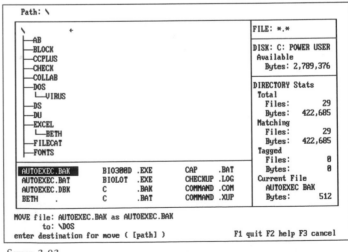

Screen 3-83

when you move it?" If you don't want to change the name, hit **<ENTER>** and the file name will remain the same. If you do want to rename the file as you move it, type in the new name and then hit **<ENTER>**. This is how you can keep different versions of the same file.

Once that is settled, you'll be asked for a destination (*where* do you want to move it to?).

In this case, let's move it to the DOS directory (Screen 3-83).

After we type in **\DOS** and hit **<ENTER>**, the file will be moved to the DOS directory.

Unless. . .there's another file there already with the same name.

■ XTREE. XTree handles the situation by asking if you want to replace the existing file, as shown in Screen 3-84. (Choose **Y** to replace the file, **N** not to replace it, or **<ESC>** to cancel.)

■ XTREEPRO. When Pro and Gold ask if you wish to replace the existing file, they display the file's stats so you can compare date, time, size, and attributes to make an *informed* decision (Screen 3-85). If one file is newer or bigger, *that* may be the version you want to keep (although

XTree PRO GOLD

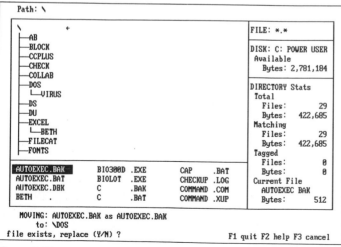

```
Path: \

\              ←                        FILE: *.*
 ├─AB
 ├─BLOCK                                DISK: C: POWER USER
 ├─CCPLUS                               Available
 ├─CHECK                                Bytes: 2,781,184
 ├─COLLAB
 ├─DOS                                  DIRECTORY Stats
 │  └─VIRUS                             Total
 ├─DS                                     Files:          29
 ├─DU                                     Bytes:     422,685
 ├─EXCEL                                Matching
 │  └─BETH                                Files:          29
 ├─FILECAT                                Bytes:     422,685
 ├─FONTS                                Tagged
                                          Files:           0
 AUTOEXEC.BAK   BIO300D .EXE   CAP    .BAT   Bytes:        0
 AUTOEXEC.BAT   BIOLOT  .EXE   CHECKUP .LOG  Current File
 AUTOEXEC.DBK   C       .BAK   COMMAND .COM    AUTOEXEC BAK
 BETH  .        C       .BAT   COMMAND .XUP    Bytes:      512

 MOVING: AUTOEXEC.BAK as AUTOEXEC.BAK
    to: \DOS
 file exists, replace (Y/N) ?              F1 quit F2 help F3 cancel
```

Screen 3-84

XTree PRO GOLD

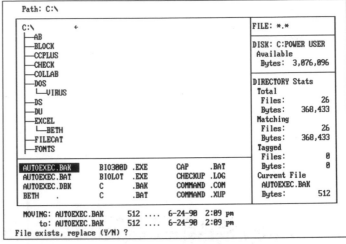

Screen 3-85

not always). In any case, hitting **Y** will continue the moving process and hitting **N** will stop it.

Pro makes it easier for you by adding the **F2** "Destination Window" option. This is a very useful feature.

After highlighting the file to be moved, type **M**, then hit **<ENTER>** to let the file keep the same file name, and you are ready to specify the file's destination. Now you can hit **F2** and the "Destination Window" pops up over what you're doing (Screen 3-86).

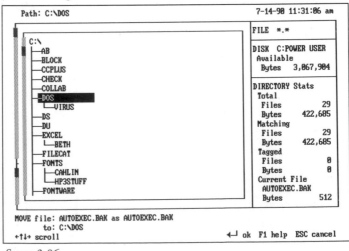

Screen 3-86

```
 Path: C:\                                    6-30-90  3:38:45 pm

 AUTOEXEC.BAK    IBMBIO  .XUP           FILE  *.*
 AUTOEXEC.BAT    ibmdos  .com
 AUTOEXEC.DBK    IBMDOS  .XUP           DISK  C:POWER USER
 BIO300D  .EXE   IMAGE   .BAK           Available
 BIOLOT   .EXE   IMA                    Bytes    2,080,768
 C        .BAT   ima
 CAP      .BAT   LOG                    DIRECTORY Stats
 CEMM     .COM   OLD                    Total
 CEMM     .EXE   PIX                      Files          35
 CHECKUP  .LOG   PR    BOMBOOK           Bytes      510,929
 COMMAND  .COM   SPI   BOMBOOK.DOC       Matching
 COMMAND  .XUP   THU   MWHELP.ORI          Files          35
 CONFIG   .BAK   TME   CAHLIN.DOC         Bytes      510,929
 CONFIG   .DBK   TO    *.BAK             Tagged
 CONFIG   .OLD   VTE   TOTAL90.WK1         Files           0
 CONFIG   .SYS   VTE   T                   Bytes           0
 CONFIG   .WRD         TOTAL9.WK1        Current File
 HIMEM    .SYS         PATCH.WS3         AUTOEXEC.BAK
 ibmbio   .com         *.*               Bytes         477


 MOVE file: AUTOEXEC.BAK as

 Enter file spec or strike enter        ↑ history  ◄┘ ok  F1 help  ESC cancel
```

Screen 3-87

Highlight the destination directory, then hit **<ENTER>**. That pesky path statement will be automatically typed in for you. Hit **<ENTER>** and (barring any file name conflicts) the file will be moved.

■ XTREEPRO GOLD. In Gold you can also use the History command, as shown in Screen 3-87 (which remembers your last choices).

After highlighting the file to be moved, type **M** to move. When you're asked "Move file as," you can hit the up (or down) arrow key to see your last thirteen choices. (Though an **<ENTER>** is all you need to let the file keep the same file name.)

Next, you'll be asked where you want to "Move file to." Again, you can press the up (or down) arrow key to display a history of your last thirteen destinations. Highlight one, press **<ENTER>** to put it on the command line (edit it if necessary), and press **<ENTER>** to let 'er rip.

■ Move more than one file

To move more than one file, it's just a matter of tagging the files to be moved, hitting **<CTRL>M** to move all tagged files, and following the same procedures as detailed above.

If you haven't looked at TAG/UNTAG and FILESPEC yet, now's a good time. It's easy to tag a whole disk,

XTree PRO GOLD

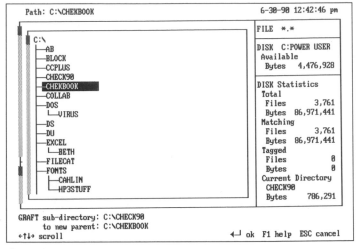

Screen 3-88

directory, portions of a directory, etc. for moving (or deleting, or whatever), and it's all spelled out in these two sections.

■ Move a directory on the tree (Graft)

Gold allows you to *Graft* a directory. This means you can take a directory (and its contents) and attach it to another directory on the tree. Here's how:

Highlight the directory to be moved and hit **<ALT>G** for Graft (Screen 3-88).

At the bottom of the screen you're asked *where* you want to move your directory to, and you're given the Destination Window so you can highlight the directory you want to move to.

In this case, we're moving the directory CHECK90 so that it will appear under the directory CHEKBOOK. When you're ready, press **<ENTER>**.

As a precaution, you'll be asked one more time if you're sure you want to do this. Just hit **Y** if you are and Gold will carry out the command.

After you graft a directory, you will have to re-log the drive (hit **L** for log) for the grafted directory to appear in alphabetical order on the tree.

Note: If you receive a "Can't Update Parent Directory" error message, you have an older version of Gold that

```
┌─────────────────────────────────────────────────────────┐   XTree PRO GOLD
│ Path: \CHECK                                              │
│ ┌──────────────────────────────┐ ┌─────────────────────┐│
│ │ \                            │ │ FILE: *.ABC         ││
│ │ ├─AB                         │ │                     ││
│ │ ├─ACCORD                     │ │ DISK: C: POWER USER ││
│ │ ├─BLOCK                      │ │ Available           ││
│ │ ├─CCPLUS                     │ │  Bytes: 3,522,560   ││
│ │ ├─CHECK                      │ │                     ││
│ │ ├─COLLAB                     │ │ DISK Statistics     ││
│ │ ├─DOS                        │ │ Total               ││
│ │ │  └─VIRUS                   │ │  Files:    2,438    ││
│ │ ├─DS                         │ │  Bytes:61,759,962   ││
│ │ ├─DU                         │ │ Matching            ││
│ │ ├─EXCEL                      │ │  Files:        0    ││
│ │ │  └─BETH                    │ │  Bytes:        0    ││
│ │ ├─FILECAT                    │ │ Tagged              ││
│ │ │                            │ │  Files:        0    ││
│ │   No Files!                  │ │  Bytes:        0    ││
│ │                              │ │ Current Directory   ││
│ │                              │ │  CHECK              ││
│ │                              │ │  Bytes:   796,701   ││
│ └──────────────────────────────┘ └─────────────────────┘│
│ DIR      Available Delete Filespec Log disk Makedir Print Rename│
│ COMMANDS ^Showall  ^Tag ^Untag Volume eXecute            │
│ ↑↓ scroll RETURN file commands  ALT menu      F1 quit F2 help│
└─────────────────────────────────────────────────────────┘
```

Screen 3-89

doesn't get along with your version of DOS. An upgrade is available to fix this. See page 285.

(See also Move in Part 5 for some new powers for XTreeGold.)

This is just another reminder that when you see "No Files!" don't have a heart attack. "No Files!" simply means that there are no files in the current directory that match the current filespec.

NO FILES!
XTree PRO GOLD

In Screen 3-89 we see a typical "No Files!" notice in the File Window. However, a glance at the File Specification Window (upper right-hand corner) reveals that we have asked XTree to display all files with an ABC extension. So in this case, the No Files! message is telling us that there are no files *with the ABC extension* in the CHECK directory.

You can prove to yourself that there are files in that directory in one of two ways:

1. Type **F** for filespec and then hit **<ENTER>** to reset the filespec to ***.*** (a/k/a "everything").
2. Or, you can take a quick peek at the bottom of the Disk Statistics Window, where it says "Current Directory." This reports that there are 796,701 bytes of files in the CHECK directory. Clearly there *are* files there. (Just none with the extension of ABC.)

XTree PRO GOLD

You can also get "No Files!" if you've got more files than XTree can count. XTree can log 2,500 files; XTreePro up to 16,000 (you may have to go into the configuration program to set the File/Directory limit); XTreePro Gold can log up to 13,000 (fewer than XTreePro because it's a bigger program that takes up more memory, and so has less space for logging files.) When you start up the program, you'll get an error message saying there are too many files and the extras will be ignored.

The average person on an average system won't run into capacity problems. However, if you start factoring in 100-megabyte hard drives and CD-ROMS, you may start to push the envelope.

(If you own XTreeGold or XTree Easy, you'll be happy to know this message now says "Dir Empty," "No Files Match," or "Dir Not Logged," depending. See Part 5.)

OPEN (AND ASSOCIATE)

See EXECUTE.

This is the Gold command that allows data files and program files to be linked (associated) by a batch file so that a program can be launched by opening a data file.

PRINT

Sure, print. But print *what?* Well... how about your directory names, your directory tree, or whatever files you've tagged? How about printing out a copy of your AUTOEXEC.BAT and CONFIG.SYS files for future reference? How about a list of those files you just copied to a floppy disk? Yep. That's what XTree can print. And, of course, more.

XTree PRO GOLD

If you are in the directory display hit **P** to Print.

You have the option of printing out a "catalog of tagged files," "pathnames," or a "tree" (Screen 3-90). Hitting the first letter of the thing you want, set the process in motion (provided, of course, your printer is turned on).

Another thing that XTree can do is print out a file. Generally it doesn't do well with files created by your word processor. (Oh, it'll try, but it'll probably come out a mess.) XTree can reliably print only simple ASCII files (see VIEW).

```
Path: \

\                                          FILE: *.*
 ├─AB
 ├─ACCORD                                   DISK: C: POWER USER
 ├─BLOCK                                    Available
 ├─CCPLUS                                     Bytes: 3,342,336
 ├─CHECK
 ├─COLLAB                                   DISK Statistics
 ├─DOS                                      Total
 │ └─VIRUS                                    Files:      2,438
 ├─DS                                         Bytes:61,822,515
 ├─DU                                       Matching
 ├─EXCEL                                      Files:      2,438
 │ └─BETH                                     Bytes:61,822,515
 ├─FILECAT                                  Tagged
                                             Files:          0
ANSI    .RTF     ASCII    .SCR     BETH   .   Bytes:          0
ANSI    .SCR     AUTOEXEC.BAK      BIO300D .EXE  Current Directory
ASCII   .DOC     AUTOEXEC.BAT      BIOLOT  .EXE  \
ASCII   .RTF     AUTOEXEC.DBK      C       .BAK  Bytes:    438,045


PRINT     Catalog of tagged files Pathnames Tree

enter print option                         F1 quit F2 help F3 cancel
```

Screen 3-90

Even so, believe it or not you do have some ASCII files
that you may want to print out. For instance, your
AUTOEXEC.BAT and CONFIG.SYS files are ASCII files.
To print a file, highlight the file to be printed and hit **P**.
Then you'll be prompted to "Press any key when the printer
is ready." (Alternatively, you can tag a bunch of files, then
hit **<CTRL>P** to print all tagged files.)

Also, whenever you get a new program, you're likely to
find a file named "READ.ME" (or README, or

```
Path: \DOS

BLANKS   .COM    DISKCOPY.COM     KEYB     .COM   FILE: *.*
CACHE    .EXE    DISKINIT.EXE     KEYBDP   .COM
CACHE    .SCR    DISPLAY .SYS     KEYBDP   .SCR   DISK: C: POWER USER
CAPSRLSE.COM     DOS33    .PAT    KEYBOARD.SYS     Available
CAPSRLSE.DOC     DOS33A   .PAT    KP       .COM      Bytes: 3,383,296
CEMM     .COM    DRIVER   .SYS    LABEL    .COM
CEMM     .EXE    EDLIN    .COM    LIST     .COM   DIRECTORY Stats
CEMMC    .SCR    ENHDISK  .SYS    MODE     .COM   Total
CEMME    .SCR    EXE2BIN  .EXE    MODE     .SCR     Files:         86
CHECKUP  .EXE    FASTOPEN.EXE     MORE     .COM     Bytes: 1,288,460
CHECKUP  .OLD    FDISK    .COM    MOUSE    .SYS   Matching
CHECKUP  .REG    FIND     .EXE    OC       .EXE     Files:         86
CHKDSK   .COM    GRAPHICS.COM     PRINT    .COM     Bytes: 1,288,460
COMMAND  .COM    GRAPHICS.SCR     READ     .ME    Tagged
CPANEL   .COM    HELP     .COM    README   .CPQ      Files:          0
DAB      .EXE    HIMEM    .SYS    RECOVER  .COM      Bytes:          0
DATECHEK.COM     HPDLBL   .EXE    REPLACE  .EXE   Current File
DAYCHEK  .BAT    INSTALL  .EXE    RESTORE  .COM     READ     ME
DEBUG    .COM    INSTALL  .SCR    ROMREV   .COM     Bytes:      1,987


PRESS ANY KEY WHEN THE PRINTER IS READY

                                           F1 quit F2 help F3 cancel
```

Screen 3-91

```
 Path: C:\DOS

 ┌─────────────────────────────────────────────────────┬─────────────────────┐
 │ CEMM    .EXE   EDLIN    .COM   LIST    .COM │ FILE: *.*           │
 │ CEMMC   .SCR   ENHDISK  .SYS   MODE    .COM │                     │
 │ CEMME   .SCR   EXE2BIN  .EXE   MODE    .SCR │ DISK: C:POWER USER  │
 │ CHECKUP .EXE   FASTOPEN .EXE   MORE    .COM │ Available           │
 │ CHECKUP .OLD   FDISK    .COM   MOUSE   .SYS │   Bytes:  3,325,952 │
 │ CHECKUP .REG   FIND     .EXE   OC      .EXE │                     │
 │ CHKDSK  .COM   GRAPHICS .COM   PRINT   .COM │ DIRECTORY Stats     │
 │ COMMAND .COM   GRAPHICS .SCR   [READ   .ME] │ Total               │
 │ CPANEL  .COM   HELP     .COM   README  .CPQ │   Files:         86 │
 │ DAB     .EXE   HIMEM    .SYS   RECOVER .COM │   Bytes: 1,288,460  │
 │ DATECHEK.COM   HPDLBL   .EXE   REPLACE .EXE │ Matching            │
 │ DAYCHEK .BAT   INSTALL  .EXE   RESTORE .COM │   Files:         86 │
 │ DEBUG   .COM   INSTALL  .SCR   ROMREV  .COM │   Bytes: 1,288,460  │
 │ DISKCOPY.COM   KEYB     .COM   ROMREV  .SCR │ Tagged              │
 │ DISKINIT.EXE   KEYBDP   .COM   SAVEDIR .COM │   Files:          0 │
 │ DISPLAY .SYS   KEYBDP   .SCR   SELECT  .COM │   Bytes:          0 │
 │ DOS33   .PAT   KEYBOARD .SYS   SETCLOCK.COM │ Current File        │
 │ DOS33A  .PAT   KP       .COM   SETUP   .EXE │ READ    .ME         │
 │ DRIVER  .SYS   LABEL    .COM   SETUP   .SCR │   Bytes:      1,987 │
 └─────────────────────────────────────────────────────┴─────────────────────┘

 Printing file: READ.ME: Number of lines per page: 55

 Enter new value, or 0 for no form feeds                    ESC cancel
```

Screen 3-92

README.1ST or some variation). READ.ME files are
generally ASCII files (unless it came with your word
processor) and they contain information and corrections
that didn't make it to the printed manual.

Even XTree came with a READ.ME file, so let's print it
out. In Screen 3-91, READ.ME is highlighted. Then
merely tap **P** to print.

In XTreePro, however, if you wanted to print out the
READ.ME file and followed the procedure above, you'd get
something like Screen 3-92 after typing **P**.

In this case, you have the option of specifying the page
length. In other words, you can "pretty up" your printout
with margins. If you don't care about top and bottom
margins, just put in a **0** (that's zero). Otherwise, experiment
to see what works for your printer. (Side note: laser printers
are *generally* set to a maximum of 62 lines a page.)

Once you find the page length of your dreams, you can go
into Pro or Gold's configuration and change the default
"Print Form Length" so that it'll always be the size you want
(see CONFIGURATION).

You can also print out a file using Pro and Gold using
1Word (the built-in text editor). To print a file, highlight

```
 ┌─────────────────────────────────Esc cancel─┐
 │ C:\DOS\READ.ME                 Size  1987  9:24:07 │
 │ Number of lines to print per page? 55       │
 │                                             │
 │                        ┌──────────────────────────┐
 │                        │      FILE COMMANDS        │
 │                        │                           │
 │                        │ Import another file  ^KR  │
 │         Quick Start    │ save As (new name)   ^KA  │
 │                        │ save and Edit        ^KD  │
 │                        │ save and eXit        ^KX  │
 │ The benefits of using TextCon may not be │→Print using PRN      ^KP  │
 │ apparent from reading the documentation.  Yo│ Quit without saving  ^KQ  │
 │ yourself a quick demonstration of its capabilit│ Save and continue    ^KS  │
 │ TEXTCON.DOC as a sample ASCII file.        │ Write marked block   ^KW  │
 │                        └──────────────────────────┘
 │ Start by loading the unmodified TEXTCON.DOC into your word │
 │ processor using the word processor's ASCII import command. │
 │ Browse through the document and you'll notice that it may │
 │ appear to be formatted correctly, but the "formatting" is │
 │ all created by use of hard returns and hard spaces. Try │
 │ editing parts of it and you'll quickly see the problems │
 │ caused by unwanted hard returns, extra blank spaces and │
 │ blank lines, and even headers and footers interspersed with │
 │ the text.                                   │
 └─────────────────────────────────────────────┘
```

XTree PRO GOLD

Screen 3-93

the victim file, hit **E** for Edit, then **<ENTER>**. Once inside
1Word, press **<ESC> <ESC> F P** to print the file. You're
still asked how many lines per page, however (Screen 3-93).

In Gold, if you hit **P** to print a file you can access the
history command to help you remember what page length
you used last time.

Hint: If you use several printers, or use different forms,
use the history command to enter several commonly used
page lengths, label them, and make them permanent (*See*
HISTORY).

QUIT

When you've finished using XTree, you can exit the
program via the Quit command.

■ XTREE. In XTree, it's a simple matter of hitting **F1** to
quit the program. You'll be asked if you're sure you want to
return to DOS — just hit **Y** for "yes" and you'll be taken
out of the program and returned to the directory you were
in when you invoked the program.

■ XTREEPRO & XTREEPRO GOLD. Pro and Gold
both use the **Q** to quit. When asked if you want to return to
DOS, hit **Y** for "yes" and you'll be out taken out of the
program and returned to the directory you were in when

XTree PRO GOLD

you invoked the program. You can also use **\<ALT\>Q** to exit Pro or Gold for slightly different results. Say you invoked Pro or Gold while in the \WP directory. Quitting would normally deliver you back there. However, if don't want to be in the \WP directory, you can go to the directory you *want* to be in (say, \GAMES) while still in Pro or Gold and then use **\<ALT\>Q** to quit. You'll find yourself out of the program and at the \GAMES prompt.

■ ALTERNATIVE WAY TO EXIT GOLD. **\<ALT\>Z** (for Zip) also exits Gold. When you quit using **\<ALT\>Z**, Gold makes a snapshot of whatever is onscreen, whatever information is logged, etc. and *saves* it. When you get into Gold the next time, it'll bypass the logging process and use the "snapshot" instead.

This is a particularly helpful option when you're in the middle of some sort of intricate operation and you're interrupted. (Say you're tagging a bunch of files to be copied to floppies when you realize you have no floppies.) If you use **Q** to exit, you'll lose all your tags. However, if you use **\<ALT\>Z** to quit, your tags will be saved. Then you can go buy your floppies (or go on vacation!). The next time you call Gold up, you'll be able to pick up where you left off when you **\<ALT\>Z**'d.

Note: When you exit using **\<ALT\>Z** and then re-enter the program, Gold *bypasses* the logging procedure and merely reinstates the environment from its "snapshot." Because of this, changes made to the disk in the interim *will not be reflected.* You must re-log the drive to see any changes.

RENAME

XTree PRO GOLD

If you want to change a file or a directory name — you can highlight the thing you want to change and then hit **R** for Rename and you can instantly swap the offensive name for something more palatable (or meaningful). Also you can rename a "volume label" with the **V** command.

■ *Rename a file*

To rename a file, highlight the file name and hit **R** for Rename. XTree will nudge you for a new name as shown in Screen 3-94. You may use any file name as long as you follow the basic rules of file names (see Part 1). Once you've typed a new name, hit **\<ENTER\>**.

XTree PRO GOLD

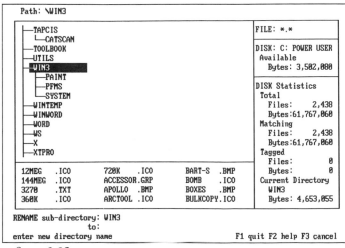

```
Path: \WIN3

12MEG    .ICO    CDRIVE2 .ICO    FLOPPY  .ICO    FILE: *.*
144MEG   .ICO    CEO     .ICO    GAMES   .GRP
3270     .TXT    CEO2    .ICO    GCICON1 .WRI    DISK: C: POWER USER
360K     .ICO    CHART   .ICO    ICONDRAW.EXE    Available
720K     .ICO    CHESS   .BMP    LABELS  .ICO    Bytes: 3,502,080
ACCESSOR.GRP     CLIPBRD .EXE    LOCK    .DOC
APOLLO   .BMP    CLIPBRD .HLP    LOCK    .EXE    DIRECTORY Stats
ARCTOOL  .ICO    CLOCK   .EXE    MACRO   .ICO    Total
BART-S   .BMP    CONTROL .EXE    MAIN    .GRP      Files:          136
BOMB     .ICO    CONTROL .HLP    MARK30  .DOC      Bytes: 4,653,055
BOXES    .BMP    CONTROL .INI    MARK30  .EXE    Matching
BULKCOPY.ICO     DIGITAL .FON    MARK30  .ZIP      Files:          136
CALC     .EXE    DOS     .ICO    METZ    .ORD      Bytes: 4,653,055
CALC     .HLP    DT1     .BMP    MINIDISK.ICO    Tagged
CALENDAR.EXE     DT2     .BMP    MOUSE   .OLD      Files:            0
CALENDAR.HLP     DT3     .BMP    MOUSE   .SYS      Bytes:            0
CARDFILE.EXE     EMAIL   .ICO    MS      .EXE    Current File
CARDFILE.HLP     EMM386  .SYS    MSAVR1  .ZIP    MOUSE    OLD
CC       .ICO    ERASE   .ICO    MSDOS   .EXE    Bytes:       31,701


RENAME file: MOUSE.OLD
         to:
 enter new file name                       F1 quit F2 help F3 cancel
```

Screen 3-94

■ Rename directory

The rules are the same to rename a directory. Just highlight the directory name to be changed and hit **R** to Rename. You'll be greeted with the type of question you would expect, "What new name do you want to give it?" (Screen 3-95.) Give it a new name and hit **<ENTER>**.

```
Path: \WIN3

├─TAPCIS                              FILE: *.*
│ └─CATSCAN
├─TOOLBOOK                            DISK: C: POWER USER
├─UTILS                               Available
├─WIN3                                  Bytes: 3,502,080
│ ├─PAINT
│ ├─PFMS                              DISK Statistics
│ └─SYSTEM                            Total
├─WINTEMP                               Files:        2,438
├─WINWORD                               Bytes:61,767,060
├─WORD                                Matching
├─WS                                    Files:        2,438
├─X                                     Bytes:61,767,060
├─XTPRO                               Tagged
                                        Files:            0
12MEG    .ICO    720K    .ICO    BART-S  .BMP    Bytes:            0
144MEG   .ICO    ACCESSOR.GRP    BOMB    .ICO    Current Directory
3270     .TXT    APOLLO  .BMP    BOXES   .BMP    WIN3
360K     .ICO    ARCTOOL .ICO    BULKCOPY.ICO    Bytes: 4,653,055


RENAME sub-directory: WIN3
         to:
 enter new directory name                  F1 quit F2 help F3 cancel
```

Screen 3-95

XTree PRO GOLD

Note: If you change a directory name that is part of any batch file — including your AUTOEXEC.BAT, the batch files should be changed accordingly. If you decided, for instance, to change your WordPerfect directory name from WORD_PRF to WP, you'd find that WordPerfect would no longer work *unless* you adjust your path statement to reflect the new directory name:

old path statement:

`path=c:\;c:\`**word_perf**`;c:\dos`

new path statement:

`path=c:\;c:\`**wp**`;c:\dos`

■ *Volume label*

Whenever you format a disk, you can give the disk a name. This name is called a label. A "volume" is a disk.

You may have seen the message "Volume has no label," which just means you didn't name the disk when you formatted it. (It has nothing to do with whether or not you put a sticker on the disk.)

Naming the volume is useful because when you log a disk, the volume name appears in the Disk Window (on the right). You'll know from the name if you have the right disk, saving you the trouble of taking the disk out of the drive to examine the sticker.

A lot of people don't bother putting labels on their

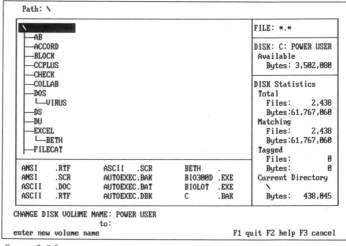

Screen 3-96

```
 Path: C:\WORD\BETH\XT                          7-13-90  7:59:23 am
┌─────────────────────────────────────────────┐ ┌──────────────────┐
│ 073A1C0C.      MC4     .DOC   X3      .DOC    │ │FILE *.*          │
│ BIGTEST .BAK   MC4     .TXT   XDUMP   .DOC    │ │                  │
│ BIGTEST .DOC   MC5     .DOC   XINTRO  .BAK    │ │DISK C:POWER USER │
│ BOOK1   .BAK   NORMAL  .BAK   XINTRO  .DOC    │ │Available         │
│ CAHLIN         .GLY   XOUT    .BAK            │ │Bytes   3,457,024 │
│ FAX            .DOC   XOUT    .DOC            │ │                  │
│ FEATURES     E .BAK   XTG     .DOC            │ │DIRECTORY Stats   │
│ IDG1         E .STY   XTP     .DOC            │ │Total             │
│ IDG2           .BAK   XTQ&A   .BAK            │ │ Files         51 │
│ IDG2           .BAK   XTQ&A   .DOC            │ │ Bytes  1,302,550 │
│ IDG3           .DOC   XTREE   .CMP            │ │Matching          │
│ IDG3           .BAK   XTREE   .DOC            │ │ Files         51 │
│ IDG4           .STY   XTREE   .ZIP            │ │ Bytes  1,302,550 │
│ IDG4           .BAK                           │ │Tagged            │
│ IDGPROP  *.*   .DOC                           │ │ Files          0 │
│ LET'S  BONBOOK      .BAK                      │ │ Bytes          0 │
│ MC1    BONBOOK.DOC  .DOC                      │ │Current File      │
│ MC2    MWHELP.ORI   .RTF                      │ │BIGTEST .DOC      │
│ MC3    CAHLIN.DOC   .BAK                      │ │Bytes       1,024 │
└─────────────────────────────────────────────┘ └──────────────────┘
 RENAME file: BIGTEST.DOC
          to:
 Enter file specification          ↑ history  ↵ ok  F1 help  ESC cancel
```

Screen 3-97

volumes. But if you want to label your volumes, XTree
provides a very simple avenue for doing so.

Just log onto the disk whose label you want to change.
Then, while in the Directory Window, hit **v** for Volume
and you'll be asked for a new volume name (Screen 3-96).
In this example, you've got a volume label of "POWER
USER." Look, ma — spaces! That's right, unlike file names,
volume names can include spaces. So, knock yourself out!

■ XTREEPRO GOLD. Gold maintains a history file for
your last responses to renaming files, directories, and even
volume labels, as shown in Screen 3-97. (*See* HISTORY.)

There are several features in XTreePro and XTreePro Gold
that help protect the data on your hard disk from prying
eyes.

Keep in mind, however, that if someone with a lot of
computer knowledge (or even *some* computer knowledge)
really wants to get what you've got on hard disk, they
probably can. It's a lot like locking the front door to your
house: No matter what, the best you can hope for is to slow
the thief down.

If you're extremely concerned about security, there are
programs that deal with that issue. However, you're still in

XTree PRO GOLD

SECURITY

the business of just slowing down the thief.

On the bright side, however, is the fact that the only people who care about what's on your computer are your co-workers. Most likely a few simple precautions on your part will be enough to discourage them from browsing through your confidential files.

The first two simple non-XTree hints.

1. Remember that most word processed files come in pairs: the original and the BAK version. If you delete one for security purposes, be sure to delete the other.
2. Many computers come with keys to lock the keyboards. If you have your key, use it.

XTree PRO GOLD

■ *Hide/Unhide a file*

There is actually no "hide a file" command. But, remember all that stuff about attributes and hidden files? (If you don't, see ATTRIBUTES.)

You can use the "hidden" attribute to render a file invisible. You can still call up the file, add to it, and save it, as long as you remember the file name

In order to render a file hidden, first highlight the file, then hit **A** for attributes. Type **+H** (translation: "add hidden" to this file's attributes) and hit **<ENTER>** (Screen 3-98).

```
Path: C:\WORD\BETH\SITCOM

BAFA6    .DOC    FINALBF .RTF    PROPOSAL.DOC    FILE: *.*
BF       .CMP    FINALPW .DOC    PW4     .DOC
BF       .DOC    FINALPW .RTF    REALWOM .DOC    DISK: C:POWER USER
BINDING  .DOC    GOLDEN  .DOC    REVWOM1 .DOC    Available
BONNIE   .DOC    GOLDEN  .STY    RON     .DOC      Bytes:  3,538,944
BONNIE   .TXT    HP_REFIL.TXT    RON     .RTG
CAST     .DOC    LUTZ    .DOC    RWA     .DOC    DIRECTORY Stats
CHARS    .DOC    LUTZ    .STY    S1A     .DOC    Total
COMMENT  .DOC    NORMAL  .GLY    S1B     .DOC      Files:        59
COMMENT  .TXT    NPW     .DOC    S1C     .DOC      Bytes: 1,139,558
DAD56    .DOC    PITCH   .DOC    SGONE   .DOC    Matching
DADDY1   .DOC    PITCH2  .DOC    SGONE   .RGF      Files:        59
DADDY2   .DOC    PITCH6  .DOC    SGONEB  .DOC      Bytes: 1,139,558
DADEND   .DOC    PITCH6  .RTF    SHERIFF .ZIP    Tagged
DADTIME  .DOC    PITCH7  .BAK    SING3   .DOC      Files:         0
DRDR     .DOC    PITCH7  .DOC    SITCOM  .STY      Bytes:         0
DUMP     .DOC    PITCH7  .RTF    TV      .DOC    Current File
FATHER   .DOC    PITCH7B .RTF    TV      .STY    BONNIE   .DOC
FINALBF  .DOC    POP1    .DOC    TV5     .STY      Bytes:     1,536

ATTRIBUTES for file: BONNIE.DOC      1,536 ....  6-02-90  7:39 pm
              : +H
Enter attribute changes (+/- R A S H)          F1 help  ESC cancel
```

Screen 3-98

```
 Path: C:\WORD\BETH\SITCOM                                  XTree PRO GOLD

 BAFA6    .DOC    FINALBF  .RTF    PROPOSAL .DOC    FILE: *.*
 BF       .CMP    FINALPW  .DOC    PW4      .DOC
 BF       .DOC    FINALPW  .RTF    REALWOM  .DOC    DISK: C:POWER USER
 BINDING  .DOC    GOLDEN   .DOC    REVWOM1  .DOC    Available
 bonnie   .doc    GOLDEN   .STY    RON      .DOC     Bytes: 3,538,944
 BONNIE   .TXT    HP_REFIL .TXT    RON      .RTG
 CAST     .DOC    LUTZ     .DOC    RWA      .DOC    DIRECTORY Stats
 CHARS    .DOC    LUTZ     .STY    S1A      .DOC    Total
 COMMENT  .DOC    NORMAL   .GLY    S1B      .DOC     Files:           59
 COMMENT  .TXT    NPW      .DOC    S1C      .DOC     Bytes:    1,139,558
 DAD56    .DOC    PITCH    .DOC    SGONE    .DOC    Matching
 DADDY1   .DOC    PITCH2   .DOC    SGONE    .RGF     Files:           59
 DADDY2   .DOC    PITCH6   .DOC    SGONEB   .DOC     Bytes:    1,139,558
 DADEND   .DOC    PITCH6   .RTF    SHERIFF  .ZIP    Tagged
 DADTIME  .DOC    PITCH7   .BAK    SING3    .DOC     Files:            0
 DRDR     .DOC    PITCH7   .DOC    SITCOM   .STY     Bytes:            0
 DUMP     .DOC    PITCH7   .RTF    TV       .DOC    Current File
 FATHER   .DOC    PITCH7B  .RTF    TV       .STY     bonnie  .doc
 FINALBF  .DOC    POP1     .DOC    TV5      .STY     Bytes:        1,536

 FILE       Attributes  Copy  Delete  Edit  Filespec  Log disk  Move  Print
 COMMANDS   Rename  Tag  Untag  View  eXecute  Quit
 ←↑↓→ scroll  ENTER tree commands    ALT menu   CTRL menu      F1 help  ESC cancel
```

Screen 3-99

To change the attributes of several files at once, tag the
files to be hidden, then use **<CTRL>A** to change the
attributes of all tagged files.

Gold and Pro will continue to display the names of the
hidden files, but in lowercase letters (Screen 3-99).
You can take this one step further if you don't want Pro
and Gold to show the files at all. Go into the configuration
program and change "System and Hidden File Access" to
"NO" (see CONFIGURATION). Once you've done so,
hidden files will not be displayed.

■ Hide/Unhide directories

Gold allows you to hide and unhide *directories* from view.
  Once designated as "hidden," the directory and its files
are, theoretically, not visible when using any program
(including DOS). Just keep in mind that there are other
utility programs with abilities similar to Gold's that allow
you to view "hidden" directories. This is not a fool-proof
security system.
  Further, anyone (like you) who knows the name of a
hidden directory can access it. Hiding does not prevent
unauthorized access. Hiding just assumes that only those
who know the directory name should have access to it.

XTree PRO GOLD

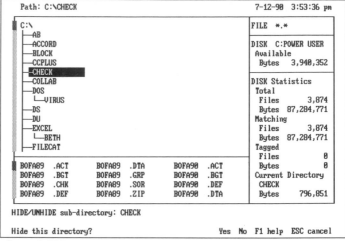

```
 Path: C:\CHECK                                     7-12-90  3:53:36 pm

┌─────────────────────────┬──────────────────────────────┐
│ C:\                     │ FILE  *.*                      │
│  ├─AB                   │                                │
│  ├─ACCORD               │ DISK  C:POWER USER             │
│  ├─BLOCK                │ Available                      │
│  ├─CCPLUS               │ Bytes    3,940,352             │
│  ├─CHECK                │                                │
│  ├─COLLAB               │ DISK Statistics                │
│  ├─DOS                  │ Total                          │
│  │ └─VIRUS              │  Files          3,874          │
│  ├─DS                   │  Bytes     87,284,771          │
│  ├─DU                   │ Matching                       │
│  ├─EXCEL                │  Files          3,874          │
│  │ └─BETH               │  Bytes     87,284,771          │
│  ├─FILECAT              │ Tagged                         │
│                         │  Files              0          │
│ BOFA89 .ACT  BOFA89 .DTA  BOFA90 .ACT │  Bytes       0  │
│ BOFA89 .BGT  BOFA89 .GRP  BOFA90 .BGT │ Current Directory│
│ BOFA89 .CHK  BOFA89 .SOR  BOFA90 .DEF │ CHECK            │
│ BOFA89 .DEF  BOFA89 .ZIP  BOFA90 .DTA │ Bytes    796,851 │
└─────────────────────────┴──────────────────────────────┘

 HIDE/UNHIDE sub-directory: CHECK

 Hide this directory?                    Yes  No  F1 help  ESC cancel
```

Screen 3-100

Let's say you've put your personal checkbook on your office computer. (Naturally you're spending time on your personal checkbook only during your lunch hour or after work.) However, you don't want the Big Boss (or even your secretary) to have access to your personal finances. So you decide to hide the directory.

The first step is to highlight the directory to be hidden, then type **<ALT>H** (for hide). You'll be presented with something like Screen 3-100.

At the bottom of the screen Gold asks you to confirm this action with a **Y** or cancel with an **N**. Naturally, we'll enter a **Y** to hide the directory.

Even though the directory is officially hidden, the directory name is still visible onscreen, though the name is now shown in lowercase.

If you wish, you can make the directory name disappear from Gold's Directory Window. You must go to the configuration program. Under Security, change "System/Hidden file and directory access" to NO.

If you should forget the names of the directories you've hidden later, just go back into the configuration and change "System/Hidden file and directory access" back to "YES" — and all will be revealed.

```
┌─────────────────────────────────────────────────────────────────┐
│ Path: C:\WORD\BETH\JC                         8-89-98  2:13:44 pm │
│                                                                   │
│         ├─COMICS                      │FILE  *.*                  │
│         ├─DOSMAN                      │                           │
│         │  └─BATCHES                  │DISK  C:POWER USER         │
│         ├─HOLLY                       │Available                  │
│         ├─INSTRUCT                    │Bytes    2,547,712         │
│         ┤JC                           │                           │
│         ├─NAMES                       │DISK Statistics            │
│         ├─PAN                         │Total                      │
│         ├─RESEARCH                    │  Files        3,877       │
│         ├─SCRIPTS                     │  Bytes   88,634,828       │
│         │  └─TREK                     │Matching                   │
│         ├─SITCOM                      │  Files        3,877       │
│         ├─STORIES                     │  Bytes   88,634,828       │
│         ├─WGABBS                      │Tagged                     │
│                                       │  Files            8       │
│  10_10   .DOC    DOSJC626.DOC  DOSJC714.DOC │  Bytes          8   │
│  DWSCRIPT.STY    DOSJC628.DOC  DOSJC717.DOC │Current Directory    │
│  DOSJC623.DOC    DOS.JC787.DOC DOSJC728.DOC │JC                   │
│  DOSJC625.DOC    DOSJC710.DOC  DOSJC722.DOC │Bytes       69,382   │
│                                                                   │
│ WASH DISK Drive C:                                                │
│                                          ←┘ ok  F1 help  ESC cancel│
└─────────────────────────────────────────────────────────────────┘
```

Screen 3-101

■ Wash disk

Deleting a file doesn't exactly delete a file. Deleting a file tells DOS that the space on the disk previously used by the "deleted" file is now free for other files to use as needed. And as long as that space has not been put to use by another file, someone can come in with Norton or Mace Utilities and *undelete* the file.

Wash Disk visits all currently unused areas on the disk and makes sure that all deleted files are no longer recoverable.

Wash Disk is very simple to do. Type **<ALT>W**, then press **<ENTER>** when you get something like Screen 3-101.

Now, go read Dear Abby for a few minutes while Gold goes to work. This could take a while.

SHOWALL WINDOW

Showall asks XTree to show *all* the files on the current drive, regardless of directory, in alphabetical order. (Or, if you prefer the files to be sorted and displayed by size or date, just hit **<ALT>S** and you can change the sort criteria to accommodate your desires. See SORT CRITERIA for details.)

To invoke Showall, start from Directory Window and type **S** for Showall. The directory and File Windows will merge into one window, the entire screen will be highlighted, and

XTree PRO GOLD | all files on the disk will be listed in alphabetical order. When a file name is highlighted, its path name is displayed above the window. Note, the box on the right now reveals "Showall Statistics."

Showall, like all file commands, works in conjunction with filespec. If you are searching for certain files on the hard disk, enter a file specification command before (or after) invoking Showall to filter out the files you don't care about.

For instance, if you want to see your BAK files, you could hit **F** for filespec and enter ***.BAK** as your file specification. Then, while in the Directory Window, hit **S** for Showall (Screen 3-102).

Then, right before your very eyes, you'll see all of the BAK files on your hard disk. (And you could type **<CTRL>T** to tag them all and then **<CTRL>D** to delete — freeing up space on your disk.)

Another approach to Showall is to use **<CTRL>S** (rather than **S**) which jumps into Showall mode showing all tagged files on the disk.

■ XTREEPRO GOLD. In Gold you can update the CTRL/Showall screen if you've untagged some of your previously tagged files. Hitting **F2** will filter out the newly untagged files from the CTRL/Showall screen.

```
Path: C:\WORD\FC

AUTOEXEC.BAK    DOC     .BAK    PITCH7  .BAK    FILE: *.BAK
BACKUP  .BAK    DOS     .BAK    PLAY2   .BAK
BATCHES .BAK    EM      .BAK    PRINT   .BAK    DISK: C:POWER USER
BIGTEST .BAK    FORMAT  .BAK    PROTEST .BAK    Available
BLU     .BAK    FRECOVER.BAK    SCROLL  .BAK      Bytes:  3,465,216
BONNIE  .BAK    FREEDOM .BAK    STAR    .BAK
BOOK1   .BAK    HERO    .BAK    SYS     .BAK    SHOWALL Statistics
C       .BAK    IDG2    .BAK    TERMS   .BAK    Total
CD      .BAK    IDG3    .BAK    THOTZ   .BAK      Files:        3,856
CHIP2   .BAK    IDG4    .BAK    TYPE    .BAK      Bytes: 86,885,572
CHKDSK  .BAK    INDEX   .BAK    X       .BAK    Matching
CONFIG  .BAK    LET'S   .BAK    X1      .BAK      Files:           55
COPY    .BAK    NORMAL  .BAK    X2      .BAK      Bytes:      707,593
DCOPY   .BAK    NORMAL  .BAK    X3      .BAK    Tagged
DEL     .BAK    OUTLINE .BAK    XINTRO  .BAK      Files:            0
DIR     .BAK    PART1   .BAK    XOUT    .BAK      Bytes:            0
DM      .BAK    PATH    .BAK    XTQ&A   .BAK    Current File
DMLETTER.BAK    PGOUT   .BAK                     DMRESME .BAK
DMRESME .BAK    PGOUT2  .BAK                       Bytes:        5,632

FILE       Attributes  Copy  Delete  Edit  Filespec  Log disk  Move  Print
COMMANDS   Rename  Tag  Untag  View  eXecute  Quit
←↑↓→ scroll  ENTER tree commands    ALT menu    CTRL menu      F1 help  ESC cancel
```

Screen 3-102

One of the great things about XTree is that when you get a list of files, they are in alphabetical order. In other words, by default the files are sorted alphabetically in ascending order.

> **SORT CRITERIA**

You don't have to settle for alphabetical order, however. **<ALT>S** allows you to select a new Sort Criteria (to assist in tagging or finding or comparing files). There are a number ways files can be sorted.

Whether you are in the Directory Window or a File Window, to invoke the Sort Criteria command, hit **<ALT>S**. Then, select which of the listed criteria you want your information sorted by hitting the highlighted letter.

XTree PRO GOLD

Pressing **<ALT>S** in XTree will give you four options, as shown in Screen 3-103.

■ Name

Lists files alphabetically by name. This is the default.

■ Ext

Groups files alphabetically by extension, and then by name within each extension. All the BAKs, all the DOCs, all the whatevers are grouped together (in alphabetical order).

■ Date & time

Lists files sorted by date of creation, then by time. The newest files at the head of the list.

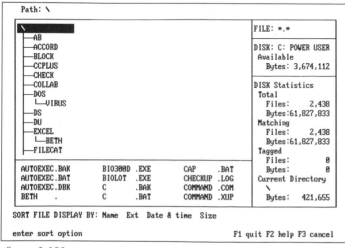

Screen 3-103

XTree PRO GOLD

■ *Size*

Lists files in order by size. The biggest files will be listed first.

As you might guess, Gold and Pro venture beyond the prosaic, and give us some new sort criteria. Also, they both allow you to change the default sort order and sort criteria through the configuration program.

You get something like Screen 3-104 when you hit **<ALT>S** in Pro and Gold programs.

While you still can select Name, Ext, Date and Time, and Size, these criteria are now modified by the Order option.

If Order is set to *ascending*, the Date and Time sorts will start with the oldest files and work up to the newest. Similarly, the Size option will start with the smallest files, and continue through the biggest.

If Order is set to *descending*, the Name and Ext options will be in reverse alphabetical order; Date and Time will start with the newest files and drop down to the oldest; Size will start with the biggest files and shrink down to the smallest.

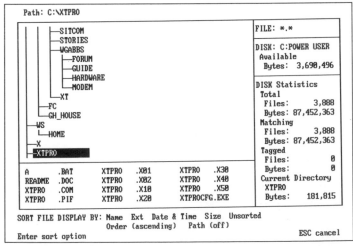

Screen 3-104

In addition to Order, you also have:

XTree PRO GOLD

■ *Unsorted*

Lists files in the real order they are actually stored on the disk by DOS. (This would be what you would see if you used DOS's DIR command.)

■ *Path*

When in Showall or Global mode, and path is turned *on* (default is *off*), the files will not be mushed together in a huge alphabetical listing. Instead the files will be grouped by directory area first, and then by the specified option section.

XTreePro Gold lets you double your fun by dividing the screen into two windows (Screen 3-105).

Whether you are in a File Window or a Directory Window, hitting **F8** will split the display into two independent windows each capable of performing any normal Gold commands. So, while either window can be manipulated as differently as you wish, only one window can function at a time.

Once split, **F8** will unsplit the windows.

In the example, the *active window* is the one on the right, because that's where the highlight is. Hitting the **TAB** key moves the highlight back and forth between windows.

SPLIT/ UNSPLIT

XTree PRO GOLD

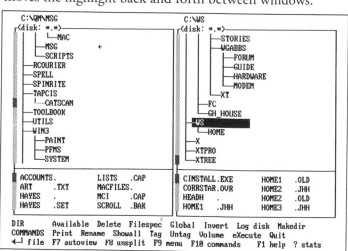

Screen 3-105

XTree PRO GOLD

NOTE: When you issue a command, it will affect only the *active* window.

In Screen 3-106, the left side is an Expanded File Window and the right side is a Directory Window. You can log onto different drives, tag different files, whatever you wish.

The main point of splitting the display into two windows is so you can compare directory trees on two different disks or compare files in two different directories. Which directory has more files? Which file is newer or bigger?

An important thing to realize is that if you delete a file on one side of the display, the inactive side will not reflect that change until it becomes the *active* window.

For example, if both windows display the same list of files and you delete a file, only the *active* screen will no longer list the file. The inactive window will still list the file until you **TAB** over to the inactive side. Once you do, it'll automatically update itself and the deleted file will disappear.

When you want to unsplit the windows **F8** will make the inactive window disappear. In the example, hit **F8** to make \RCOURIER the current directory.

While in split mode, you might create a situation in which you are viewing the same directory in both windows, with a different set of files tagged (all your BAKs on the left and all your DOCs on the right).

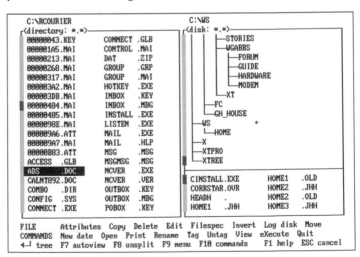

Screen 3-106

Normally when you unsplit the windows, the tagging in the active window stays and the tagging in the inactive window disappears.

XTree PRO GOLD

As an alternative, you can use **<CTRL>F6** (while in a File Window only) to transfer the tags from the active window to the inactive window so that both windows have the same tags. (You'd end up with both DOCs and BAKs tagged, for instance.) Press **<CTRL>F6**, then **TAB** over to the other window for the new, "merged tagging" to take effect.

No one will deny that we live in a "bottom-line" kind of era. XTree accommodates type-A personalities by providing a box (window), on the right of your screen, filled with your *current statistics*. That's why the window on the right is called the Statistics Window.

STATISTICS

As you travel up and down the directory tree, go into a directory, enter filespecs, tag files, and so forth, the statistics window is continually being updated to reflect your actions. How many files are on this disk? How many are in this directory? Are tagged? Match the filespecs? How big is this file? This directory? How much space do the tagged files take up? Etc. All this stuff is right there on your screen. Pretty impressive, huh?

XTree PRO GOLD

If your cursor is in the Directory Window, the statistics window becomes a DISK Statistics window. The Total, Matching, and Tagged files and bytes reflect what's going on with the whole disk (Screen 3-107).

But when your cursor is in one of the File Windows, the statistics box becomes a DIRECTORY Statistics box and reflects the Total, Matching, and Tagged statistics of the *current directory* only (Screen 3-108).

By the same token, if you're in Showall or Global mode, the window transforms into a SHOWALL or GLOBAL Statistics window with statistics for the current drive, or all logged drives (Screen 3-109).

■ Extended statistics

Just when you think it couldn't get any better, XTreePro Gold presents *another* box of statistics for you insatiable number-crunchers. The Extended Statistics box gives you

XTree PRO GOLD

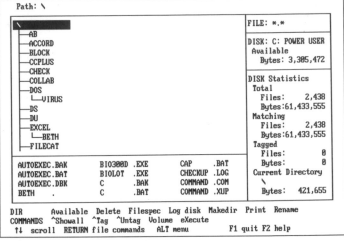

Screen 3-107

even more detail about the files on your disk. (Bet you're dying to know the average file size on your hard disk, right?)

While in the Directory Window, just type a **?** (a question mark) and you'll get something like Screen 3-110.

Since some of this stuff is pretty technical, we're not going to go through it here (read Chapter 7 of your operations manual if you're intrigued by this kind of stuff).

Hint: Normally, you can see the **?** in the lower right-hand

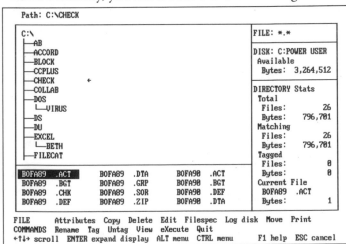

Screen 3-108

```
Path: C:\WORD\BETH

01REC89D.ZIP    00000317.MAI    10_10   .DOC    FILE: *.*
$$$$$$$$.FS     00003A2.MAI     11      .TXT
$DEFAULT.F1     000003DB.MAI    12      .TXT    DISK: C:POWER USER
$DEFAULT.F10    00000404.MAI    123SETUP.DOC     Available
$DEFAULT.F2     00000485.MAI    12MEG   .ICO      Bytes:  3,264,512
$DEFAULT.F3     0000098E.MAI    12_191D .DOC
$DEFAULT.F4     00009A6.ATT     12_22PRM.DOC    GLOBAL Statistics
$DEFAULT.F5     00009A7.MAI     144MEG  .ICO     Total
$DEFAULT.F6     000B03.ATT      1STTZPAR.DOC      Files:    3,896
$DEFAULT.F7     8B340959.       1WORD1  .PIX      Bytes: 87,866,372
$DEFAULT.F8     1        .DOC   1WORD2  .PIX     Matching
$DEFAULT.F9     1        .TXT   1WORD3  .FST      Files:    3,896
$UPDATE .IFS    10       .BAT   1WORD3  .PIX      Bytes: 87,866,372
(C)ALDUS.'88    10       .TXT   1WORD4  .PIX     Tagged
(C)BITS .'89    18391438.       2       .TXT      Files:         0
00000043.KEY    183B164D.       22BLOCKS.DOC      Bytes:         0
000001A5.MAI    10MAM    .CMP   22BLOCKS.PM3     Current File
00000213.MAI    10MAM    .DOC   2S1-WARN.DOC     01REC89D.ZIP
00000268.MAI    10MAM    .STY   2GUYS   .DOC      Bytes:  106,479

FILE    Attributes  Copy  Delete  Edit  Filespec  Log disk  Print
COMMANDS  Rename  Tag  Untag  View  eXecute  Quit
↑↓→ scroll  ENTER tree display    ALT menu  CTRL menu    F1 help  ESC cancel
```

Screen 3-109

corner of the screen as a reminder of this option. Once
you've logged more than one drive, however, the **+/–**
prompt appears in that spot. Even though the **?** may not be
visible on the screen, you can always type it to get your
statistics.

```
                                      7-13-90  11:19:13 am

DISK STATISTICS                  FILE STATISTICS

Disk drive    C:POWER USER       File spec *.*

Capacity        100,835,328 bytes   Total files        3,898 files
Available space   3,252,224 bytes                  87,938,229 bytes

Used space       97,583,104 bytes   Matching files     3,898 files
Slack space       9,644,875 bytes                  87,938,229 bytes

Cluster size          4,096 bytes   Tagged files           0 files
Sector size             512 bytes                          0 bytes

Total sectors       196,944         Displayed files       52 files
Total clusters       24,618                        1,368,086 bytes

Sectors/cluster           8         Average size      22,559 bytes

                                              ↵ ok
```

Screen 3-110

SUBSTITUTE

XTree PRO GOLD

Note: This section is "rated R" and may be too intense for newer users. If the following feels way over your head, skip it for now. However, it's quite a time-saver if you have a large, complex drive.

If you're daydreaming about a way to force XTree to log just one directory and ignore the rest of the drive, then DOS's substitute command will come to the rescue. Substitute will let you trick XTree into thinking that your favorite directory is actually a drive.

To do *that*, however, requires two things:
1. DOS version 3.1 or higher. (See page 190 to learn how to determine what version of DOS you have.)
2. A willingness to change your CONFIG.SYS file. (Be sure to *back up* your present CONFIG.SYS file before you make any changes to it.)

Here's our old CONFIG.SYS file:

```
files=20
buffers=30
device=\dos\ansi.sys
```

Before we edit this file, be sure to back it up first. Then you need to determine two simple things:
1. What's the name of the directory you want to be able to log on to? (In this case, we'll use the WORD directory.)
2. Currently, what is your last disk drive? (C:? D:? E:?) In this case, the last drive is **C:**. Knowing the last drive is important because the next drive after that is what we're going to assign to our directory. In this case, the WORD directory will become drive D:.

Okay, now we're ready to edit the CONFIG.SYS file (*if* you've already backed it up, that is).

Given the above information, the CONFIG.SYS file needs to end up looking like this:

```
files=20
buffers=30
device=\dos\ansi.sys
lastdrive=f:
```

All we did was add the "**lastdrive=f:**" line. If you already have a drive F, you'll have to say "lastdrive=g:". And so forth.

(If you don't know how to edit your CONFIG.SYS file, see Edit.) Briefly, however, if you're using Pro or Gold,

XTree PRO GOLD

highlight the CONFIG.SYS file in the root (\) directory
and hit **E** for Edit. Add the "lastdrive" line to the file and
then hit **<ESC>** and **S**ave the file.

After the file is edited, you need to reboot your computer
and get to a system prompt.

Now, if you type: **subst d: c:\word <ENTER>** you
will be tell DOS to pretend that C:\WORD is Drive D.
You can now **D: <ENTER>** and you'll be on your new D
drive. If you engage XTree from the D prompt, it'll log only
that "drive."

Please note that when you're in substitute mode, you
cannot rename or delete a directory or subdirectory that is
part of the substitution. Also, you cannot change the
volume label.

If you are want to void the substitution, quit XTree, go
back to your *real* drive and type: **subst d: /d <ENTER>**.
This means delete the D: drive substitution.

If you just *love* substituting directories for drives, you may
want to put the subst command in the AUTOEXEC.BAT
file so that it will take effect automatically when you turn
on your computer.

Naturally, each version of XTree handles substitution
differently:

■ XTREE. In the "DISK" box, you'll see that XTree
simply reports the fact that we're on drive D (Screen 3-111).

■ XTREEPRO. Pro also is completely fooled. The path at
the top of the screen shows we're on drive D (Screen 3-112).

■ XTREEPRO GOLD. Gold properly reports that we're
actually on the C: drive, though it keeps statistics on D: as
though it were a drive (Screen 3-113).

When you wish to perform an operation on a file (or files or
directories) there are two ways of indicating to XTree which
file to copy, delete, or whatever. One selection method is to
simply highlight the file (or directory). However, if you
wish to perform an operation on a group of files, you must
use the second method, called "tagging."

**TAG/
UNTAG**

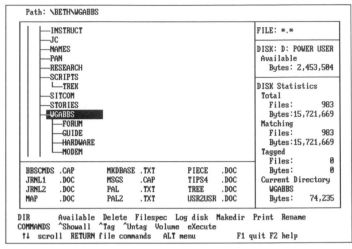

Screen 3-111

There are two ways to tag files.

One is to simply highlight the file and press **T** for tag.

The second way to tag files, usually groups of files, is to use the filespec command to display a set of files then hit **<CTRL>T** to tag them. For instance, enter a filespec of ***.BAK** to display all the files that end with BAK. Then hit **<CTRL>T** and all files displayed will become tagged.

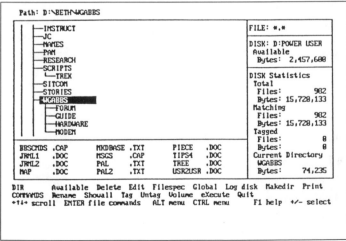

Screen 3-112

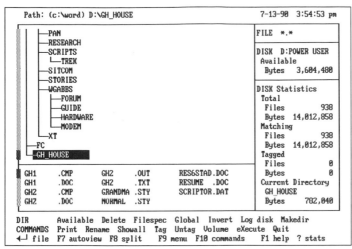

```
Path: (c:\word) D:\GH_HOUSE              7-13-90  3:54:53 pm

   ├─PAN                          FILE  *.*
   ├─RESEARCH
   ├─SCRIPTS                      DISK  D:POWER USER
   │ └─TREK                       Available
   ├─SITCOM                       Bytes    3,604,480
   ├─STORIES
   ├─WGABBS                       DISK Statistics
   │ ├─FORUM                      Total
   │ ├─GUIDE                       Files        938
   │ ├─HARDWARE                    Bytes   14,012,858
   │ └─MODEM                      Matching
   └─XT                            Files        938
   └─FC                            Bytes   14,012,858
   └─GH_HOUSE                     Tagged
                                   Files          0
 GH1    .CMP   GH2    .OUT   RES6STAD.DOC  Bytes        0
 GH1    .DOC   GH2    .TXT   RESUME  .DOC  Current Directory
 GH2    .CMP   GRANDMA.STY   SCRIPTOR.DAT  GH_HOUSE
 GH2    .DOC   NORMAL .STY                  Bytes      702,040

DIR      Available Delete Filespec Global Invert Log disk Makedir
COMMANDS Print Rename Showall Tag Untag Volume eXecute Quit
↵ file  F7 autoview F8 split   F9 menu F10 commands  F1 help ? stats
```

Screen 3-113

If you have tagged a file in error, highlight the file and hit **U** for Untag. If you want to untag all the currently tagged files, **<CTRL>U** will do the job.

XTree PRO GOLD

■ Tag/Untag a file

To tag a file, highlight the file to be tagged and press **T** (for tag) and a diamond will appear next to the file name indicating that the file is tagged. In Screen 3-114, DAB.EXE is tagged (see the little diamond to the right of the file name) and SCAN.EXE is highlighted, but not tagged (no diamond).

If you were to hit **T** while the highlight was on SCAN.EXE, then it would be tagged also.

(To tag several files in a row, hold the **T** down and don't let go. The cursor will automatically move to the next file and tag it.)

If you change your mind about tagging DAB.EXE you could highlight it and hit **U** to untag (and remove the diamond).

■ Tag/Untag all files in a directory

There are two approaches to tagging all files in a directory.

First, while in a Directory Window, highlight a directory name and hit **T** to tag every file in that directory (Screen 3-115). You can see some of the tagged files in the Small File Window.

Typing **U** while highlighting the directory name would

XTree PRO GOLD

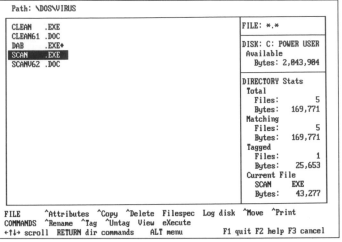

Screen 3-114

untag (and remove all the files in the directory.

The second approach to tagging all files requires that you first get into a *File Window*. Now typing **<CTRL>T** tags *all* files displayed in the current directory. Conversely, **<CTRL>U** will untag all tagged files.

■ Tag/Untag the whole disk

You may tag all files by typing **<CTRL>T** while in a Directory Window. **<CTRL>U** will untag all tagged files.

■ Tag/Untag and filespecs

Using **<CTRL>T** in conjunction with the filespec command is a powerful way to tag a particular group of files. In Screen 3-116, we hit **F** for filespec and then entered ***.BAK** and **<ENTER>**. XTree then shows all those files that match the filespec (in other words, only the files ending in BAK). *Then* we hit **<CTRL>T** to tag all files. This tags all the BAK files. (Now we can copy or delete or perform whatever operation we wish on them.)

In a different case, lets say you've got some DOC files along with other files in a directory. You want to keep all the DOC files and delete the rest. **Note:** In Gold there's an easier way to do this.) Here's how to do it in XTree and Pro: First go to the directory and **<CTRL>T** (tag) all the files.

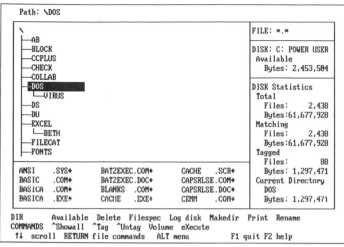

Screen 3-115

Then you'd enter filespec of ***.DOC**. Once you've got the
DOC files on screen, you can hit **<CTRL>U** to untag the
DOC files. Next, change your filespecs back to ***.*** and
you'll see that all files *except* the DOC files are tagged! Now,
use **<CTRL>D** to delete all tagged files. (If you can't "see"
this in your brain — try it out on your computer.)

(Just remember, the art of this program is in the mixing
and matching of all the tools [i.e. commands] you are
given.)

```
Path: C:\WS

HEADH   .BAK♦                          FILE: *.BAK
HOUSE   .BAK♦
SMOU90A .BAK♦                          DISK: C:POWER USER
SMOU90B .BAK♦                          Available
SMOU90C .BAK♦                          Bytes: 2,158,592
SMOU90D .BAK♦
TEST    .BAK♦                          DIRECTORY Stats
TITLE   .BAK♦                          Total
                                       Files:       73
                                       Bytes: 2,351,530
                                       Matching
                                       Files:        8
                                       Bytes:  227,584
                                       Tagged
                                       Files:       16
                                       Bytes:  455,168
                                       Current File
                                       HEADH   .BAK
                                       Bytes:      128

FILE      Attributes Copy Delete Edit Filespec Log disk Move Print
COMMANDS  Rename Tag Untag View eXecute Quit
←↑↓→ scroll  ENTER tree commands  ALT menu  CTRL menu    F1 help ESC cancel
```

Screen 3-116

XTree PRO GOLD

■ *Showall tagged files*

There may be times when you have files tagged in different directories over your hard disk and you'd like to display them all.

Typing **<CTRL>S** from the Directory Window will show all tagged files on the disk. It operates just like the regular Showall Window, except the statistics box on the right reads, "Showall Statistic."

■ *XTreePro Gold goodies*

Note: In case you're curious about the easier way to tag all files except the DOC files, Gold allows the use of an exclusionary filespec. Entering **-*.DOC** would display all files *but* the DOC files. Then a simple **<CTRL>T** and **<CTRL>D** would delete the files. Or you could have used Invert.

■ *Invert*

In the previous example we entered a filespec of ***.BAK** so that all the files ending with BAK would be displayed.

Pretend we did all the things we wanted to do with the BAK files and now we want to do something to the other files — the ones that don't end in BAK. Instead of entering in a new filespec, wouldn't it be great if you could just say "Reverse the tags" and everything that was tagged is now untagged and vice versa?

That's what Invert does.

With all the BAK files still tagged, and our filespecs set to *.*, hitting **<CTRL>I** (to invert all tagged files) nets us the question shown in Screen 3-117.

Do we want to invert the File Specification or the Tags? In this case, hit **T** and instantly the BAKs are untagged and the other files are tagged.

■ *Tag by attributes*

In Gold, you can even tag files based on their *attributes* (read-only, archive, system, or hidden).

In the following example, we hit **<ALT>A** to tag all files in the current window with certain attributes. Naturally, Gold wants to know *which* attributes we want to use as our criteria for tagging.

In Screen 3-118, we are asking to tag all files that have

```
Path: C:\WS                                          8-09-90  2:28:30 pm

 CINSTALL.EXE      PERSONAL.DCT      SMOU90A .          FILE  *.*
 CORRSTAR.OVR      RESET   .PTR      SMOU90A .BAK◆
 HEADH   .         SCRIPTOR.001      SMOU90A .OLD       DISK  C:POWER USER
 HEADH   .BAK◆     SCRIPTOR.002      SMOU90B .          Available
 HOME1   .JHH      SCRIPTOR.003      SMOU90B .BAK◆      Bytes    2,117,632
 HOME1   .OLD      SCRIPTOR.004      SMOU90B .OLD
 HOME2   .JHH      SCRIPTOR.005      SMOU90C .          DIRECTORY Stats
 HOME2   .OLD      SCRIPTOR.DAT      SMOU90C .BAK◆      Total
 HOME3   .JHH      SCRIPTOR.FMT      SMOU90C .OLD        Files             73
 HOME3   .OLD      SCRIPTOR.MSG      SMOU90D .           Bytes    2,351,530
 HOMETIT .DOC      SCRIPTOR.PRD      SMOU90D .BAK◆      Matching
 HOUSE   .         SKBATCH .COM      SMOU90D .OLD        Files             73
 HOUSE   .BAK◆     SMOU    .DOC      SMOU9_17.ZIP        Bytes    2,351,530
 INSTALL .COM      SMOU    .DTX      SMOUH   .ZIP       Tagged
 INTERNAL.DCT      SMOU    .ICF      SMOUOLD .ZIP        Files              8
 LASER   .EXE      SMOU    .ZIP      SMOUP   .DOC        Bytes      227,584
 MAILMRGE.OVR      SMOU2   .DOC      SMOUTIT .DOC       Current File
 MAIN    .DCT      SMOU89  .ZIP      TEST    .          CINSTALL.EXE
 MAKE-ICF.EXE      SMOU90  .ICF      TEST    .BAK◆       Bytes       16,384

INVERT    File specification  Tags

                                                    F1 help  ESC cancel
```

Screen 3-117

their *archive attribute* turned on (translation: they haven't been backed up yet). **+A** means the archive attribute is positive (turned on). (See ATTRIBUTES if you need a refresher on this topic.)

You can also tag all files on the disk by attribute using the above method as long as you start from the Showall Window.

```
Path: C:\WS                                          8-09-90  2:29:24 pm

 CINSTALL.EXE      PERSONAL.DCT      SMOU90A .          FILE  *.*
 CORRSTAR.OVR      RESET   .PTR      SMOU90A .BAK
 HEADH   .         SCRIPTOR.001      SMOU90A .OLD       DISK  C:POWER USER
 HEADH   .BAK      SCRIPTOR.002      SMOU90B .          Available
 HOME1   .JHH      SCRIPTOR.003      SMOU90B .BAK       Bytes    2,117,632
 HOME1   .OLD      SCRIPTOR.004      SMOU90B .OLD
 HOME2   .JHH      SCRIPTOR.005      SMOU90C .          DIRECTORY Stats
 HOME2   .OLD      SCRIPTOR.DAT      SMOU90C .BAK       Total
 HOME3   .JHH      SCRIPTOR.FMT      SMOU90C .OLD        Files             73
 HOME3   .OLD      SCRIPTOR.MSG      SMOU90D .           Bytes    2,351,530
 HOMETIT .DOC      SCRIPTOR.PRD      SMOU90D .BAK       Matching
 HOUSE   .         SKBATCH .COM      SMOU90D .OLD        Files             73
 HOUSE   .BAK      SMOU    .DOC      SMOU9_17.ZIP        Bytes    2,351,530
 INSTALL .COM      SMOU    .DTX      SMOUH   .ZIP       Tagged
 INTERNAL.DCT      SMOU    .ICF      SMOUOLD .ZIP        Files              0
 LASER   .EXE      SMOU    .ZIP      SMOUP   .DOC        Bytes              0
 MAILMRGE.OVR      SMOU2   .DOC      SMOUTIT .DOC       Current File
 MAIN    .DCT      SMOU89  .ZIP      TEST    .          CINSTALL.EXE
 MAKE-ICF.EXE      SMOU90  .ICF      TEST    .BAK        Bytes       16,384

TAG ALL MATCHING FILES BY ATTRIBUTES
                   : +A
 Enter attributes (+/- RASH)          ↑ history  ←┘ ok  F1 help  ESC cancel
```

Screen 3-118

XTree PRO GOLD

```
┌─────────────────────────────────────────────────────────────────────┐
│ Path: C:\UTILS                                      8-09-90  2:34:19 pm │
├─────────────────────────────────────────────────────────────────────┤
│ 10      .BAT♦  CONFIG   .  ♦   GLOBAL  .EXE♦   FILE *.*                 │
│ 3D      .BAT♦  CONFIG  .828♦   GUIDE   .BAT♦                           │
│ AUTOEXEC.IMP♦  CONFIG  .CAH♦   IN      .BAT♦   DISK C:POWER USER       │
│ AUTOEXEC.MEM♦  CONFIG  .DUM♦   INSTRUCT.BAT♦   Available               │
│ AUTOEXEC.OLD♦  CONFIG  .EG  ♦  JC      .BAT♦    Bytes   2,088,960      │
│ AUTOEXEC.SAV♦  CONFIG  .IMP♦   LJZUP   .EXE♦                           │
│ AUTOEXEC.STD♦  CONFIG  .NOW♦  │LZESHELL.EXE♦│  DIRECTORY Stats         │
│ AUTOEXEC.WIN♦  CONFIG  .OLD♦   LZEXE   .EXE♦   Total                   │
│ BETH    .  ♦   CONFIG  .STD♦   MALE    .BAT♦    Files          107     │
│ BETH    .BAT♦  CONFIG  .UNI♦   MC      .BAT♦    Bytes      804,642     │
│ BLANKS  .COM♦  CONFIG  .WIN♦   MENU    .BAT♦   Matching                │
│ BLU     .BAT♦  CONFIGTS.EXE♦   MSG     .BAT♦    Files          107     │
│ BUFFERS .RPT♦  DEF     .COM♦   MYMENU  .DAT♦    Bytes      804,642     │
│ BUFFERS1.RPT♦  DESET   .BAT♦   MYMENU  .EXE♦   Tagged                  │
│ CAT     .BAT♦  DL      .BAT♦   NUKEBAK .EXE♦    Files          107     │
│ CHECKS  .BAT♦  E       .BAT♦   OLDAUTO .BAT♦    Bytes      804,642     │
│ CIM     .BAT♦  EXAMPLE .BAT♦   OLDZIP  .EXE♦   Current File           │
│ CLASSES .BAT♦  FC      .BAT♦   ORG     .BAT♦   LZESHELL.EXE           │
│ COMICS  .BAT♦  FFEED   .COM♦   PDAILY  .DAT♦    Bytes       18,746     │
├─────────────────────────────────────────────────────────────────────┤
│ COPYING: LZESHELL.EXE as LZESHELL.EXE                                  │
│    to: B:\JUNK                                                         │
│ DESTINATION DISK FULL:      F2 format diskette  ↵ continue copy  ESC cancel │
└─────────────────────────────────────────────────────────────────────┘
```

Screen 3-119

■ Partial untag

Okay, here's the setting. You've tagged a slew of files and you're in the middle of copying them to another disk and halfway through you hear a familiar beep to let you know that the destination disk is full (Screen 3-119).

We have a few choices at this point: put another disk in the B drive and hit **<ENTER>**. We can format a disk, then continue copying. Or even hit **<ALT>Z** to exit and save our tags.

However, let's say we decide to do something different. We want to put the rest of the files on a disk in the A drive. The first step is to hit **<ESC>** to cancel the current operation.

At this point, all the files up to LZESHELL.EXE have been copied. When we start copying again, we want to *start* with LZESHELL.EXE. Normally, if we pressed **<CTRL>C** to copy, Gold would begin copying with the first tagged file. To pick up copying where we left off, we have to go back and untag all the files up to LZESHELL.EXE.

Fortunately, there's a way to automatically do this. **<ALT>F8** is the *partial untag* command. **<ALT>F8** tells Gold to untag all the files that have *already* been operated on (Screen 3-120).

This saves you the bother of untagging files one by one. (Neat, huh?)

```
Path: C:\UTILS                              8-09-90  2:35:06 pm

  18   .BAT    CONFIG  .       GLOBAL  .EXE   FILE *.*
  3D   .BAT    CONFIG  .828    GUIDE   .BAT
  AUTOEXEC.IMP CONFIG  .CAH    IN      .BAT   DISK  C:POWER USER
  AUTOEXEC.MEM CONFIG  .DUM    INSTRUCT.BAT   Available
  AUTOEXEC.OLD CONFIG  .EG     JC      .BAT   Bytes   2,000,768
  AUTOEXEC.SAV CONFIG  .IMP    LJ2UP   .EXE
  AUTOEXEC.STD CONFIG  .NOW    LZESHELL.EXE♦  DIRECTORY Stats
  AUTOEXEC.WIN CONFIG  .OLD    LZEXE   .EXE♦  Total
  BETH   .      CONFIG  .STD    MALE    .BAT♦  Files              107
  BETH   .BAT    CONFIG  .UNI    MC      .BAT♦  Bytes          804,642
  BLANKS .COM    CONFIG  .WIN    MENU    .BAT♦  Matching
  BLU    .BAT    CONFIGTS.EXE    MSG     .BAT♦  Files              107
  BUFFERS .RPT   DEF     .COM    MYMENU  .DAT♦  Bytes          804,642
  BUFFERS1.RPT   DESET   .BAT    MYMENU  .EXE♦  Tagged
  CAT    .BAT    DL      .BAT    NUKEBAK .EXE♦  Files               63
  CHECKS .BAT    E       .BAT    OLDAUTO .BAT♦  Bytes          683,786
  CIM    .BAT    EXAMPLE .BAT    OLDZIP  .EXE♦  Current File
  CLASSES .BAT   FC      .BAT    ORG     .BAT♦  LZESHELL.EXE
  COMICS .BAT    FFEED   .COM    PDAILY  .DAT♦  Bytes           18,746

FILE      Attributes  Copy  Delete  Edit  Filespec  Invert  Log disk  Move
COMMANDS  New date  Open  Print  Rename  Tag  Untag  View  eXecute  Quit
◄┘ tree  F7 autoview  F8 split    F9 menu  F10 commands    F1 help  ESC cancel
```

Screen 3-120

Are you convinced that a gremlin of some sort gets into your computer at night and creates files with unrecognizable names? "Where did *that* file come from?" you wonder. "*I* didn't create that file! No siree!"

Then you call the file up in your word processor or spreadsheet program and realize, "Oh yeah...I *need* this," vowing never to forget that file name again.

Sound familiar?

XTree's incredible View command will allow you to take a quick peek at a file *without leaving* XTree.

View will work on any file. However, trying to view program files (files with EXE and COM extensions) will give you a screen full of unrecognizable characters. It's best to stick with Viewing files that you created.

■ XTREE. To View a file, highlight it and hit **V** for View. In Screen 3-121, we went to the root (\) directory, highlighted the CONFIG.SYS file and hit **V** for View.

As you can see, the top line displays the available commands. If the whole file doesn't fit on the screen, you can move around with cursor keys and **<PgUp>** and **<PgDn>** keys.

(If you were to view a file created by a word processor or

VIEW

XTree PRO GOLD

Page 177

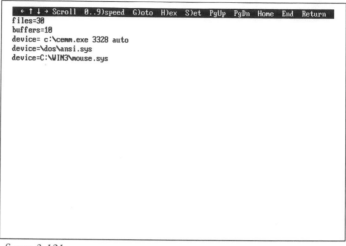

```
← ↑ ↓ → Scroll  0..9)speed  G)oto  H)ex  S)et  PgUp  PgDn  Home  End  Return
files=30
buffers=10
device= c:\cemm.exe 3328 auto
device=\dos\ansi.sys
device=C:\WIN3\mouse.sys
```

Screen 3-121

other program, your display would not be as easy to read as in the example.)

When you're finished viewing, hit **<ENTER>** and you'll be returned to your normal File Window.

Note: We are not going to worry about Hex mode or stuff like that in this book.

■ XTREEPRO. To View a file, highlight it and hit **V** for View. If the whole file doesn't fit on the screen, you can move around the file using the cursor keys and **<Pg Up>** and **<Pg Dn>** keys.

In Screen 3-122, however, we're looking at a word processed file. Any time you view a file created by another program, you may have unpredictable results (but you should see enough to recognize the file).

Hitting **<ENTER>** will take you out of View mode and you'll be returned to your normal File Window.

■ XTREEPRO GOLD. Highlighting a file and hitting **V** in Gold gives you something like Screen 3-123.

Here's a Microsoft Word file in View mode. Note the extraneous characters in the upper left-hand corner. The reason for this is that we are viewing the file without being in Word or using Gold's formatted mode.

XTree PRO GOLD

```
File: C:\WS\HOME\HOME1
←↑↓→ Scroll   0..9)speed   G)oto   S)et   M)ask   D)isplay mode: NORMAL
trudges forward, only slightly revived by the cooling
evening air.

                  ANNA
             (to herself)
        This is it.  I've got to get a car...
        no matter what...

Her thoughts are broken when she hears the excited
BARKS of a small, black COCKAPOO. Anna sees the dog
a short distance down the road, on the other side of
a small bridge over a now-dry creek.  The dog is
running back and forth over the bridge barking down
at the creek bed and then stopping to stare and
listen, only to whimper and begin barking again

                  ANNA
        How'd you get out again, Muffin?
        They shouldn't let a little boy like
        you wander around out here...
        Whatcha doing?  You smell something
        down there?
```

Screen 3-122

Gold comes with some file format filters (with more in the works) to allow files to be viewed in a way that more closely resembles how it would look in the file's native program.

When you enter Gold's view mode, Gold automatically recognizes and formats dBASE, 1-2-3, and some word processed files for easier viewing.

Other file formats may need you to hit **F** to prompt Gold to put the file in formatted viewing mode. Depending on

```
File: C:\WS\HOME\HOME1                          ASCII (no mask)
─────────────────────────────────────────────────────────────
trudges forward, only slightly revived by the cooling¦
evening air.

                  ANNA
             (to herself)
áááááááááThis is it.  I've got to get a car...¦
ááááááááno matter what...

Her thoughts are broken when she hears the excited¦
BARKS of a small, black COCKAPOO. Anna sees the dog¦
a short distance down the road, on the other side of¦
a small bridge over a now-dry creek.  The dog is¦
running back and forth over the bridge barking down¦
at the creek bed and then stopping to stare and¦
listen, only to whimper and begin barking again

                  ANNA
áááááááááHow'd you get out again, Muffin?¦
ááááááááThey shouldn't let a little boy like¦
═════════════════════════════════════════════════════════════
VIEW     ASCII Dump Formatted Gather Hex Mask Wordwrap
COMMANDS F2 F3 F4 F5 F6 goto bookmark F9 search F10 search again
↑↓ scroll ALT SHFT menus                    F1 help  ESC cancel
```

Screen 3-123

XTree PRO GOLD

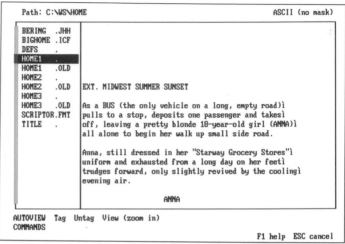

```
Path: C:\WS\HOME                                      ASCII (no mask)

  BERING   .JHH
  BIGHOME  .ICF
  DEFS     .
  HOME1    .
  HOME1    .OLD
  HOME2    .
  HOME2    .OLD   EXT. MIDWEST SUMMER SUNSET
  HOME3    .
  HOME3    .OLD   As a BUS (the only vehicle on a long, empty road)ì
  SCRIPTOR.FMT    pulls to a stop, deposits one passenger and takesì
  TITLE    .      off, leaving a pretty blonde 18-year-old girl (ANNA)ì
                  all alone to begin her walk up small side road.

                  Anna, still dressed in her "Starway Grocery Stores"ì
                  uniform and exhausted from a long day on her feetì
                  trudges forward, only slightly revived by the coolingì
                  evening air.

                                    ANNA

  AUTOVIEW  Tag  Untag  View (zoom in)
  COMMANDS
                                              F1 help  ESC cancel
```

Screen 3-124

the size of the file, the process of turning an unformatted
file into a formatted file may not be instant. (It may not be
worth the bother — or it may. You have to decide.)

■ Search

Once you are viewing a file (regardless of format), you may
hit **F9** to search for a particular phrase or word. This may
reduce some **<Pg Up>** and **<Pg Dn>** keystrokes.

■ View tagged files

If you wish to view a group of files, tag them and then press
<CTRL>V (to view all tagged files). The first tagged file will
be shown in a normal view screen. When you're ready to
view the next tagged file, press **N**. You can continue through
the list, cycling back to the first file after viewing the last file
in the group.

Note: When you are using **CTRL/V**, you cannot use the
format command.

■ AutoView

Hitting **F7** puts you in AutoView mode (Screen 3-124).
As you cursor up and down the list of files on the left, the
currently highlighted file is automatically shown as a view
file on the right. This allows you to look at the contents of a
file and then tag or untag the file.

Whenever you like, you can *zoom* in on a file by pressing   XTree PRO GOLD
v. The View Window will expand so you can get a better
look at your file. When you're done, press **<ENTER>** or
<ESC> and you'll return to AutoView. (If you wish to enjoy
a formatted view of a file, you must first zoom in first.)

Hitting **<ENTER>** (or **<ESC>**) when you're finished
browsing in AutoView will put you back in a File Window.

(If you are an XTreeGold or XTree Easy owner, go to View
in Part 5 and see all the nifty new viewers and handy added
options you get with your version!)

The 5th Wave

"NAAAH - HE'S NOT THAT SMART. HE WON'T BACK UP HIS HARD DISK, FORGETS TO CONSISTENTLY NAME HIS FILES, AND DROOLS ALL OVER THE KEYBOARD."

Hard Disk Management In a Nutshell

4

There's a saying that "anything that can fit in a nutshell belongs there." At the risk of proving that axiom, we shall break hard disk management down into two basic categories: maintenance and operation.

"Maintenance" covers all the issues that have to do with efficient functioning of the hard disk and increasing the longevity of the drive. "Operation" includes those issues that make data and programs easy for you to get to and use.

Five key guidelines for hard disk maintenance are:
1. Keep related files together. Keep the WordPerfect files in the appropriateWordPerfect directory, and so forth.
2. Delete files and directories when obsolete.
3. Back up regularly.
4. Be aware of the amount of free space on your drive (and repeat guideline number two often).
5. Optimize your hard disk (explained below).

If you own XTree, you already have the ability to easily perform all these tasks — except the last one.

Optimizing your hard disk (the fifth guideline) requires some special action and some additional software. Read on.

■ Hard Disk Optimization

Hard disk optimization means one thing: *do whatever you can to make sure the hard disk isn't working any harder than necessary.*

More work equals more wear and tear, which leads to a shorter hard disk life. When you make things easy on the hard disk, the by-product is not only longer life, but faster "access time." Granted, "access time" is measured usually in seconds or portions thereof, but every time you get a file and save a file, you're sitting through access time. Anytime you see your hard disk light go on, that's access time. Over the years, it all adds up in wasted time and in hard disk wear and tear.

The methods you can use to optimize your hard disk fall into two basic categories: what you can do for free and what costs money.

Free options Let's start with the free stuff.

■ RUN CHKDSK. Your hard disk already contains a program called "CHKDSK" (a/k/a "check disk"). You should run this program at least once a month.

CHKDSK does two things: it gives you a "bottom line" total of all files stored on the disk and the amount of available space and memory, and it makes a search for hard disk errors called "lost and cross-linked clusters."

A *cluster* is just a piece of a file. A lost cluster is a piece of a file that has become disconnected from the rest of the file. Everybody gets lost clusters every now and then. It's not a big deal. Clusters get "lost" when you don't exit a program properly and DOS doesn't have a chance to put things away neatly.

A *cross-linked cluster* is a lost cluster that has become embedded in another file. This is slightly more serious, but it's not necessarily a big problem *if* you have no more than a half dozen cross-linked clusters.

If you run CHKDSK once a month, you'll prevent lost and cross-linked clusters from accumulating.

Fortunately, running CHKDSK is a simple procedure. First make sure you have exited any program. Then, at the system prompt, type **chkdsk** and press **<ENTER>**.

If you *do* have cross-linked clusters, the computer can fix them for you by collecting them together for disposal. All you have to do is type **chkdsk /f** and hit **<ENTER>**. The "**/f**" says "fix it" to DOS.

DOS takes all your lost and cross-linked clusters and puts them in files with a CHK extension. You can then delete the CHK files.

If, however, you have lots of cross-linked clusters, do not try to fix them with CHKDSK /F.

Excessive cross-linked clusters can be a symptom of impending computer failure. If you have lots of cross-linked clusters, back up your system on a fresh set of floppies. Then run CHKDSK /F.

■ EFFICIENT DIRECTORY STRATEGIES. The way directories are structured on your hard disk has a definite effect on hard disk performance and longevity.

The four key points for directory creation are:

1. **Keep programs in one directory, data in another.** Make a directory for each of your programs, and sub-directories for the data belonging to each program.

2. **Keep your root as empty as possible.** Your root is your entryway, not your storage area. All that *really* needs to be in the root are your special files (COMMAND.COM, CONFIG.SYS, AUTOEXEC.BAT, and the two hidden files).If you find you've got a lot of stuff in your root, be sure to back everything up before you start moving and deleting things.

3. **Make many small directories (versus a few large ones).** Stay aware of how many files are in a directory, and make more directories when things get too full. One hundred is recommended — 200 is clogging your arteries!

4. **Keep directory names simple.** The longer the name, the harder it is to type. Life is difficult enough — make it easy on yourself when you can.

· ·
Here are some true-or-false questions:

1. The root should not be used as a storage area.
2. Give directories long and complex names.
3. Keep the file count under 200 in each directory.

For the answers, see Appendix D.

Pop Quiz

· ·

Proper system config- uration

The contents of your CONFIG.SYS file and AUTOEXEC.BAT file can affect your hard disk perfor- mance. Although you should already have a CONFIG.SYS and an AUTOEXEC.BAT on your computer, you might want to compare it to the following example files (which reflect the suggested *minimum* setup for running XTree):

■ CONFIG.SYS.

```
files=20
buffers=30
device=\dos\ansi.sys
```

The *files* and *buffers* commands speed up memory and directory access. If your files and buffers numbers are greater, that's okay. ANSI.SYS is a DOS file that handles your screen display, among other things.

■ AUTOEXEC.BAT.

```
prompt $p $g
path c:\;c:\dos;c:\wp;c:\xtgold
```

The *prompt* command above ensures that your system prompt will always tell you what directory you are in.

The *path statement* tells your operating system where to look for your *program* files.

Let's assume that your hard disk has the above AUTOEXEC.BAT file and that you're in your WP directory. Let's say you type **xtgold <ENTER>** to start XTreePro Gold.

However, XTreePro Gold is not stored in the WP directory. You should, therefore, be told by DOS that **xtgold** is a "bad command or file name."

Before DOS chastises you, however, DOS *first* "follows the yellow-brick road" — it searches for XTGOLD in each of the directories specified by the path statement.

In this example, DOS would look in the root for XTGOLD, then in the DOS directory, then in the WP directory, and finally the XTGOLD directory. XTGOLD is stored in the XTGOLD directory and so DOS is able to launch the program. All this hunting and searching takes place in the blink of an eye.

Another example would be that you have your WordPerfect program stored in a directory area called "WP." All your data/work is stored in a directory called "LETTERS."

Usually, when you want to work, you would go to the "LETTERS" directory (to use the files stored there). Then you type **wp** and hit **<ENTER>** to engage your WordPerfect software. But WordPerfect is not stored in the "LETTERS" directory.

Luckily, because "WP" is in the path statement, the computer can track down the program and crank it up.

It is not necessary to include the location of every piece of software on your hard disk in the path statement. If you've got a game, for instance, you don't need to include it in the path.

If you have a program you wish to use, no matter which directory you're in, then include it in your path statement.

Note: The amount of information you can put in a path statement is finite. Put only those things you are actually using *throughout your hard disk* in the path statement.

If you don't know how to view and edit CONFIG.SYS and AUTOEXEC.BAT, see VIEW (page 177) and EDIT (page 97) in the "Quick Reference Guide." *However*, before you begin experimenting with these two key files, please be sure to back them up *first.*

Optimization for sale

In addition to the above, you can also buy software to assist you in your search for hard disk longevity and peak performance.

■ BACKUP PROGRAMS. XTree will back up your hard disk.

There are, however, programs made specifically for the task. The advantage of buying one of these programs is that they will back up your computer faster and with less mental effort. Fastback and Norton Backup are two programs dedicated to this procedure.

PC Tools is another program that performs several hard disk maintenance operations, including backing up.

Another (expensive) alternative is the purchase of a piece of hardware called a "tape backup unit." It truly makes backing up a mindless, *fast* process. If you need to do daily system backups, or you've got a large hard disk, or you like to spend your money on cool stuff, this is highly recommended.

■ DISK DEFRAGGERS. When DOS saves your files, it puts them in the "next available space" on your hard disk. Later, when you add to an existing file, DOS is generally forced to put that new piece of the file some place else on the hard disk. Whenever you call up (or save) a file, DOS must search through the drive to collect all the pieces. (Your file is "to-be-continued" all over the drive). This, of course, increases access time and promotes wear and tear on the drive.

A disk defragger goes through the drive and puts all the pieces of the file next to each other. OPTune and Vopt are two simple programs designed specifically to handle this chore although both Norton and Mace Utilities will do this also.

■ DISK SCRUBBERS. After you've owned a hard disk for a while, entropy (and evil electromagnetic fluctuations) starts to take their toll on your disk's magnetic fields. Really. This isn't "Lost In Space" double-talk.

The only cure for this problem is to reformat the hard disk. Of course, formatting has the unfortunate side effect of *erasing* everything on the disk. Most people don't have the time or inclination to spend a day backing up, formatting, and restoring their data all for the sake of strengthening their magnetic fields.

What a disk scrubber does is reformat and test your hard disk *without* disturbing (i.e. erasing) the data on it. SpinRite II and Disk Technician handle this unique job. Regular reformatting will extend the life of your hard disk, perhaps indefinitely.

SpinRite II and Disk Technician (and OPTune) also check to make sure your hard disk is set to the proper *interleave* (a problem found mostly in older hard disks). Proper interleave can seriously increase disk performance. And save you-know-what (wear and tear).

■ CACHING. Most computers, these days, come with at least one megabyte of memory and a cache program. A cache program works on the theory that you are likely to keep using the commands that you've just used. The cache program keeps track of the most recently employed commands. If you do repeat a command, the cache already knows how to proceed, instead of having to ask the hard disk for the instructions. If you didn't get a cache program with your computer, PC-Kwik is the program to try.

■ UNERASE AND DISASTER RECOVERY. Although disaster recovery isn't exactly part of hard disk optimization, any book on hard disks would be incomplete without *some* mention of this important topic.

A disaster is when you delete something by mistake. A disaster is when you accidently reformat your hard disk, or delete a directory. There are even more (technical) things that can go wrong, but let's not dwell on the subject of disasters.

Suffice it to say that Peter Norton's Advanced Utilities and The Mace Utilities can save the day in all these situations.

Norton and Mace will also do defragging. (As will PC Tools.)

In addition to XTree, of course, you should have either Norton or Mace Utilities and SpinRite II. Next a backup program. Then PC-Kwik for caching if your computer didn't come with a cache program. (Norton Utilities also comes with a cache program.) Go to your local friendly computer or software store and look at the boxes — talk to the professionals — and make a selection.

The wish list

The point of all these programs is not so much to save you money by making your hard disk last a long, long time. If you buy *everything*, you'll be spending as much as the cost of a new 40-megabyte hard disk. The point is to put off and to reduce the tragedy of a hard disk crash. The loss of data is the critical issue.

On the other hand, prolonging the life of your drive might actually save you thousands of dollars. The death of a drive often precipitates the rationalization of the purchase of a whole new computer system.

Anyway, when you are considering the purchase of any software, be sure to note the "system requirements" on the box before shelling out cash. You'll need to know how much memory your computer has (see CHKDSK on page 184) as well as what version of DOS you own.

■ DOS VERSION. It easy to determine which version of DOS is installed in your computer.

At any system prompt, type **VER <ENTER>**. The version number of DOS will be displayed.

If you have version 2.0 or 2.11 of MS-DOS and are toying with the idea of upgrading to 3.1 or higher, you may want to take several things into consideration.

There are good reasons to upgrade, and silly reasons to upgrade. Good reasons to upgrade are that you want to use a program that requires a higher version of DOS, or you want to exchange work with someone who has a higher version of DOS, or your laptop has a higher version than your desktop, or you want to repartition your hard disk. If any of these cases is true for you, it is wise to upgrade.

If you do upgrade, a low-level and high-level format of your hard disk *may* be required. (That means you need to back up everything, reformat, and restore your system.)

If this makes you squeamish, you may want to find a friend, a consultant,or computer store you feel comfortable dealing with to help you out.

You may not be missing a thing by not having the hippest version of DOS. In fact, stepping up the DOS's evolutionary ladder exacts a price in disk space and memory.

Some older computers will also require a chip upgrade to accommodate the new DOS. Some software also requires adjustments in the CONFIG.SYS to accommodate the new DOS.

Translation: Upgrading DOS is not recommended as a "fun thing to do."

■ Step-by-Step Hard Disk Maintenance

This small section is devoted to listing the commands needed to perform the two things you *must* do to maintain your hard disk (and your sanity):

1. Back up your files.
2. Delete what you don't need.

If these two lessons are all you get from this book, we'll both sleep easier at night.

All of the commands used below are described in detail elsewhere in this book. Where possible, this section just tells you what keys to hit and in what order. Period. No muss, no fuss.

■ Backup

One of the greatest conveniences of a hard disk — everything being in one place — is also the most dangerous aspect of a hard disk — everything being in one place! To soften the blow of a hard disk failure (the inevitable hard disk failure), you should duplicate (back up) the contents of your hard disk onto a set of floppy disks at least once a month. In addition, every day you should be backing up any edited or newly created file.

Although your word processor may make BAK backup files as you work, they don't count as a backup because both original and backup are in the same place. The point of backing up is to avoid dependence on one device as the guardian of *all* your data.

Unfortunately, learning to back up regularly is a lesson most people choose to learn the hard way. When you do experience the sheer terror of a hard disk failure (without a back up) you, too, will become a staunch, born-again backer-upper.

Backup strategies There are several different backup strategies. You'll probably end up using all of them in various combinations.

■ DAILY. The first backup strategy is the simple daily backup. At the end of the day you have to remember which files you created or edited that day and copy them onto a floppy disk. To back up only a few files, just use XTree's Copy command (see page 70).

■ SYSTEM. A system backup copies your data, your programs, and your directory structure setup onto a big stack of floppy disks. You may wonder why you should copy the programs when your master program disks are sitting safely in their boxes. What you're backing up is the program *including* whatever hard-fought customizations have been performed by you or your brother-in-law.

It's recommended that you perform a system backup once a month. Further, you should have two complete copies of your computer system which should be "rotated." In January, say, use one set of backup disks. In February, the second. In March, use the first set of disks again, and so forth.

If you're using a database, a point-of-sale system, a complex accounting system, or any kind of software that updates dozens of individual files every day, you probably need to do a system backup once a day.

■ INCREMENTAL. In between your daily backups and your monthly system backups are incremental backups. This is when you back up everything that hasn't been backed up since the last system backup. This is an interim just-to-be-sure backup.

System backup Let's do a full system backup first.

Since a full system backup requires a slew of floppies, the first step is to determine the number of floppies needed. Just get into XTree and look at the DISK Statistics box on the right. It'll tell you the "Total Bytes" used on your hard disk.

How many disks will you need? If you have 18,000,000 bytes used and you use high density 5¹/₄-inch floppy disks (which hold 1,200,000 bytes), you'd need at least 15 floppy disks. (Divide 1,200,000 into 18,000,000.) If you have low density 5¹/₄-

inch disks (which hold 360,000 bytes), you'd need at least 50 floppy disks. (High density 3¹/₂-inch disks hold 1,400,000 bytes, and low density 3¹/₂-inch disks hold 720,000 bytes.) **Note:** If you calculate that you need seven disks to back up your system, you should also be prepared with a few extra disks, because XTree may not fill up each disk.

If you have a 2,500-byte file to be copied, and only 2,000 bytes of disk space left over on your backup disk, XTree will determine that the 2,500-byte file won't fit and ask that you put a new floppy disk in the drive. That 2,000 bytes of disk space is then just left blank.

Also, XTree cannot back up a file if it is larger than a floppy disk. If you have a disk with a 360,000-byte capacity and a file that is 425,000 bytes big, XTree cannot copy that file onto your disk (and you should explore some of the other backup-specific software available).

Once you've determined how many disks you need, then you must format them (see page 117).

1. Get into XTree and from the Directory Window, hit **S** (for Showall).
2. Press **<CTRL>T** to tag all files.
3. Press **<ALT>C** to copy all tagged files and the directory structure.
4. Press **<ENTER>** to maintain the same name of the files.
5. When prompted, type the name of the destination drive and hit **<ENTER>**. XTree will start backing up your system.
6. When a disk is full, XTree will prompt you to feed the computer another formatted floppy disk.

Back up everything in six easy steps

After you've finished your system backup, there's one last small task: While your files are still tagged, hit **<CTRL>A** (for attribute), then type **-A <ENTER>**. This turns *off* the archive bit on each of the tagged files. Any file you create or edit from this point foward will automatically have its archive bit turned *on*.

You can use these turned-on archive bits as "flags" when it comes time to do an incremental backup. Only those files

Keep track of what you've backed up

with their archive bits turned on need to be backed up —
you'll see how to do that next.

Incremental   An incremental backup (backing up any files that haven't
backups   been created or edited since the last backup) should be
performed between system backups.

If you've done a system backup and you turned off the
archive bit on the backed up files (as instructed above), you
can perform an incremental backup as follows:

1. Get into XTree and from the Directory Window, hit **S**
   (for Showall).
2. Press **<ALT>T** (to tag by attributes).
3. Type **+A <ENTER>** to tag all files that have the archive
   bit turned on. (These are the files that have changed
   since your last system backup.)
4. Press **<ALT>C** to copy all tagged files (and preserve
   your directory structure).
5. Press **<ENTER>** to maintain the same name of the files.
6. When prompted, type the name of the destination
   drive and tap **<ENTER>**.
7. After you finish backing up (while your files are still
   tagged), hit **<CTRL>A** for attributes, and type
   -A<ENTER> to turn off the archive bit.

Backup   You can use XTree's ability to sort files by date to isolate files
by date   created or updated during any period of time (weekly, or
since last Tuesday, for example).

1. Get into XTree and from the Directory Window. Hit **S**
   (for Showall).
2. Hit **<ALT>F-F** to change File display to include the
   date and time each file was last saved.
3. Hit **<ALT>S-D** to sort the files by date and time.
4. Look at the date and time next to the file names, and
   tag those files within the dates you want.
5. Hit **<CTRL>C** to copy all tagged files (or **<ALT>C** to
   copy the files and their directory structures).
6. Press **<ENTER>** to maintain the names of the files.
7. When prompted, type the name of the destination
   drive and press **<ENTER>**.

■ Delete Unneeded Files

Every now and then, you should do some housecleaning on your hard disk. Take a look at the files on your disk. Anything growing mold? If a file is obsolete, either delete it or copy it to a floppy disk if you think you may want to use it again someday.

In addition to these familiar files, however, there may be some additional junk files that have accumulated on your hard disk. Junk files are created in a few ways: Some programs deposit stray files on your disk when you quit by turning of your computer, or doing a reboot, instead of exiting normally. In MS Word these junk files end with TMP; in Wordstar they end with $?$.

Word processors create BAK files which you may want to delete to keep things clean and save space.

Here are some ways to get rid of unwanted files.

1. Get into XTree and from the Directory Window, hit **S** (for Showall). All files will be displayed in alphabetical order. Files with the same names will, therefore, be listed next to each other.

2. To help you decide which file to keep and which to tag for deletion, you can use one of the following methods:

   A. Highlight a file and look at its directory path (displayed at the top of the screen). This will tell you where the file is stored, which may be a deciding factor.

   B. Press **<ALT>F-F** to change File display to include the size and the date and time the file was last saved. Whichever is the newer or the bigger *may* be the one to keep.

   C. View the file's contents. Just highlight the file and type **V** to see what's in the file (see page 177).

3. Once you've tagged all the files you want to delete, then a **<CTRL>D** will delete them.

Note: Remember not to delete any of the following files from the root: AUTOEXEC.BAT, CONFIG.SYS, COMMAND.COM, IBMBIO.SYS, and IBMDOS.COM.

Remove duplicate files

Remove BAK and TMP files in four easy steps

1. Get into XTree and from the Directory Window type **F** for filespec. Type ***.BAK** (or ***.TMP** or any other filespec) and press **<ENTER>**.
2. Type **S** (for Showall). All files matching the filespec you entered (***.BAK**) will be displayed.
3. **<CTRL>T** will tag all files.
4. **<CTRL>D** deletes them.

Remember, when you have deleted all the tagged files, XTree will report NO Files! in the File Window. When you change your Filespec back to ***.***, you'll see the rest of your files.

Retire some files

You may decide to take some rarely used files off your hard disk and store them on floppies. One approach is to have XTree list files by extension (using DOC or WK1 or DBF, or whatever extension your software generates). Examine the list, using View as necessary, and tag those which can be copied to a floppy (and deleted from your hard disk).

1. Get into XTree and from the Directory Window, type **F** for filespec. Type ***.DOC** (or ***.XLS** or ***.DBF** or whatever) and **<ENTER>**.
2. Type **S** (for Showall). All files matching the *.DOC filespec will be displayed. Now for a trip down memory lane.
3. Look at each file name or type **V** to view the file (see page 177).
4. Tag each file that can be removed from the hard disk and copied to a floppy.
5. When finished tagging, type **<CTRL>C** to copy all tagged files.
6. When finished copying, type **<CTRL>D** to delete the tagged files.

Continuing The Evolution Of XTree: A "Greenprint" For The Future

By King Lee
President
XTree Company

We'reeeeee back. And this time I can honestly tell you that we really do have it all planned! From XTreeNet to XTreeGold, from the just released XTree Easy to the series of environmental programs we're calling Project Green, we put our heads together and looked down the road. Each program represents hundreds of hours of planning, programming, testing, tweaking, and pizzas. (Without pizza, no software would ever be created.)

And we're not finished. Far from it. As a result of our groundwork in years past, in 1991 XTree Company is branching out into a variety of different environments, and not all of them have to do with computers.

For example in 1989, we wanted to expand the XTree concept of managing information on a single computer in the DOS environment to managing information on many computers on a Novell network. We named it right off — XTreeNet. We wanted to see what would happen if we named it first, then went to work on it. It turned out not to make a difference. We still had to learn all about the special challenges administrators face working on a network.

So we interviewed network managers and listened to their beefs. We found out exactly what they liked in our XTree products, what they didn't, and what special features they needed to tame their unique problems. To be honest, the first time we didn't get it all right. So in 1990 we went back to the famous drawing board, dusted off our Klingon curses, and in August, 1990, released XTreeNet 2.0.

We must be doing something right because in less than seven months, XTreeNet 2.0 was awarded LAN Times' prestigious Reader's Choice Award for Best Network Software of 1990.

THEN THERE'S THE new XTreeGold. This is the product I'm most proud of in my four years at the helm of XTree Company. Which is saying something since every incarnation of XTree has won awards from major computer publications.

Our goal was to make XTreePro Gold even easier and more intuitive. So again, we talked to you, our users. And with your help I think we've succeeded. Since its release in January, 1991, XTreeGold has consumers, reviewers, and our industry peers talking.

Reviewers are praising Gold's new features like the pull down-menus, undelete feature, and application menu that actually searches your hard disk and builds a customized menu for you automatically.

As I write this, XTreeGold is currently a candidate and finalist for the Software Publisher's Association's (SPA) Best Software Utility. Even if we don't win — and we're up against some pretty impressive products including Adobe Type Manager Windows Version, PC Tools Deluxe, PC Kwik PowerPak, and Norton Utilities — this nomination is particularly gratifying because it's voted on by members of the SPA who are other software publishers. And your peers are always a tough crowd to please.

BUT EVEN TOUGHER were some of the behind-the-scene decisions we made concerning XTreeGold. These decisions not only impact our entire product line, forever, but we hope they will change the way other software publishers manufacture their software as well.

There's a bumper sticker you see every now and then. It reads: THINK GLOBALLY, ACT LOCALLY. Certainly the right thought for any time, especially so considering the state of things today. But, as is the case with most slogans, the slogan is the easy part. That's what we found out back in September, 1990, when we decided to embark on a series of environmental programs under the umbrella name of PROJECT GREEN.

Now XTree Company is no stranger to change. In 1985, we revolutionized PC use with a simple hard disk management utility called XTree. In 1989, we launched the U.S. market's first-ever software amnesty program. In 1991, with the release of the new XTreeGold, we wanted to become the first major software publisher to produce and ship products using recycled or environmentally sensitive materials wherever possible.

The result is Project Green.

Starting with XTreeGold, every product component except the floppy disk and the shrink-wrap are made from recycled and recyclable materials. (And we're still looking for alternatives to shrink-wrapping.) All future products will be designed to meet this new Project Green standard and that includes the just-released XTree Easy.

THE NEW XTREE EASY is sort of an XTreeGold Jr., designed for new/novice/and beginner users. This product replaces the original XTree. As fate — well, careful planning — would have it, XTree Easy is being released, along with this book, almost six years to the day that the first XTree was released at the West Coast Computer Faire. (Call me crazy, but Cahlin is still handling the public relations for product introductions as well as the entire Project Green Program!)

But we're not stopping there.

We formed an alliance with The American Forestry Association. Neil Sampson, the AFA's Executive Vice President, showed us how to shift gears from "acting locally" to "thinking globally". With the help of Global ReLeaf — a public awareness and tree planting campaign started by the AFA — XTree Company has introduced a "groundbreaking" Plant-A-Tree Program that involves all of our registered users.

An invitation to join Global ReLeaf is included in every XTreeGold. Every time a new user sends in their XTreeGold registration card, XTree Company will contribute funds to have one tree planted in Global ReLeaf's efforts to restore abused and neglected lands. Every time a current user upgrades to XTreeGold, we will also contribute funds to have trees planted. Our goal is to help Global ReLeaf plant 100 million new trees in the United States by 1992.

These Return-A-Registration Card/Plant-A-Tree Programs will also be added to our other product lines and we are in the process of launching them internationally by the end of 1992.

Now everyone, not just XTree users, is invited to participate. So if you're reading this in a bookstore and have no intention of ever purchasing one of our products, you can still get involved by calling Global ReLeaf at 900/420-4545. Five bucks will be charged to your phone bill, and you'll get a packet of Global ReLeaf materials and a tree will be planted in your name in a Global ReLeaf Heritage Forest.

FRANKLY WE'D LIKE to see everyone in the computer industry become more environmentally aware. MAGEE Enterprises, Inc., The Financial $oftware Company, and others are already printing their manuals on recycled paper. Progress has a price, and the price of the PC has been paper. Which is why we encourage everyone in our industry to investigate other ideas, including the possibility of distributing upgrades in the future via modem, saving disks and paper both.

We're also hoping that our Project Green Program will become a blueprint — or "greenprint," if you will — for the entire computer industry. To help other companies facing these same issues, XTree Company has created a "Greenprint" which lists suggestions for moving toward increased environmental responsibility. We have also compiled a "Green Pages" of environmentally sensitive vendors that have helped us turn over a new leaf. Both lists are available at no charge. Interested parties should send a stamped self-addressed envelope to: Green Pages, XTree Company, 4330 Santa Fe Road, San Luis Obispo, CA 93401. Since we're still learning, and always open to new suggestions, if you have sources or ideas to contribute, please send them to the same address.

Although only a few software-related companies have announced environmental programs, the movement is growing. IDG Books Worldwide, a division of IDG Communications, publishers of InfoWorld and PC World, recently became the first major publisher of computer books to print on recycled paper — and it happened with the first edition of this book. This second edition is also printed on recycled paper. In July of 1990, PC Connection, Inc./ MacConnection of Marlow, NH, the leading mail-order supplier of software and peripherals for IBM personal computers and the Apple Macintosh, began printing their catalogs on recycled paper and are now using recycled tissue instead of foam peanuts to pack orders.

Think about it. If other software publishers join us and begin offering Plant-A-Tree Programs, and printing their manuals on recycled paper, and start using recycled, recyclable and environmentally sensitive materials in their packaging, we really have a chance to change the world for the better. How many times do you get to do that?

Introduction

Find a need and fill it, they say. Looks like we did: The Official XTree MS-DOS and Hard Disk Companion *(this book, silly!) jumped onto the computer book bestsellers list the day it came out and has been there ever since. It rang a bell with all those XTree owners, both old and new, who were happy for a chance to get more out of their old friend, XTree, (and get a clearer idea of how MS-DOS and their hard disks work).*

Glad to be of service. But nothing stands still for long in the computer business. Even as this volume was leaping onto the bestseller charts, the developers at XTree Company were busily at work upgrading, updating, crossing new frontiers, and generally not leaving well enough alone. Hey, it's a competitive business!

So here we are with two new versions of XTree newly on the market. And in answer to your cards and letters, there is a command-key list for each and every XTree product. (That reminds me, please go fill out the reader registration card in the back of the book right now — we're already gathering ideas for the next edition!)

■ Quick Update Guide to The New XTrees: XTree Easy & XTreeGold

Updating a much-beloved product is tough. (Just ask Coca Cola.) Changing XTree had its own set of problems. On the one hand, any major change would upset old-timers. On the other hand, new-timers are expecting to see the emerging (easier to use) graphical interface standards. It turns out that the complex mission of making everyone happy is very simple — just give everyone what they want.

XTreeGold (and its baby brother, XTree Easy) have the traditional XTree interface and the more hip "pull-down menus." You can use either command system, or both. In addition to the pull-down menus, many other subtle changes are in the new software to make it more responsive.

In essence, XTreeGold is XTreePro Gold (as described in Part 3) plus the changes documented in this section. If there have been no changes to a particular feature, it will not be included in this Update section.

For instance, XTreeGold handles the issue of Attributes exactly as XTreePro Gold did, so there is no need to rehash a topic already covered in the Quick Reference Guide.

XTree Easy is basically XTree, plus the changes noted below. In addition, XTree Easy has been given a couple of powers formerly the sole domain of its big brothers: one is the ability to edit ASCII files (as described on page 97), format a floppy disk, (page 119) and it will collapse down to 7K when you **<ALT>X** (eXecute) a program (page 105).

(Added features. See page 50.)

If you loved the idea of XTreePro Gold's application menu, but found yourself hiding under the desk when it came time to actually figure out how to set up the menu, welcome to

APPLICA-TION MENU

XTree
EASY GOLD

XTreeMenu — the revamped application menu now found in the new XTrees.

You have only to ask (at installation) and XTree will search your hard disk and, all by itself, build a sophisticated menu system for you (like the one in Screen 5-1) in a matter of seconds.

Just keep in mind that the menu builder is not omniscient. It will recognize over 700 programs, but it still may miss something on your system or mistake one program for another. (For instance, on my system a monitor saver program was mistaken for a game called Mean Streets since both programs use the same file name — **MS.EXE**.)

So come on out from under the desk and look at XTreeMenu.

Once the XTreeMenu has been built, it can be popped up from within XTree by hitting **F9**. As illustrated in Screen 5-1, XTree groups the programs found on your hard disk into categories such as "Business" and "Communications" to make programs easier to locate. (If you don't like those category titles, we'll see how to rename them shortly.)

If you want to use a program on the menu, just highlight it with the cursor and hit **<ENTER>**. For instance, if you want to activate Excel, just highlight it and hit **<ENTER>** and after a few seconds, you'll be in Excel. At the conclusion

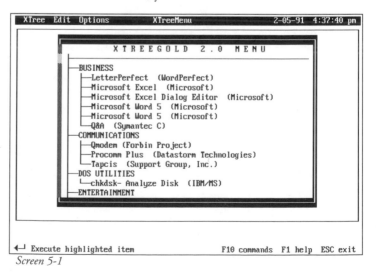

Screen 5-1

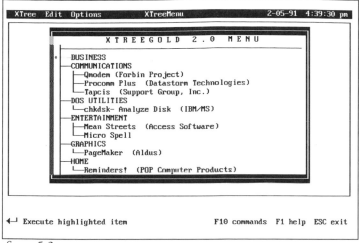

Screen 5-2

of your Excel session, you'll be delivered right back to XTreeMenu.

The previous version of XTreeMenu had a limit of thirteen listings. Now, however, no such restrictions apply. You can have screenful after screenful of menu listings if you wish.

If, however, you end up with too much of a good thing and your menu gets too long, you can collapse portions of the menu so that just the group titles, for instance, are visible.

In Screen 5-2 only the "Business" group title remains — all the sub-listings are gone. This was accomplished simply by highlighting the group title (in this case "Business") and pressing the minus key (**-**). All listings beneath the title disappear from sight. (The "+" to the left of "Business" tells you there's "more.") To bring back the sub-listings, just highlight the title and press the plus key (**+**) (or you can just hit **<ENTER>**).

Let's say there are a few things about the XTreeMenu you'd like to modify — delete a listing here, rename a group title there — that sort of thing. If so, the first step is to highlight the menu listing you want to alter and then hit **F10.**

Hitting **F10** (or clicking at the top of the screen with the mouse) activates the new pull-down menu system at the top of the screen (see "Pull-Down Menus" later in this chapter).

XTree
EASY GOLD

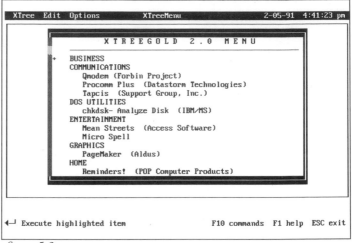

Screen 5-3

Then use your arrow keys to highlight the menu category you want. The options appear underneath allowing you to highlight the command you want to execute. Hit **<ENTER>**. (Alternately you can hit the letter highlighted in the word you wish to use.)

Take a deep breath and start with a simple but sort of dramatic change. As illustrated in Screens 5-1 and 5-2, the XTreeMenu is organized in a "tree display" (much like how the directories and sub-directories are laid out in XTree). You can, however, turn off XTreeMenu's tree (as in Screen 5-3) for an exciting change of pace.

To turn off the tree, hit **F10** to activate the menu bar, then hit the right arrow key to highlight Options. At this point you can hit either highlight Graphics Toggle and hit **<ENTER>** or simply hit **G** (for Graphics Toggle) and the tree display will vanish. Repeat the procedure to toggle the tree back on.

More tools can be found under the Edit menu (Screen 5-4), which allow you to Add, Delete, Move and Rename items in your XTreeMenu.

To delete rarely-used (or sensitive) programs from the XTreeMenu, highlight the item to be deleted, hit **F10** (for the commands), arrow-key over to highlight Edit, then either hit **D** or highlight the word Delete and hit **<ENTER>**.

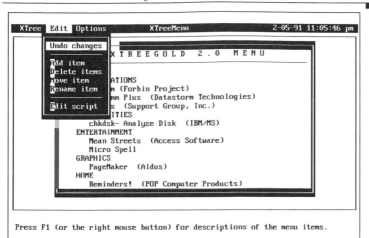

XTree
EASY   GOLD

Screen 5-4

You'll be asked to verify that you want the item deleted. Confirm with an **<ENTER>**.

Note: If you delete an item that has sub-listings (i.e. items indented underneath it), the sub-listings will be deleted as well.

If you make a mistake, immediately use the "Undo changes" command, also found under Edit, to "throw away changes" made to the menu. Be sure to use this *before* you exit the menu — otherwise it's too late.

The Move command lets you change the assigned position of a listing. This lets you customize the menu to your needs. Move, in addition to moving menu items up and down (with the up and down arrow keys), also lets you indent (or outdent) items using the left and right arrow keys. To move, highlight the item to be moved, hit **F10**, highlight Edit, hit **M** (for move) and move the item to its new home and hit **<ENTER>** to lock it into position.

When you use Move, you'll find that you cannot move an item from one group to another (from underneath "ENTERTAINMENT" to underneath "BUSINESS" for example) *unless* you outdent it first (use your left arrow key to move the item to the left). Once you get the listing in the proper group, use the right arrow to indent the item to its correct position (then hit **<ENTER>** to complete the operation).

XTree
EASY GOLD

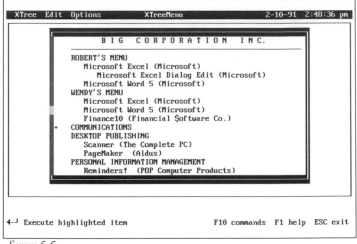

```
 XTree  Edit  Options          XTreeMenu                2-10-91  2:48:36 pm

              B I G   C O R P O R A T I O N   I N C.

        ROBERT'S MENU
           Microsoft Excel (Microsoft)
              Microsoft Excel Dialog Edit (Microsoft)
           Microsoft Word 5 (Microsoft)
        WENDY'S MENU
           Microsoft Excel (Microsoft)
           Microsoft Word 5 (Microsoft)
           Finance10 (Financial Software Co.)
     +  COMMUNICATIONS
        DESKTOP PUBLISHING
           Scanner (The Complete PC)
           PageMaker  (Aldus)
        PERSONAL INFORMATION MANAGEMENT
           Reminders!  (POP Computer Products)
```

←┘ Execute highlighted item   F10 commands F1 help ESC exit

Screen 5-5

If you want to rework the XTreeMenu, you'll quickly realize that editing listings via the pull-down menu is somewhat tiresome. Fortunately, there's a secret shortcut: All highlighted key commands in the pull-down menu can be used whether you're in the pull-down menu or not.

For instance, while looking at your application menu, just press **G** to turn the graphics toggle on and off. Want to move an item? Hit **M** and move away. Expand or collapse the tree — hit **+** or **-**. It is quite a frustration-saver.

Screen 5-5 is one example of an edited XTreeMenu. You may also wish to replace "XTreeGold Menu" at the top with an appropriate company name. If you have other people using your computer, giving them their own sub-menus (like "Robert" and "Wendy") can save time and frustration. (Remember, using the History command when editing repetitive menus will save some keystrokes.) You may add more indented levels as needed.

Once you have edited the menu *display*, selecting Edit Script — the final option underneath Edit — allows you to create (or edit) XTreeMenu's underlying instructions for a given menu item. If a menu item works (i.e., it executes the program) then you don't have to edit the script. But if you move a program from one location to another on your hard disk, or if you add an item on the menu, you must

XTree
EASY GOLD

```
 XTree  Edit  Item              XTreeMenu              2-08-91  3:11:24 pm

 Scanner (The Complete PC)

 01 C:
 02 cd\scan
 03 scan.exe
 04
 05
 06
 07
 08
 09
 10
 11
 12
 13
 14
 15
 16
 17

 EDIT      Copy  Delete  Edit  Insert  Move  cOpy to scrap  Paste from scrap
 COMMANDS  Rename item  TAB next item  BACKTAB previous item  Quit
 ↑↓ scroll through command script            F10 commands  F1 help  ESC menu
```

Screen 5-6

create/edit a "script" for that item that tells the computer where the program resides on the hard disk and what command activates it.

To edit a script, highlight the menu listing to be edited, hit **F10**, highlight Edit, then highlight Edit Script and hit **<ENTER>**. (Or just hit **E** for Edit.) You'll get a display something like Screen 5-6.

This is the script for the highlighted menu item. If you've ever created a DOS batch file (like AUTOEXEC.BAT, the automatic-startup file, for instance) you'll see that this is nothing more than a fancy, more convenient way to create a batch file. At this point, some of you may be again experiencing that urge to crawl back under the desk. Others, however, may be happy to see that several new options have been added here, reducing the amount of typing required and making it possible to copy a script from one menu listing to another.

In Screen 5-6, we are editing the script for the Scanner menu item. (In Screen 5-5 you can see Scanner is listed under the "DESKTOP PUBLISHING" group title.)

One of the fun new commands in Editing a script is the mysterious "TAB Next item" and "BACKTAB previous item." The word "item" refers to a menu listing (like Scanner). This means that, in this case, once you finished

**XTree
EASY GOLD**

editing the Scanner script, hitting **<TAB>** will save your edits and move you on to the script for the next item on the menu (the PageMaker listing, in our example). If instead you hold down the **<SHIFT>** key while hitting **<TAB>**, you'll be taken to the previous item, the "DESKTOP PUB-LISHING" group title.

The other handy additions are the "Copy to scrap" and "Paste from scrap" commands. "Scrap" does not mean thrown away (as in scrap heap). In computers, scrap is another name for a "clipboard" or temporary storage space.

In the menu in Screen 5-5, both Robert and Wendy's menus contain Microsoft Word. While each menu listing needs its own script, chances are the scripts Robert and Wendy use to invoke Word will be nearly identical. With Copy and Paste you can take a script from one menu item and duplicate it into another. Then you can make whatever minor edits are necessary rather than starting from scratch.

To copy the script you are currently editing, hit **O** (to Copy to scrap). Then **<TAB>** or **<BACKTAB>** (i.e **<SHIFT><TAB>**) to display the other menu item's script screen and hit **P** to Paste from scrap. The script will magically appear on screen.

Note: If you already had some information in script "B," pasting script "A" into script "B" will wipe it out, replacing it the contents of script "A."

Once you are editing a script, there's yet another pull-down menu (accessed by **F10**) waiting to help you out. As with most pull-down menus, it offers basically the same choices as what you see at the bottom. With one important exception: Undo. The pull-down menu lists Undo — though you don't have to pull down the menu to use it (just hit **U**).

Note: As with XTreePro Gold, the configuration program for XTreeGold will let you set XTreeMenu to automatically pop up whenever XTree is activated. Also, as a security measure, you can make it impossible for anyone to make changes to the menu (except you, of course). Also, if you're the office guru, you can set up menus for your disciples and be free from concern about anyone accidently changing anything.

(Added features.)

XTreeGold now also supports the Zip archive format. For more detail (a whole chapter, in fact) see Archiving in the appendix starting on page 263.

ARCHIVING

(New command.)

AVAIL

This tells you how much space is AVAILable on the disk drive. Generally you can discover how much space is left on the current drive just by looking at the upper right hand corner where the "Available Bytes" are always displayed.

XTree
EASY GOLD

Where Avail becomes helpful is when you have a floppy and you just want to know how much free space is on the disk without going through logging and relogging.

Just hit **A** (for Avail) and when prompted, type in the name of disk drive in question and hit **<ENTER>**. In a flash, XTree will give you an answer.

(New command.)

BRANCH FILE

A new command now appearing at the bottom of local XTreeGold screens everywhere is "Branch." The Branch command is a local or "mini Showall" command. When you hit Showall, every single file on your entire hard drive is listed, usually alphabetically, one after the other. Branch, however, displays all the files in the current directory *and* its children directories (the indented directories) in one list.

XTree
EASY GOLD

It's just another way to simplify finding and copying files, identifying duplicates and so forth.

In the directory window, highlight a parent directory and hit **B**. All files (matching the current file specifications, of course) will be listed as though they were in one mega-directory.

If you hit **<CTRL>B** only those files currently *tagged* will be displayed.

COMPARE

XTree
EASY GOLD

(New command.)

One of the great features of XTreePro Gold was the split window command. *Two* directories side by side! That was great. New vistas opened up — along with new problems. Why did the directory on the left have more files than the one on the right — what was missing? Which one had the newest version?

Now, Compare will tag the matches and the mismatches *for* us. It will not only compare two directories on one drive, but also two directories on *different* drives.

To compare two directories highlight the first (source) directory and hit C for Compare. You'll be asked to specify the name of the second directory. Type in the directory name (or better yet, use Point or History) and hit **<ENTER>**. In Screen 5-7, we're just about ready to compare the Express directory with the Excel directory.

At the bottom of the screen, Gold is asking *which* files to tag — i.e. "what are you looking for?"

Your options are:

Identical — asks that any files in the source directory that have the same name, date, size and attributes as the files in the compare directory be tagged.

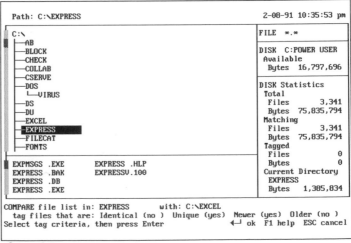

```
Path: C:\EXPRESS                               2-08-91 10:35:53 pm

 C:\                                     FILE  *.*
  ├─AB
  ├─BLOCK                                DISK  C:POWER USER
  ├─CHECK                                Available
  ├─COLLAB                               Bytes   16,797,696
  ├─CSERVE
  ├─DOS                                  DISK Statistics
  │  └─VIRUS                             Total
  ├─DS                                    Files        3,341
  ├─DU                                    Bytes   75,835,794
  ├─EXCEL                                Matching
  ├─EXPRESS                               Files        3,341
  ├─FILECAT                               Bytes   75,835,794
  ├─FONTS                                Tagged
                                          Files            0
 EXPMSGS .EXE     EXPRESS .HLP            Bytes            0
 EXPRESS .BAK     EXPRESSV.100           Current Directory
 EXPRESS .DB                              EXPRESS
 EXPRESS .EXE                             Bytes    1,385,834

COMPARE file list in: EXPRESS      with: C:\EXCEL
   tag files that are: Identical (no )  Unique (yes)  Newer (yes)  Older (no )
Select tag criteria, then press Enter                ←┘ ok  F1 help  ESC cancel
```

Screen 5-7

Unique — asks that any files in the source directory that do not exist in the compare directory be tagged.

Newer — asks that any files in the source directory that are newer (by date/time) than files in the compare directory be tagged.

Older — asks that any files in the source directory that are older (by date/time) than files in the compare directory be tagged.

Each of these options can be turned on and off by hitting the highlighted key (**I** for Identical, for instance). The options are not mutually exclusive. Mix and match to get what you want.

Back in Screen 5-7, we've chosen Unique/Newer. This will tag those files in the source directory that are *not* in the compare directory *or* that were newer.

Once your options are set, another **<ENTER>** will trigger the appropriate files in the source directory to be tagged.

Imagine your disappointment when you realize that Compare is presented as an option only when you're in a directory window. Do not despair: **<ALT>F4** will activate Compare from other windows.

What's *really* fun (if you think you can handle it) is to start Compare (using **<ALT>F4**) from a Branch, Showall, or Global file window. You even get a few extra options (Screen 5-8, next page).

The choices at the bottom of the screen are:

Duplicate — lists files with the same names

Unique — files that are one-of-a kind

Identical dates — duplicate names and same dates

Newest dates — newest version of files with the same name (if more than one file shares the same date, they are all listed)

Oldest dates — oldest version of files with the same names (if more than one file shares the same date, they are all listed)

Scope — used when in the Global window. The three options for Scope are:

XTree
EASY GOLD

```
Path: c:\word\docs\bbs\modem                      2-14-91 12:51:42 pm

  1        .TXT      GOLD1    .DOC          FILE  *.*
 10        .TXT      GOLD2    .DOC
 11        .TXT      GOLD2    .DOC          DISK  C:POWER USER
 12        .TXT      INDEX    .DOC          Available
  2        .TXT      INDEX    .DOC            Bytes   11,051,008
  3        .TXT      INST     .CAP
  4        .TXT      SLIDE    .BAT          BRANCH Statistics
  5        .TXT      THATSA   .EXE          Total
  6        .TXT                               Files              27
  7        .TXT                               Bytes       1,674,246
  8        .TXT                             Matching
  9        .TXT                               Files              27
 BBSTALK   .DOC                              Bytes       1,674,246
 BBSWKSHT  .DOC                             Tagged
 BIGX      .BAK                               Files               0
 BIGX      .BAK                               Bytes               0
 BIGX      .DOC                             Current File
 BIGX      .DOC                               1           .TXT
 GOLD1     .DOC                               Bytes             274

Show files with:  Duplicate names   Unique names
                  duplicates with: Identical dates  Newest dates  Oldest dates
                  global Scope (n/a)                     F1 help  ESC cancel
```

Screen 5-8

- All (files with the same names),
- Across drives (files with same names on different drives),
- Matching paths (files with the same names and same paths, but on different disks).

After you hit the highlighted letter, XTreeGold redisplays the list.

Using **<ALT>F4** allows you, in essence, to compare files from more than one drive and from more than one disk.

Compare can also be used in your backup scheme. Compare the source directory with your backup disk and then copy only the tagged ("unique/newer") files onto your backup disk.

COPY

(Added features. See page 70.)

XTree
EASY GOLD

<ALT>Copy (which copies files and their paths) now allows you to specify a *directory* as a destination. The source directory structure is duplicated underneath the destination directory. You can choose to either duplicate the full source path name, or just the portion of the path name where the files are actually stored.

DIR EMPTY/ DIR NOT LOGGED

See NO FILES! on page 225.

FILESPEC

(Added features. See page 108.)

XTree
EASY   GOLD

The only news about File specification is that there is space for more of them. You can now you have up to 232 characters (up to 28 files) in your File specification command.

FUNCTION KEYS

(Added features. See page 120.)

Only one function key has changed from XTreePro Gold to XTreeGold: F10. F10 now activates the pull-down menu system (previously it activated The Quick Reference Guide, which has been eliminated.)

HISTORY

(Added features. See page 130.)

XTree
EASY   GOLD

The history command now saves the last sixteen responses (up from thirteen).
  History is very handy and can be found at almost every command window, remember to make use of it. It saves keystrokes (and reduces silly typos).

LAPTOP CONFIG- URATION

(Added features. See page 133.)

XTree
EASY   GOLD

Usually the hard disk on your laptop is smaller than your desktop system and disk space is at a premium. After installing Gold or Easy, you can delete files that support unneeded functions. For example, if you are an experienced user, you can delete all the Help system files and save yourself 200K or so of disk space. XTree will still run, but you will not be able to call up help.

XTREE EASY

REQUIRED:

XTREE.COM	(1K)	The XTree Easy program and loader
XTR.EXE	(75K)	The auxiliary program file

OPTIONAL:

XTR_CFG.EXE	(24K)	The configuration program. Once you have configured your program, you no longer need it.
XTR_HELP.XTR	(6K)	Part of the Help system. If you don't need Help, you can live without this and all of the Help system files.
XTR_HELP PD0	(10K)	Help text files
XTR_HELP X10 *through*		
XTR_HELP XD0	(14K each)	Parts of the Help system. The exact number of these Help files varies as the programmers add material in later revs, but they're always called XTR_HELP.X-something and they run 14-15K apiece.

The following files control various features and functions. If you don't need the feature or function, you can delete the file:

XTR_EDIT.XTR	(25K)	1Word text editor module
XTR_FORM.XTR	(12K)	Format diskette module (ALT+F2)
XTR_MENU.XTR	(6K)	Application Menu module (F9)
XTR_VIEW.XTR	(39K)	View file module

These files are needed to run Easy under Windows:

README.WIN	(9K)	Helpful information for running Easy in Windows.

			XTree
			EASY GOLD

XTREE.PIF   Files required to run Easy under Windows.

XTREE.ICO   The XTree Easy icon for Windows.

Miscellaneous files:

README.DOC   (17K)   Addendum to the manual.

XTREE.HST   History file. (A new one is created as you use the program.)

XTREEGOLD:
REQUIRED:

XTGOLD.COM   (1K)   The XTreeGold program and loader

XTG.EXE   (80K)   The auxiliary program file

XTGOLD.CFG   The configuration file

OPTIONAL:

XTG_CFG.EXE   (40K)   The configuration program. Once you have configured your program, you no longer need it.

XTG_HELP.XTP   (6K)   Part of the Help system. If you don't need Help, you can live without this and all of the Help system files.

XTG_HELP PD0	(10K)	Help text files
XTG_HELP X10	(14K)	Part of the Help system
XTG_HELP X20	(14K)	Part of the Help system
XTG_HELP X30	(15K)	Part of the Help system
XTG_HELP X40	(14K)	Part of the Help system
XTG_HELP X50	(15K)	Part of the Help system
XTG_HELP X60	(15K)	Part of the Help system
XTG_HELP X70	(15K)	Part of the Help system
XTG_HELP X80	(14K)	Part of the Help system
XTG_HELP X90	(14K)	Part of the Help system
XTG_HELP XA0	(15K)	Part of the Help system
XTG_HELP XB0	(14K)	Part of the Help system
XTG_HELP XC0	(15K)	Part of the Help system

XTG_HELP XD0   (8K)   Part of the Help system

The following files control various features and functions. If you
don't need the feature or function, you can delete the file:

XTG_EDIT.XTP   (25K)   1Word text editor module
XTG_FIND.XTP   (8K)   Search file module
(CTRL+S)
XTG_FORM.XTP   (12K)   Format diskette module
(ALT+F2)
XTG_HEXX.XTP   (15K)   View Hex editor module
XTG_MENU.XTP   (6K)   Application Menu module
(F9)
XTG_MOVE.XTP   (5K)   Graft module (ALT+G)
XTG_OOPS.XTP   (23K)   Undelete module
XTG_VIEW.XTP   (39K)   View file module
XTG_V_TO.XTP   (26K)   Word processor conversion
utility (for all formats)
XTG_WASH.XTP   (7K)   Wash disk module (ALT+W)
XTG_WBAT.XTP   (9K)   Write batch file module
XTG_ARC1.XTP   (32K)   Archive Manager PKarc
compression module
XTG_ARC2.XTP   (42K)   Archive Manager PKarc
open module
XTG_AZIP.XTP   (14K)   Archive Manager loader
XTG_ZIP1.XTP   (32K)   Archive Manager Zip
compression module
XTG_ZIP2.XTP   (52K)   Archive Manager Zip
open module

The following files are used with the View system. Delete
the ones you don't need.

XTG_VDBF.XTP   (72K)   View Database file module
XTG_VWKS.XTP   (85K)   View Spreadsheet file
module
XTG_VFFT XTP   (20K)   View FFT files
XTG_VMSR XTP   (28K)   View Microsoft RTF and
MS Word 3.0, 3.1, 4.0, 5.0
XTG_VPFS XTP   (32K)   PFS: First Choice 1.0, 2.0
and Write Version C
XTG_VWP4 XTP   (20K)   WordPerfect 4.0

XTG_VWP5 XTP	(29K)	WordPerfect 5.0		XTree
XTG_VWS2 XTP	(26K)	WordStar 2000		EASY GOLD
XTG_V_DC XTP	(27K)	View DCA file module		
XTG_V_EN XTP	(22K)	Enable 1.0, 2.0, 2.15		
XTG_V_LM XTP	(50K)	Lotus Manuscript 2.0, 2.1		
XTG_V_MM XTP	(26K)	MultiMate 3.3, 4 and Advantage I, II, 3.6, 3.7		
XTG_V_MW XTP	(29K)	Microsoft Windows Write 3.0		
XTG_V_QA XTP	(20K)	Q&A Write		
XTG_V_WS XTP	(31K)	WordStar		
XTG_V_XY XTP	(27K)	XyWrite		
XTG_VFRM XTP	(21K)	Framework III 1.0, 1.1		
XTG_VIBM XTP	(20K)	IBM Writing Assistant		
XTG_VOFF XTP	(24K)	Office Writer 4.0, 5.0, 6.0, 6.1		
XTG_VRAP XTP	(18K)	RapidFile (Memo) 1.0, 1.2		
XTG_VSAM XTP	(24K)	Samna Word IV & Word IV Plus		
XTG_VVK2 XTP	(16K)	Volkswriter Deluxe 2.2		
XTG_VVK3 XTP	(28K)	Volkswriter 3, 4		
XTG_VWNG XTP	(16K)	Wang PC Version 3		

Information on running Gold under Windows:

README.WIN	(9K)	Helpful information for running Gold in Windows
XTGOLD.PIF		Files required to run Gold under Windows
XTGOLDF.PIF		

Miscellaneous files:

README.DOC	(17K)	Addendum to the manual
XTGOLD.HST		History file. (A new one is created as you use the program.)

The following files are needed only if you want to use the Open and associate (see EXECUTE) command to start BAT, COM and EXE files. (However, they are so small in size that they will have little impact on your system.)

BAT.BAT	Association batch file for .BAT files.
COM.BAT	Association batch file for .COM files.

EXE.BAT   Association batch file for .EXE files.

LOG

(Added features. See page 137.)

XTree
EASY GOLD

A few changes have been made in this area — mainly to accommodate people with big disks who are running out of memory.

The first change is in the configuration program (see page 66). Screen 5-9 illustrates your opportunity to limit what directories will be automatically logged when XTreeGold is invoked.

Once you're in XTreeGold, just highlight the directory (or directories) you *want* to log and hit the plus key (**+**). You probably won't be too surprised to learn that a minus key (**-**) will unlog a directory.

Note: In previous versions of XTree, the "**+**" and "**-**" were used to cycle through the logged disks. Now the "**>**" and the "**<**" handle that task (or the comma and period — you don't have the use the shift key, thank goodness). If, however, you don't have a big hard disk and have never had a memory problem and want XTreeGold to work like it always has, then add "/XT" to the command when starting XTreeGold. (i.e. **XTGOLD /XT <ENTER>**.) If you do use the /XT switch, the Insert and Delete keys will become your "log and

```
XTreeGold - Configuration Items                              Page 1

Application Menu
    1 Opening screen is the Application Menu              NO
    2 Pause after application program execution           NO

Directories
    3 Program path:                                       C:\X
    4 Editor program:

Disk logging
    5 Disk logging method                                 QUICK
    6 Log disk commands only read the root directory      NO
    7 Log disk commands only read the directory tree      NO




  Next page     Main menu

Show the next screen of configuration items.

  ↑↓ Select item    ENTER Change item          ESC Return to main menu
```

Screen 5-9

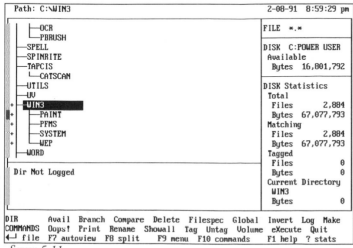

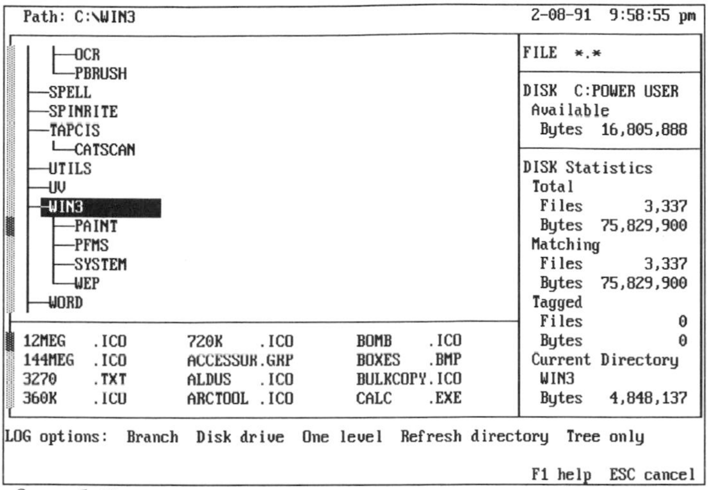

```
Path: C:\WIN3                          2-08-91  9:58:55 pm        XTree
┌─────────────────────────────┐┌─────────────────────────┐   EASY  GOLD
│      ┌─OCR                   ││FILE  *.*                │
│      └─PBRUSH                ││                         │
│    ─SPELL                    ││DISK  C:POWER USER       │
│    ─SPINRITE                 ││Available                │
│    ─TAPCIS                   ││Bytes  16,805,888        │
│      └─CATSCAN               ││                         │
│    ─UTILS                    ││DISK Statistics          │
│    ─UU                       ││Total                    │
│    �─WIN3                     ││  Files       3,337      │
│      ┌─PAINT                 ││  Bytes  75,829,900      │
│      ┌─PFMS                  ││Matching                 │
│      ┌─SYSTEM                ││  Files       3,337      │
│      └─WEP                   ││  Bytes  75,829,900      │
│    ─WORD                     ││Tagged                   │
│                              ││  Files           0      │
│ 12MEG  .ICO  720K   .ICO  BOMB    .ICO ││  Bytes           0      │
│ 144MEG .ICO  ACCESSOR.GRP BOXES   .BMP ││Current Directory        │
│ 3270   .TXT  ALDUS  .ICO  BULKCOPY.ICO ││WIN3                     │
│ 360K   .ICU  ARCTOOL .ICO CALC    .EXE ││Bytes   4,848,137        │
└─────────────────────────────┘└─────────────────────────┘
LOG options:  Branch  Disk drive  One level  Refresh directory  Tree only

                                           F1 help  ESC cancel
```
Screen 5-10

unlog" keys.

Additional logging options for those with mega-hard disks are accessible from **<ALT>L** (for log) as in Screen 5-10.

At the bottom of the screen are your various options to log only the current branch, drive, only one level of directories, or relog the current directory. The last option, "Tree only," will log only the tree structure (without the files) in the current directory and its children directories.

```
Path: C:\WIN3                          2-08-91  8:59:29 pm
┌─────────────────────────────┐┌─────────────────────────┐
│      ┌─OCR                   ││FILE  *.*                │
│      └─PBRUSH                ││                         │
│    ─SPELL                    ││DISK  C:POWER USER       │
│    ─SPINRITE                 ││Available                │
│    ─TAPCIS                   ││Bytes  16,801,792        │
│      └─CATSCAN               ││                         │
│    ─UTILS                    ││DISK Statistics          │
│    ─UU                       ││Total                    │
│  +  ▮WIN3                    ││  Files       2,884      │
│  +   ┌─PAINT                 ││  Bytes  67,077,793      │
│  +   ┌─PFMS                  ││Matching                 │
│  +   ┌─SYSTEM                ││  Files       2,884      │
│  +   └─WEP                   ││  Bytes  67,077,793      │
│    ─WORD                     ││Tagged                   │
│                              ││  Files           0      │
│  Dir Not Logged              ││  Bytes           0      │
│                              ││Current Directory        │
│                              ││WIN3                     │
│                              ││Bytes             0      │
└─────────────────────────────┘└─────────────────────────┘
DIR       Avail  Branch  Compare  Delete  Filespec  Global  Invert  Log  Make
COMMANDS  Oops!  Print  Rename  Showall  Tag  Untag  Volume  eXecute  Quit
◄┘ file  F7 autoview  F8 split   F9 menu  F10 commands   F1 help  ? stats
```
Screen 5-11

XTree
EASY GOLD

In Screen 5-11, the WIN3 directory was highlighted, then we hit **<ALT>L** then **<T>** (for "Tree only"). The result is that WIN3 and its subdirectories were instantly "unlogged".

Note: The issue of logging and partial logging becomes important only when you start receiving "out of memory" messages while logging drives, or if you hate waiting for a big drive to log.

MENU

See either PULL-DOWN MENUS (for details on the new XTree interface) on page 228 or APPLICATION MENU on page 205 (for your own customized menus).

MOVE

(Added features. See page 141.)

XTree
EASY GOLD

XTree has, yet again, overcome DOS's shortcomings by expanding the power of "Move." **<ALT>M**ove lets you move files from one disk to another (as well as to another directory).

What's more, if you wish, **<ALT>M**ove will also duplicate the source directory structure.

NO FILES!

XTree
EASY GOLD

```
Path: C:\PLOTS                              2-08-91  4:37:58 pm

   ├─NUWORD                          FILE   *.DOC
   ├─OB2
   ├─OPTUNE                          DISK  C:POWER USER
   ├─PCLFONTS                        Available
   ├─PCPLUS                            Bytes  16,838,656
   ├─PD
   ├─PLOTS                           DISK Statistics
   ├─PM                              Total
   ├─POP                              Files       3,337
   ├─QA                               Bytes  75,803,720
   ├─QEMM                            Matching
   ├─QM                               Files         458
   │   ├─DOWNLOAD                     Bytes   7,086,985
   │   ├─COMP                        Tagged
                                      Files           0
 No Files Match                       Bytes           0
                                     Current Directory
                                     PLOTS
                                      Bytes   1,682,078

DIR       Avail  Branch  Compare  Delete  Filespec  Global  Invert  Log  Make
COMMANDS  Oops!  Print  Rename  Showall  Tag  Untag  Volume  eXecute  Quit
←┘ file  F7 autoview  F8 split    F9 menu  F10 commands   F1 help  ? stats
```

Screen 5-12

(Added features. See page 147.)

The infamous "No Files!"-induced panic attack has been eliminated. "No Files!" has been replaced by three more reassuring, and meaningful, messages as follows:

"DIR EMPTY" means there are no files in the current directory at all.

"NO FILES MATCH" means that there *are* files in the current directory, but none of them meet the current File Specification. In Screen 5-12, the File Specification (upper right hand corner) is set to show *.DOC (all "DOC" files). There are no "DOC" files in the PLOTS directory, hence the "No Files Match" warning (the File Specification must be set to *.* to see all files).

"DIR NOT LOGGED" means that, for some reason, the directory you're pointing at has, well, not been logged. A directory doesn't get logged for two basic reasons: You ran out of memory before the hard disk was finished logging; or you have "unlogged" the directory (by hitting the minus key).

All things being equal, you won't run out of memory unless you're logging a bunch of floppies, or you have a CD-ROM or something that has so many files on it that it demands a lot of memory. One way to get XTree to log the directory is to tell XTree to forget all the other disks you've logged so far (with the Release — **<ALT>R** — command) and then try logging the directory with the plus key (or the whole drive with **L**).

(New command.)

OOPS!

There's nothing worse than the moment when horrified realization strikes: You've just deleted files you really didn't want to delete. Perhaps you even say something like "oops!" when you imagine the consequences of your error. Perhaps you say something worse.

To the rescue is XTree's new Oops! command which lets you bring your files back from the dead... sometimes.

The "sometimes" qualifier is necessary because of the way

XTree
EASY GOLD

```
Path: C:\123                                    2-04-91  3:00:17 am

 ?AN92   .WK1    37  **  2-04-91  2:59:02 am   FILE  *.*
 ?EB92   .WK1    37  ...  2-04-91  2:59:02 am
 ?AR92   .WK1    37  ...  2-04-91  2:59:02 am   DISK  C:
                                                Available
                                                Bytes  10,260,480

                                                UNDELETE Stats
                                                Total
                                                 Files          3

                                                Matching
                                                 Files          3

                                                Conflicting
                                                 Files          0

                                                Current File
                                                 ?AN92   .WK1
                                                 Bytes         37

UNDELETE   Undelete   Sort criteria
COMMANDS
                                                F1 help  ESC exit
```

Screen 5-13

DOS saves and deletes files. A so-called "deleted" file can be recovered only because the computer doesn't erase the file when you order it to do so. Instead of actually exterminating the file, the computer *reclassifies* the space that the file occupies as "available" (rather than "reserved"). After the "deleted" file's space becomes "available," it's only a matter of time before another file uses the space for itself (like a VCR recording over a previously-used tape).

So, if you decide to undelete a file that you deleted a month ago, chances are quite high that the space has since been used by another file and your file is lost. If, however, you want to undelete a file you deleted ten minutes ago, your chances for recovery are excellent.

Note: If you plan on undeleting a file, be sure you *do not* use Wash (page 84) or a Disk Defragger (page 188) prior to undeleting. Running either of these types of programs will render all deleted files *permanently* unrecoverable (by recording over the deleted file's space). If your computer is set up to automatically run a disk defragger as part of its daily "start up" activities, be sure to take care of your undeletes before turning your computer off (and on) again.

For now, let's assume that all aspects are favorable.

The first step is to highlight the directory containing the file (or files) to be retrieved. Now hit **O** (for Oops!) and

```
                                                                       XTree
 Path: C:\123                              2-04-91  3:01:12 am      EASY  GOLD

│ ?AN92    .WK1     37 .**. 2-04-91  2:59:02 am │  FILE  *.*
│ ?EB92    .WK1     37 .... 2-04-91  2:59:02 am │
│ ?AR92    .WK1     37 .... 2-04-91  2:59:02 am │  DISK  C:
                                                  Available
                                                  Bytes  10,260,480

                                                  UNDELETE Stats
                                                  Total
                                                   Files            3

                                                  Matching
                                                   Files            3

                                                  Conflicting
                                                   Files            0

                                                  Current File
                                                   ?AN92    .WK1
                                                   Bytes           37

UNDELETE file: ?AN92.WK1
          as: JAN92.WK1
Enter new file name              ↑ history  ←┘ ok  F1 help  ESC cancel
```

Screen 5-14

Gold will give you a list files in the current directory that are recoverable (Screen 5-13).

In this example, there are three deleted Lotus 1-2-3 files that can be recovered. To the right of the first file listed (after the file size), are two asterisks ("**"). The two asterisks indicate that *if* this is one of the files you want to undelete, you should start with it first. If you undelete one of the other files first, they will "record over" the first file's space, making it unretrievable. (If you don't want the "**" file, then go forth and undelete the other files.)

To undelete, highlight the file you want and hit U (for undelete). Next, XTreeGold will ask you what to call the file to be undeleted. (You may have noticed that each of the "undeletable" file names begins with a question mark. A question mark at the beginning of a file name is DOS's signal to itself that the file is "erased.")

To satisfy XTreeGold's request for a filename you can do one of two things: Simply type that missing *first letter* (like **J**) or type in a whole file name (as in Screen 5-14) and hit **<ENTER>**. XTreeGold will undelete the file (and remove it from the "undelete" file list).

After the last file in the list is undeleted, an error message will sound telling you there are no more files to undelete. Just hit **<ENTER>** and you'll be conducted back to a directory window.

OPEN

Open can refer either to Open and Associate (launching a program by pointing to file used by that application), see page 148 or opening Zip and Arc files (see Appendix A, page 263, for the Arc and the new Zip features).

PULL-DOWN MENUS

XTree
EASY GOLD

(New feature.)

So what's all the brouhaha about pull-down menus? Other than the fact that they are very cute, pull-down menus present XTree's command structure in a more logical way (by subject) making things easier to find. You can say goodbye to searching for a command by first hitting CTRL to reveal the CTRL commands and then ALT to reveal the ALT commands and so forth. All the standard, CTRL, and ALT commands are organized by subject in the pull-down menu. Whenever there are several levels of commands (standard, CTRL and ALT), a pull-down menu will be available to make things easier.

Whenever you see "F10 Commands" at the bottom of the screen, you can use the pull-down menu system.

To actually see the pull-down menus, just hit function key

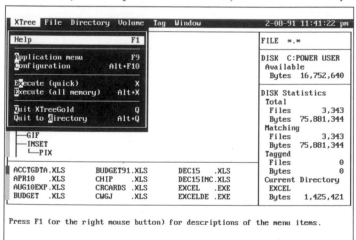

Screen 5-15

XTree
EASY GOLD

```
 XTree  File  Directory  Volume  Tag  Window          2-11-91 11:27:22 am
   ┌─JC                        Autoview           F7
   ├─PAN                       Split on/off       F8
   ├─PRSTUFF                   Video mode       Alt+F9  WER USER
   ├─RESEARCH
   ├─SAFEH                     Directory files    Enter  4,241,792
   ├─SCRIPTS                   Branch files       B
   ├─SITCOM                    Branch tagged    Ctrl+B  stics
   └─DRDR                      Disk files (Showall)  S
   ├─STORIES                   Disk tagged      Ctrl+S      3,416
   ├─WGABBS                    Global             G   8,229,342
   ├─FORUM                     Global tagged    Ctrl+G
   ├─HARDWARE                                                3,416
   └─MODEM                     File specification...  F  8,229,342
  ─XT                          File display columns
                              Sort criteria...   Alt+S        0
                                                             0
  BIGX   .BAK    INDEX    .DOC    MCNOTES .DOC    Current Directory
  BIGX   .DOC    MACNOTE  .BAK    NORMAL  .GLY    XT
  BIGXINDX.BAK   MACNOTES .BAK    UPDATE  .BAK    Bytes   2,873,695
  BIGXINDX.DOC   MACNUTES .DOC

  Press F1 (or the right mouse button) for descriptions of the menu items.
```

Screen 5-16

F10, (or click the top line with the mouse).

A menu bar at the top of the screen and several major topics will be displayed. By highlighting a topic, that topic's options are revealed. When you first hit **F10**, the first topic in the menu is highlighted and its options underneath are exposed.

If you're in a directory window when you strike F10, you'll get the same menu bar as in Screen 5-15 with the cursor highlighting the first topic in the menu ("XTree"). Below the first topic the pertinent "XTree" command options are automatically disclosed.

"Application menu" is one of the items in the list. If you want to enter the Application Menu, you may either hit **A** (the highlighted letter in Application menu) or use the down arrow key to highlight the words Application menu and then hit **<ENTER>**. Alternatively, as suggested on the same menu, you may simply press **F9** at any time (whether the pull-down menu is up or not). *Or*, if you've got a mouse, you can even click on it.

If the XTree topic isn't what you want, hitting the right arrow key will move the highlight from XTree and to the next topic, "File," revealing the File command options underneath. You may continue moving to the right, to reveal other commands, or back to the left.

XTree
EASY GOLD

Screen 5-17

Did you notice that some of the commands have ellipses (you know, the three dots: "...") next to them? That's your hint that when you ask XTree to perform that command, XTree will require some additional input from you at the bottom of the screen. In Screen 5-16, for instance (previous page), File specification (which has ellipses) is chosen (highlighted). Once you hit **<ENTER>**, XTree will ask you what file specification you want.

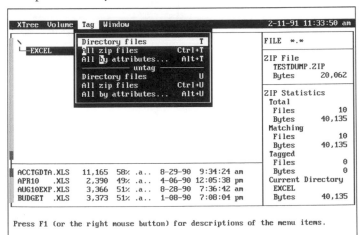

Screen 5-18

On the other hand, you can predict that XTree will be able to carry out the next command — File display columns — without human intervention because there are no ellipses. If you were to hit **<ENTER>** (or **<ALT>F**), XTree would proceed to adjust the display.

Just as XTree's commands change depending upon which window you're in, the pull-down menu also matches your current "window" location within XTree.

Screen 5-16 showed the pull-down menu while in the directory window. Screen 5-17, however, shows the pull-down menu while in the small file window. Notice the topics and the commands change to fit the situation.

And Screen 5-18 displays commands appropriate to working with "Open archive."

The pull-down menu system makes it easy to browse through commands, find what you want, and be reminded of what you forgot. (In fact, the pull-down system is so helpful, they decided to eliminate the "Quick Reference Guide" in XTreeGold.)

SEE *Applications Menu*, page 205.

XTree
EASY GOLD

XTREE MENU

VIEW

XTree
EASY GOLD

(Added features. See page 177.)

XTree sports tons o' new file viewers including spreadsheet and database viewers as well as most popular word processor formats. If you haven't been using View before, it's worth another look. Before you know it, you'll wonder how you ever got along without it.

First, the complete list of formats supported are (take a deep breath):

Spreadsheets: Lotus 1A, 2.0, 2.2 and compatibles, Excel, Quattro and Quattro Pro

Databases: dBASE III, IV and compatibles, and Paradox.

Word processors now include FFT files, Microsoft RTF and MS Word 3.0, 3.1, 4.0, 5.0; PFS: First Choice 1.0, 2.0 and Write Version C; Word Perfect 4.0; Word Perfect 5.0;

XTree
EASY GOLD

```
File: C:\EXCEL\ACCTGDTA.XLS
F60:

            C           D        E       F           G              H
59    H29250     $342.47    -    vram vga 512, ret'd 8/28 via R0182800
60    H31359     $281.40    P
61    H35392     $818.81    -    NHE/MGE/256 color board-- ret'd 8/28 via
62    H41485     $310.74    -    paid check 12648
63    H43548      $47.26    -    paid check 12648
64    H53558     $232.49    P
65    927450    ($307.00)   -    taken via 7/17/90 ck #12562 (copy of
66                               statement enclosed)
67    927917   ($1,225.07)  -    taken via 7/17/90 ck #12562 (copy of
68                               statement enclosed)
69    H76729   $1,593.45    -    paid check 12704 - 8/28/90
70    H76730     762.38     -    paid check 12704 - 8/28/90
71    931391    ($890.00)   P
72    H89435     $761.47    P
73    H93531       $8.64    P
74    I05668     $176.24    P
75    I14341      $72.28    P

VIEW 123  ASCII  Dump  Gather  Hex  Wordwrap                    version 1.7
COMMANDS  F2 go to cell  F9 search  SPACE search again
↑↓ scroll                                    F10 commands  F1 help  ESC cancel
```

Screen 5-19

WordStar 2000; View DCA file module; Enable 1.0, 2.0,
2.15; Lotus Manuscript 2.0, 2.1; MultiMate 3.3, 4 and
Advantage I, II, 3.6, 3.7; Microsoft Windows Write 3.0;
Q&A Write; WordStar; XyWrite; Framework III 1.0, 1.1;
IBM Writing Assistant; Office Writer 4.0, 5.0, 6.0, 6.1;
RapidFile (Memo) 1.0, 1.2; Samna Word IV and Word IV
Plus; Volkswriter Deluxe 2.2; Volkswriter 3, 4; Wang PC
Version 3; HP AdvanceWrite Plus.

Being able to examine/see the information in a file created
by a program that you do not own and are not likely to
learn can be quite useful. If a co-worker gives you an Excel
spreadsheet, you don't have to know a single word of
accounting to View (or print out!) the file.

Just highlight the file to be viewed and hit **V** for View and,
voila, the spreadsheet will appear (as in Screen 5-19). (If all
you see on screen is a bit of garbage, hit **F** for Formatted
and within seconds, you'll see a spreadsheet.)

At the bottom of the screen you'll see, as usual, your
current options. (Including **F10** to pop up the pull-down
command menu at the top.) When you're finished viewing a
file, **<ESC>** will take you back to the normal XTree view.

Once you're viewing a file, there are a couple of things you
can do to it: you can save it as an ASCII file (which can be
called up in any word processor for editing or merging into

```
┌─────────────────────────────────────────────────────────┐        XTree
│ File: C:\EXCEL\BUDGET91.XLS                              │     EASY  GOLD
│ D13: (formula)                                          │
│                                                         │
│         A          B         C         D        E       │
│  1  Monthly Budget                                      │
│  2                                                      │
│  3                                                      │
│  4  Rent                                2500            │
│  5  Cat Food                             200            │
│  6  Insurance - Auto                     150            │
│  7  Insurance - House                     75            │
│  8  Lawyer                               165            │
│  9  Dry Cleaning                          75            │
│ 10  Entertainment                        450            │
│ 11  Clothes                              750            │
│ 12                                                      │
│ 13                                      4365            │
│ 14                                                      │
│ 15                                                      │
│ 16                                                      │
│ 17                                                      │
│─────────────────────────────────────────────────────── │
│ Append marked text to file:                             │
│                                                         │
│ Enter file name          ↑ history  ↵ ok  F1 help  ESC cancel │
└─────────────────────────────────────────────────────────┘
```

Screen 5-20

another document) or print it out on your printer.

Using another Excel file as an example, in Screen 5-20 that section of the viewed file to be printed out has been highlighted with the Gather command. (You just hit **G** for Gather then hit **<ENTER>** to start highlighting the material to be "gathered." Then, using your arrow/cursor keys, move to the end of the material to be "gathered" and hit **<ENTER>** again.)

You'll see the message, like the one at the bottom of Screen 5-20 saying "Append marked text to file." Here's where you decide between printing the file out on a printer or saving it on your hard disk.

If you want to print the file out, type **PRN** — the computer's secret code for "printer" — and hit **<ENTER>**. (If you have a laser printer, you may have to take the printer off-line and press the form feed button to get the page to come out.) If you want to save what's on screen as an ASCII file, type a file name (something other than the file's current name) and **<ENTER>**. In the blink of an eye, you'll have a file.

(New feature.)

This isn't a command... it's just a thing that happens.

WIGGLE

XTree
EASY GOLD

When you issue a command via the pull-down menus, the cursor flashes on the selected item (as confirmation) before carrying it out. (If you've got a fast computer, you probably won't even notice it.) If you don't want the cursor to flash/wiggle, having your Scroll-Lock key "on" while in XTree will put the wiggle to rest.

If you do use Scroll-lock to turn off the wiggle, be sure to un-Scroll-lock when you exit XTree or your screen and cursor will behave oddly.

■ XTreeNet Guide –Easy Network File Management

6

In the beginning, there were individual, standalone computers (well, actually, there were rocks... but let's move on) — and XTree was there to manage them. Then, in the course of time, someone said "Hey, isn't there some way to connect these suckers so we all could share our data?" — and lo, the local area network (LAN) was born!

And shortly thereafter XTreeNet burst forth to manage them as well.

If you don't have a LAN, you can just skip this section because it details the network-related features provided by XTreeNet. (Unless you've got a network, you can't use XTreeNet.)

If you have a network, it's not recommended that you just slap your old tried and true XTree on it. There are more differences between a standalone computer and a network of computers than just the number of computers.

Since the main "goal" of a network is to have lots of people using the system at the same time, and since DOS can only handle one person at a time, other operating environments were created by various vendors. The most popular network operating environment (and the one that XTreeNet works with) is Novell's NetWare.

Why not use XTreeGold on your LAN?

Although the vision of everyone on a network sharing and caring may give you the warm fuzzies, the bottom line is that most businesses don't really want all information equally available to all employees, for two main reasons: confidentiality (for instance, only certain people should have access to payroll records); and security (whether by malice or ignorance, the ability to change a file on a computer is also the power to destroy).

Neither of these issues are relevant on a PC where the owner is the user/creator/owner of the work on the system. In a network, however, a system administrator (or supervisor) has to be selected to handle the care and feeding of the network and to dole out user rights.

A network, therefore, needs a file-management program that not only copies and deletes — but also understands who has the *right* to copy and delete. Further, since NetWare keeps track of what files and directories people are creating and using a network file management system must keep on top of that information as well — no blundering about the network deleting and moving files other people are busy working on! XTreeNet handles all these feats and more. (If you know networks, you'll be happy to know that XTreeNet can substantially replace SYSCON.)

Basics Congratulations! If you know XTreePro Gold on the PC, you are up and running on XTreeNet. The basic difference between the PC version and the network version is in the area of attributes and rights. XTreeNet goes beyond NetWare by being able to directly connect two computers on the network, attach and detach from file servers, and more, as we'll see in the pages ahead.

We'll run through some of the commands that are new or behave differently in XTreeNet. (You can use XTreePro Gold instructions to cover most of the rest of what XTreeNet does.) Please note, because of the, er, uh, "robust" nature of the NetWare system, this is going to get a little technical — but there's no way around it.

■ New Concepts

Peer-to-peer file management Although networks are designed so that each computer in the system can share data on a file server, peer-to-peer communication allows two computers on the system to connect directly. The purpose of this connection is not to "share data," but usually it is so that files can be copied or deleted. Basically, this feature exacerbates the already sedentary lifestyle of the system supervisor by allowing the supervisor to carry out network maintenance on another computer in the system without ever leaving his chair.

To connect with another computer on the system, hit **<ALT>M** (for map), then **R** (remote map), then the workstation name and drive (e.g. **CHRIS\C:**) and press **<ENTER>**. You will then see the **CHRIS\C:** disk added as another volume. Tedious updates, file transfers, etc., can be handled without endangering shoe leather.

(By the way, the remote computer has got to be running the Host program, XTSERV *first* — before you try to map it. XTSERV can be put in AUTOEXEC.BAT files so it is automatically loaded. Finally, you must either have supervisory rights or know Chris's password to have access to that computer.)

Not only can you map onto another computer in the system to copy and delete and stuff, you can actually *take control* of the other computer and use it as though you were sitting in front of it. (If you're the one providing help to other people on the system, this can be very handy.)

Peer-to-peer remote control

Hitting **<ALT>F7** begins the remote control process (see Screen 6-1). Once you have attached to the other computer, you may continue your work. **<CTRL><ALT>** will return you to the Remote Control screen and allow you to detach.

```
                                        2-12-91  3:29:48 pm




            ┌─────────────────────────────────────┐
            │ When attached to remote machine press: │
            │            CTRL+ALT                    │
            │       to return to this menu.          │
            └─────────────────────────────────────┘




 REMOTE CONTROL   Attach  Reboot  Time display off  Update interval
 COMMANDS
                                    ←┘ ok  F1 help  ESC cancel
```

Screen 6-1

Directory information mode

A flick of the key (**<ALT>I** to be specific) will coax the statistics window into revealing more data about the directory including: effective and maximum rights, owner, and creation date.

File information mode

While in the file window, **<ALT>I** will reveal these additional facts about the current file: file flags, last modified and accessed dates, owner, creation date, and last archived date.

Trustee information mode

Another **<ALT>I** will bring up the trustee information window, which displays the current directory trustee information.

Pick list

To select an item from a group of items known to XTreeNet (like "pick a drive") **F2** says "show me the list to pick from."

■ Network Commands

ATTACH/ DETACH

Pressing **<ALT>A** activates the attach command to let you log onto another file server. After activating Attach, you'll select from Attach, Detach, and Server List (to find out "what's out there"). When attaching, you'll be prompted for your "username" and password.

ATTRIBUTES (DIRECTORY)

We're used to attributes for files, but in NetWare there are also attributes for directories. From the directory window of the drive in question, you may modify directory rights as follows (by hitting **A**):

Creation Date	A directory's New Date command.
Flags	**S**ystem, **H**idden, **P**rivate. (Private renders the contents of a directory invisible, unless you have "search" rights.)
Owner	Each directory can be assigned to an owner (for tracking).
Rights mask	The use of the following rights establishes the maximum rights any user will have to a directory.

(These rights apply to what can be done on a directory-wide basis.)

Read	open and look at files
Write	open and save files
Open	can read, save, and change attributes
Create	save a new file
Delete	remove the directory
Parental	create, rename and delete subdirectories
Search	list files and subdirectories
Modify	change file attributes
Trustees	People can be designated as "Trustees" of a directory. A Trustee may not have more rights than those assigned to the directory have.

From the file window, you may assign/modify one or more of the following file attributes (by first hitting **A**):

> **ATTRIBUTES (FILE)**

Accessed date	New date and time
Creation date	Creation date
Flags	
Read-only	open and look at files
Archive	has it been backed up
System	protects file as important
Hidden	won't appear in DOS listing
Network shareable	can be accessed by more than one user at a time
e**X**ecute-only	COM or EXE files can't be copied, changed, rename, or deleted
Transactional	(for supervisors only)
Indexed	(for supervisors only)
Modified date	Change the "modified date" attribute
Owner	Change the owner name of files

```
Path: XTREE\SYS:PUBLIC                            2-12-91  3:18:25 pm
┌<showall: >───────────────────────────────────────────────────────
 VIEWER   .EXE   75,907 r...n...  5-25-90 12:46:02 pm  FILE  *.*
 VOLINFO  .EXE  142,235 r...n...  4-26-90  3:39:06 pm
 VOLINFO  .HLP    8,521 ....n... 11-06-90  3:06:14 pm  NETWARE VOLUME
 WANGTEK  .EXE   22,950 r...n... 12-08-89  3:19:46 pm  SYS
 WBROLL   .EXE   20,608 r...n...  3-15-90 11:24:38 pm  Space   10,186,752
 WBTRCALL .EXE   27,628 r...n...  3-22-90  3:51:06 pm
 WHOAMI   .EXE   25,723 r...n...  5-18-90 11:05:04 am  FILE Information
 WIND     .BAT      380 ........ 11-12-90 10:59:58 am  Current File
 WIND     .MIS      380 ........ 11-12-90 10:59:58 am  WHOAMI    .EXE
 WINSET   .BAT      414 ........ 11-12-90 10:54:26 am  Bytes       25,723
 WINWORD  .           73 ....n... 10-18-90  1:20:34 pm  Flags   [r...n...]
 WINWORD  .BAT      788 ........ 11-12-90 10:46:28 am  Last Modified
 WORD     .           57 ....n... 10-17-90  6:58:10 am   5-18-90 11:05 am
 WORD     .BAK      146 ........  1-23-91  5:25:04 pm  Owner
 WORD     .BAT      525 ........  1-23-91  5:25:28 pm  SUPERVISOR
 WORDTMS  .BAT      146 ........  1-23-91  5:25:22 pm  Accessed  2-12-91
 XM       .BAK      999 ........ 11-15-90  7:03:30 am  Created   1-01-85
 XM       .BAT      466 ........ 11-19-90  8:26:02 am  Last Archived
 XM$16    .BAT       16 ....n... 10-03-90  4:45:06 pm  No Date

 FILE      Attributes Copy Delete  Edit Filespec Invert Log volume Move
 COMMANDS  Open Print  Rename Tag  Untag View eXecute Quit
 ←┘ tree  F7 autoview  F8 split   F9 menu  F10 commands    F1 help  ESC cancel
```
Screen 6-2

aRchived date   Enables you to change the
                       archived date stamp

In Screen 6-2 is an example of a file in the expanded file
display mode.

Note there are eight dots next to the file name, as place
markers for each of the flags listed above.

WARNING! Use the execute-only flag with *extreme*
caution. You may get the idea to set all your programs to
execute-only as a hedge against deletion, or for virus protection. The problem is that during the normal course of
usage, many programs alter their own executable (COM
and EXE) files. If you add the execute-only flag, you may be
rendering the program useless. Further, there is *no way* to
remove this flag. Once it's set to execute-only, it is set
forever. The only solution is to delete the file and reinstall
it. So — use carefully.

TAG/UNTAG BRANCH

You may tag/untag a Branch with **<CTRL>F7** and
<CTRL>F8.

When you want to tag/untag by attributes in Net
(**<ALT>T**) there are (as you may have surmised) more
attributes than in DOS:

**TAG/UNTAG
BY
ATTRIBUTES**

Accessed date	Tags files with accessed dates that fall between the dates you're looking for.
Created date	Tags files with creation dates that fall between the dates you're looking for.
Flags	Tags those files that match the flag settings you enter.
Modified date	Tags those files changed between the dates you enter.
Owner	Tags files owned by the specified owner.
a**R**chived date	Tags files not backed up between the dates you enter.

Map is NetWare's "path" command... It's different from
DOS's path in two ways: It's cumulative (in DOS's path, the

MAP

```
Path: (BRK/C:) R:\                          2-12-91  3:29:10 pm

 R:\                              FILE *.*
 + ─$MENU
 + ─AP                           REMOTE VOLUME
 + ─BRIEF                        R:BOB
 + ─DOCS                         Space     10,991,616
 + ─DOS
 + ─FW3                          VOLUME Statistics
 + ─FWL                          Total
 + ─MENUWRKS                      Files            82
 + ─PERSDATA                      Bytes     1,558,989
   ─PSFONTS                      Matching
 +    ─AFM                        Files            82
 +    ─PFM                        Bytes     1,558,989
 + ─SHOW                         Tagged
                                  Files             0
 $HOT$UM$.    214,032 .a......  3-08-90  8:57:40 am   Bytes             0
 $STATE  .     28,750 .a......  3-08-90  8:57:40 am  Current Directory
 ADDRESS .BAK      42 .a......  2-20-90 11:41:30 am  R:\
 ADDRESS .BAT      42 .a......  2-20-90 11:41:34 am  Bytes       684,115

DIR          Attributes Delete Filespec Global Invert Log volume Makedir
COMMANDS    Print Rename Showall Tag Untag Volume eXecute Quit
 ←┘ file  F7 autoview  F8 split    F9 menu  F10 commands    F1 help  < > select
```
Screen 6-3

last path statement is the active path — in NetWare each path is *added* to the previous paths); and you assign a letter to each path.

When you use **<ALT>M**, you will be offered a choice between **D**elete (to remove a map), **R**emote (to add another computer as a volume), and **S** (to add a network volume).

In Screen 6-3 we have mapped drive C of the remote workstation BRK as R:

VOLUME

Although there's a Volume command on PC/XTree, the one on Net does more. Pressing **V** from the directory window offers these options: **A**vailable (amount of space available on the volume), **F**ormat (formats a floppy disk), **L**abel (changes the name of the current volume), **W**ash (makes sure that deleted files are deleted).

Final thought

Clearly, a successful LAN is the result of careful thought, planning, and subtle fine-tuning. The preceding commands, coupled with XTreePro Gold commands, makes XTreeNet an extremely powerful ally in any LAN.

■ Shortcuts: Command Keys/ Function Keys

7

On the following pages you'll find lists of the *most often* used command keys in each of the various versions of XTree. Following that, I've repeated the list of function key commands from page 120.

The lists are intended as cheat sheets... quick refreshers. All these commands have been detailed in earlier chapters. However, if you come across something you don't recall, the index and table of contents will point you in the right direction.

Keep in mind that in XTree where you are in the program is as important as what you hit. For instance, hitting **F** can mean "File specification" or "Formatted" depending on whether you're in the directory window or the view window.

The charts work as follows:

First of all, a heading states "directory window" or "file window" to establish where you must be to get the commands to work as listed.

Secondly, the "Key" is the letter of the alphabet you hit to activate a function. For the most part, there is a *word* in the "key" column with a highlighted letter. The highlighted letter is the key you actually strike. The word is the definition of what the key will do. (i.e. hit **A** to get the amount of space "Available.") The descriptions to the right tell you exactly what it does by itself (Standard), in combination with the Control key (CTRL) and in combination with the Alt key (ALT).

Sometimes, however, you'll just see a letter by itself (like "F") in the "key" column. In that case, check the three columns labeled Standard, CTRL, and ALT to reveal what command that key will perform by itself, when you hit it together with the Control key, and when you combine it with the Alt key. (For example, "**F**" by itself gives you the Filespec command, as **<ALT>F** it gives you the File display.)

When an entry in one of those columns just says "current file" or "tagged files" or "all files," that means that the command (described in the key column) will be carried out on the current file or on all tagged files or on all files.

Finally, if there is an empty space in one of the "Standard/CTRL/ALT" columns, it means that there is no command for that key in that window. For example, hitting the letter "**A**" will give you "available space," if you're in the directory window, but **<CTRL>A** or **<ALT>A** won't do anything at all.

Following the command key list for each version of XTree is the function key list for the same version. It's organized more simply, since there are fewer options: the first column lists the function key, the second column gives the explanation, including whether you have to be doing a specific operation for the command to be active. Where it says "See," that means you can get more detail in the alphabetized listing in Part Three, the Quick Reference Guide, of this book.

■ XTree

Directory Window

KEY	STANDARD	Ctrl	alt
[A]vailable	free space		
[D]elete	current directory		
[F]	filespec		file display
[L]og disk	log new disk		
[M]akedir	make directory		
[P]rint	files/paths/tree		
[R]ename	current directory		
[S]	showall	tagged files	sort criteria
[T]ag	all files in directory	all files on disk	by attribute
[U]ntag	all files in directory	all files on disk	by attribute
[V]olume	renames disk		
e[X]ecute	runs program		runs program

File Window

KEY	STANDARD	Ctrl	alt
[A]ttributes	add or remove	to tagged files	
[C]opy	current file	tagged files	tagged files/paths to another disk
[D]elete	current file	tagged files	
[F]	filespec		file display
[L]og disk	log disk		
[M]ove	current file	tagged files	
[P]rint	current file	tagged files	
[R]ename	current file	tagged files	
[S]ort			sort criteria
[T]ag	current file	all displayed files	by attribute
[U]ntag	current file	tagged files	by attribute
[V]iew	view		
e[X]ecute	runs program		runs program

■ Function Keys — XTree

F1	Quit XTree (see QUIT).
F2	Help (see HELP).
F3	Cancel (see CANCEL).
F4	Makes the Directory and File Commands disappear from the bottom of the screen. Fun! Try it (see DIRECTORY).
F5	Keep Filespec. Normally, if you log another drive, the filespec defaults back to *.*. If you set a filespec, then hit F5, then log another drive, the filespec will not default back to *.*. This is useful when hunting through several disks for a file (see FILESPEC and FIND).
F10	ALT lock. An alternative to holding down the ALT key. Hitting and releasing F10 leaves you in the ALT menu. You may peruse the ALT menu without the physical exertion of holding down the ALT key.

■ XTreePro

Directory Window

KEY	STANDARD	Ctrl	alt
[A]vailable	free space		
[D]elete	current directory		
[E]dit	edit file		
[F]	filespec		file display
[G]lobal	files on logged disks	tagged files on logged disks	
[L]og disk	log new disk		log new disk/ release logged disks
[M]akedir	make directory		
[P]rint	files/paths/tree		
[Q]uit	exit program		exit to current directory
[R]	rename directory		release disk
[S]	showall	showall tagged files	sort criteria
[T]ag	all files in directory	all files on disk	by attribute
[U]ntag	all files in directory	all files on disk	by attribute
[V]olume	renames disk		
e[X]ecute	runs program		unlogs disk on launch

File Window

KEY	STANDARD	Ctrl	alt
[A]ttributes	add or remove	to tagged files	
[C]opy	current file	tagged files	tagged files/paths to another disk
[D]elete	current file	tagged files	
[E]dit	current file		
[F]	filespec		file display
[L]og disk	log new disk		log new disk/release logged disks
[M]ove	current file	tagged files	

Page 247

■ XTreepro (Cont.)

KEY	STANDARD	[Ctrl]	[alt]
[P]rint	current file	tagged files	
[Q]uit	exit program		exit to current directory
[R]	rename file	rename tagged files	release disk
[S]ort			sort criteria
[T]ag	current file	all displayed files	by attribute
[U]ntag	current file	tagged files	by attribute
[V]iew	current file		
e[X]ecute	runs program		XTree goes to 7K on launch

■ Function Keys — XTreePro

[F1] Help (see HELP).

[F2] Destination Directory Window. When in COPY or MOVE mode, pressing F2 pops up the Destination Window, allowing you to merely point to where you want to copy or move your files to (see COPY and MOVE).

[F9] CTRL lock. An alternative to holding down the CTRL key. Hitting and releasing F9 leaves you in the CTRL menu. You may peruse the CTRL menu without the physical exertion of holding down the ALT key.

[F10] ALT lock. An alternative to holding down the ALT key. Hitting and releasing F10 leaves you in the ALT menu. You may peruse the ALT menu without the physical exertion of holding down the ALT key.

■ XTreePro Gold

Directory Window

KEY	STANDARD	Ctrl	alt
[A]vailable	free space		
[D]elete	current directory		
[E]dit			edit file
[F]	filespec		file display
[G]	files on current disk	tagged files on logged disks	graft
[H]ide/unhide			directory
[I]nvert	reverse tags on directory		reverse tags on disk
[L]og disk	log new disk	switch to logged disk	log new disk/unlog current disk
[M]akedir	make directory		
[P]	print files/paths/tree		prune
[Q]uit	exit XTree		exit to current directory
[R]	rename directory		release disk
[S]	showall	showall tagged files	sort criteria
[T]ag	all files in directory	all files on disk	by attribute
[U]ntag	all files in directory	all files on disk	by attribute
[V]olume	renames disk		
[W]ash disk			wash disk
e[X]ecute	runs program		XTree goes to 7K on launch
[Z]			quit and save structure

■ XTreePro Gold (Cont.)

File Window

KEY	STANDARD	[Ctrl]	[alt]
[A]ttributes	add or remove	to tagged files	
[C]opy	current file	tagged files	tagged files/paths to another disk
[D]elete	current file	tagged files	
[E]dit	current file		
[F]	filespec		file display
[I]nvert	reverse tag on file	on tagged files	
[L]og disk	log disk	switch to logged disk	log new disk/unlog current disks
[M]ove	current file	tagged files	
[N]ew date	on current file	tagged files	
[O]pen	launches program associated w/file		XTree goes to 7K upon launch
[P]rint	current file	tagged files	
[Q]uit	exit XTree		exit to current directory
[R]	rename file	rename tagged files	release disk
[S]		search tagged files for text	sort criteria
[T]ag	current file	all displayed files	by attribute
[U]ntag	current file	tagged files	by attribute
[V]iew	current file	tagged files	
e[X]ecute	runs program		XTree goes to 7K upon launch
[Z]			quit and save structure

■ Function Keys — XTreePro Gold

F1	Help (see HELP).
F2	Destination Directory Window. When in COPY MOVE or GRAFT mode, pressing **F2** pops up the Destination Window, allowing you to merely point to where you want to copy or move your files to (see COPY and MOVE).
F2	Screen Update. When in CTRL/Showall, hitting **F2** redisplays the screen, eliminating those items which have been untagged since CTRL/Showall was invoked (see SHOWALL).
alt F2	Formats a floppy disk (see FORMAT).
F3	When entering text, displays last response.
alt F3	Re-logs the current directory (see LOG).
F4	Menu toggle. Cycles through the standard CTRL and ALT menus. Hit **F4** once and the CTRL menu will be displayed. Hit it again, and the ALT menu will be displayed. Hit it again and you'll cycle back to the standard Menu.
F5	Collapses or expands directories two levels below the current directory (see DIRECTORY).
alt F5	Opens an arc file (see "Archiving," Appendix A).
Ctrl F5	Archives tagged files (see "Archiving," Appendix A).
F6	Collapses or expands directories below the current directory (see DIRECTORY).
Ctrl F6	Merges tags between two file windows (see SPLIT/UNSPLIT).
F7	Autoview. Can see the contents of a file (see VIEW).
F8	Splits/unsplits the display into two directories (see SPLIT/UNSPLIT).
alt F8	Untags all tagged files that have been operated on (see TAG/UNTAG).
Ctrl F8	Same as <ALT>F8.
F9	Pops up the Application Menu (see APPLICATION MENU).
alt F9	Toggles between the 25-line and 51-line modes for EGA and VGA systems (see CONFIGURATION).
F10	Pops up the Quick Reference Help Window (see HELP).
alt F10	Starts the configuration program (see CONFIGURATION).

■ XTreeGold

Directory Window

KEY	STANDARD	Ctrl	alt
[A]vail	free space		
[B]ranch	display branch	tagged files in branch	
[C]ompare	current directory		
[D]elete	current directory		
[E]dit			edit file
[F]	filespec		file display
[G]	files on current disk	tagged files on logged disks	graft
[H]ide/unhide			directory
[I]nvert	reverse tags on directory	reverse tags on disk	
[L]og disk	log new disk	switch to logged disk	log new disc/ unlog current
[M]ake	make directory		
[O]ops!	undeletes files		
[P]	print files/paths/tree		prune
[Q]uit	exit program		exit to current directory
[R]	rename directory		release disk
[S]	showall	showall tagged files	sort criteria
[T]ag	all files in directory	all files on disk	by attribute
[U]ntag	all files in directory	all files on disk	by attribute
[V]olume	renames disk		
[W]ash			wash
e[X]ecute	runs program		XTree goes to 7K upon launch
[Z]			quit and save structure

■ XTreeGold (Cont.)

File Window

KEY	STANDARD	[Ctrl]	[alt]
[A] ttributes	add or remove	to tagged files	
[C] opy	current file	tagged files	tagged files/paths to another disk/directory
[D] elete	current file	tagged files	
[E] dit	current file		
[F]	filespec		file display
[I] nvert	reverse tag on file	reverse tagged files	
[L] og disk	log new disk	switch to logged disk	various logging options
[M] ove	current file	tagged files	tagged files/paths to another disk/directory
[N] ew date	current file	tagged files	
[O] pen	launches program associated w/file		XTree goes to 7K upon launch
[P] rint	current file	tagged files	
[Q] uit	exit program		exit to current directory
[R] ename	current file	tagged files	
[S]		search tagged files for text	sort criteria
[T] ag	current file	all displayed files	by attribute
[U] ntag	current file	tagged files	by attribute
[V] iew	current file	tagged files	
e[X] ecute	runs program		XTree goes to 7K upon launch
[Z]			quit and save structure

■ Function Keys — XTreeGold

`F1`	Help (see HELP).
`F2`	Destination Directory Window. When in COPY, MOVE, COMPARE, or GRAFT mode, pressing **F2** pops up the Destination Window, allowing you to merely *point* to where you want to copy or move your files to (see COPY and MOVE).
`F2`	Screen Update. When in CTRL/Showall, hitting **F2** redisplays the screen, eliminating those items which have been untagged since CTRL/Showall was invoked (see SHOWALL).
`alt` `F2`	Formats a floppy disk (see FORMAT).
`F3`	When entering text, displays last response.
`alt` `F3`	Re-logs the current directory (see LOG).
`F4`	Menu toggle. Cycles through the standard CTRL and ALT menus. Hit **F4** once and the CTRL menu will be displayed. Hit it again, and the ALT menu will be displayed. Hit it again and you'll cycle back to the standard Menu.
`alt` `F4`	Compare directory (available in File window) (see COMPARE).
`F5`	Collapses or expands directories two levels below the current directory (see DIRECTORY).
`alt` `F5`	Opens an archive file (when you're in the File window) (see "Archiving," Appendix A).
`Ctrl` `F5`	Archives tagged files (ditto) (see "Archiving," Appendix A).
`F6`	Collapses or expands directories below the current directory (see DIRECTORY).
`Ctrl` `F6`	Merges tags between two file windows (see SPLIT/UNSPLIT).
`F7`	Autoview. Can see the contents of a file (see VIEW).
`F8`	Splits/unsplits the display into two directories (see SPLIT/UNSPLIT).
`alt` `F8`	Untags all tagged files that have been operated on (see TAG/UNTAG).
`Ctrl` `F8`	Same as **<ALT>F8**.

■ Function Keys — XTreeGold (Cont.)

F9	Pops up the Application Menu (see APPLICATION MENU).
alt F9	Toggles between the 25-line and 51-line modes for EGA and VGA systems (see CONFIGURATION).
F10	Activates the pull-down menus for currently available commands.
alt F10	Starts the configuration program (see CONFIGURATION).

■ XTree Easy

Directory Window

KEY	STANDARD	[Ctrl]	[alt]
[A]vailable	free space		
[D]elete	current directory		
[E]dit	edit file		edit file
[F]	filespec		file display
[L]og disk	log new disk		
[M]akedir	make directory		
[P]rint	files/paths/tree		
[Q]uit	quit		to current directory
[R]ename	current directory		
[S]	showall	showall tagged	sort criteria
[T]ag	all files in directory	all files on disk	by attribute
[U]ntag	all files in directory	all files on disk	by attribute
[V]olume	renames disk		
e[X]ecute	runs program		runs program
[Z]			quit and save structure

File Window

KEY	STANDARD	[Ctrl]	[alt]
[A]ttributes	add or remove	to tagged files	
[C]opy	current file	tagged files	tagged files/paths to another disk/directory
[D]elete	current file	tagged files	
[E]dit	edit file		
[F]	filespec		file display
[L]og disk	log disk		
[M]ove	current file	tagged files	tagged files/paths to another disk/directory
[P]rint	current file	tagged files	
[Q]uit	quit		to current directory
[R]ename	current file	tagged files	

■ XTree Easy (Cont.)

KEY	STANDARD	Ctrl	alt
[S]ort			sort criteria
[T]ag	current file	all displayed files	by attribute
[U]ntag	current file	tagged files	by attribute
[V]iew	view		
e[X]ecute	runs program		runs program
[Z]			quit and save structure

■ Function Keys — XTree Easy

[F1]	Help (see HELP).
[F2]	Destination Directory Window. When in COPY or MOVE, pressing **F2** pops up the Destination Window, allowing you to merely *point* to where you want to copy or move your files to (see COPY and MOVE).
[F2]	Screen Update. When in CTRL/Showall, hitting **F2** redisplays the screen, eliminating those items which have been untagged since CTRL/Showall was invoked (see SHOWALL).
[alt][F2]	Formats a floppy disk (see FORMAT).
[F3]	When entering text, displays last response.
[alt][F3]	Re-logs the current directory (see LOG).
[F4]	Menu toggle. Cycles through the standard CTRL and ALT menus. Hit **F4** once and the CTRL menu will be displayed. Hit it again, and the ALT menu will be displayed. Hit it again and you'll cycle back to the standard Menu.
[alt][F4]	Compare directory (available in File window) (see COMPARE).
[F6]	Collapses or expands directories below the current directory (see DIRECTORY).
[F9]	Pops up the Application Menu (see APPLICATION MENU).
[alt][F9]	Toggles between the 25-line and 51-line modes for EGA and VGA systems (see CONFIGURATION).
[F10]	Activates the pull-down menus for currently available commands.
[alt][F10]	Starts the configuration program (see CONFIGURATION).

■ XTree Net

Note: You may not have access to all these commands unless you have the necessary rights.

Directory Window

KEY	STANDARD	[Ctrl]	[alt]
[A]	attributes		attach/detach
[D]elete	current directory		
[E]dit			edit file
[F]	filespec		file display
[G]	files on current disk	tagged files on logged disks	graft
[I]	reverse tags on directory	reverse tags on disk	info display
[L]og volume	log new disk	switch to logged disk	log new disk/ unlog current disk
[M]	make directory		map drive
[P]	print files/paths/tree		prune
[Q]uit	exit XTree		exit to current directory
[R]	rename directory		release disk
[S]	showall	showall tagged files	sort criteria
[T]ag	all files in directory	all files on disk	by attribute
[U]ntag	all files in directory	all files on disk	by attribute
[V]	volume commands		
e[X]ecute	runs program		XTree goes to 7K on launch

■ XTree Net (Cont.)

File Window

KEY	STANDARD	Ctrl	alt
[A] [C]opy	add or remove current file	to tagged files tagged files	attach/detach tagged files/paths to another disk
[D]elete	current file	tagged files	
[E]dit	current file		
[F]	filespec		file display
[I]nvert	reverse tag on file	on tagged files	
[L]og disk	log disk	switch to logged disk	log new disk/ unlog current disks
[M]ove	current file	tagged files	map drive
[O]pen	launches program associated w/file		XTree goes to 7K upon launch
[P]rint	current file	tagged files	
[Q]uit	exit XTree		exit to current directory
[R]	rename file	rename tagged files	release disk
[S]		search tagged files for text	sort criteria
[T]ag	current file	all displayed files	by attribute
[U]ntag	current file	tagged files	by attribute
[V]iew	current file	tagged files	
e[X]ecute	runs program		XTree goes to 7K upon launch
[Z]			quit and save structure

■ Function Keys — XTree Net

`F1`   Help (see HELP).

`F2`   Destination Directory Window or Pick List. When in COPY, MOVE or GRAFT mode, pressing **F2** pops up the Destination Window, allowing you to merely point to where you want to copy or move your files to (see COPY and MOVE).

`F2`   Screen Update. When in CTRL/Showall, hitting **F2** redisplays the screen, eliminating those items which have been untagged since CTRL/Showall was invoked (see SHOWALL).

`alt` `F2`   Formats a floppy disk (see FORMAT).

`alt` `F3`   Re-logs the current directory (see LOG).

`F4`   Menu toggle. Cycles through the standard CTRL and ALT menus. Hit **F4** once and the CTRL menu will be displayed. Hit it again, and the ALT menu will be displayed. Hit it again and you'll cycle back to the standard Menu.

`alt` `F5`   Opens an arc file (see "Archiving," Appendix A).

`Ctrl` `F5`   Archives tagged files (see "Archiving," Appendix A).

`Ctrl` `F6`   Merges tags between two file windows (see SPLIT/UNSPLIT).

`F7`   Autoview. Can see the contents of a file (see VIEW).

`Ctrl` `F7`   Tag branch.

`F8`   Splits/unsplits the display into two directories (see SPLIT/UNSPLIT).

`Ctrl` `F8`   Untag branch.

`F9`   Pops up the Application Menu (see APPLICATION MENU).

`alt` `F9`   Toggles between 25-line and 51-line modes for EGA and VGA systems (see CONFIGURATION).

`Ctrl` `F9`   From File Window, updates tags (untags files that have been operated on) (see TAG/UNTAG).

`F10`   Pops up the Quick Reference Help Windows (see HELP).

`alt` `F10`   Starts the configuration program (see CONFIGURATION).

The 5th Wave

"I ALWAYS BACKUP EVERYTHING."

Appendix

A

■ Archiving —
The Shocking Truth!

Only XTreePro Gold and XTreeGold have built-in archiving powers — the options in the two programs are not the same (XTreeGold has more).

However, before we get into the differences between XTreePro Gold and XTreeGold archive options, it might be best to explain what the heck archiving and compressing files is in the first place.

In normal English, the word *archives* refers to either the place where public documents are stored, or to the documents themselves.

Archiving basics

In computers, *file archiving* has little to do with the public, but a lot to do with storing documents. Archiving (also known as "Arcing") is a special method of file creation and storage.

Archiving does two unique things to your files:
1. Groups files together into one megafile (like packing clothes in a suitcase).
2. *Compresses* your files so they take up less space (not unlike freeze-drying). Arcing can reduce the size of your files by at least fifty percent (programs will shrink less than data, generally).

Any file (programs, data, etc.) can be archived. Generally, files are archived for the purpose of convenient storage on a floppy disk (the originals are then deleted from the hard drive to free up space). Another use for archiving is for simplified (and speedier) file transmission over a modem.

An archived file is good for storage, but is about as useful

as a handful of freeze-dried coffee granules. As with freeze-
dried coffee, you have to "add water" before you can use it
again. In the case of archived files, you have to un-compress
(or unpack) the files before you can use them again.
Since archiving involves several new concepts, let's take a
quick overview of the process. Let's say you've written
seventeen letters to Mr. Steven Laff. Now that you're
finished doing business with Mr. Laff, you don't need the
letters on your hard disk. You decide to "Arc" them, and put
the "Arced" file on a floppy for storage.

To do this you'd invoke XTree, tag the seventeen files, tell
Gold you want to Arc them, and then name the archive file.
In this case, you might want to call the file **LAFF**.

At this point, XTree packs (and *simultaneously* compresses)
the seventeen files. Because of the compression, the size of
the **LAFF** megafile will actually be smaller than the sum
total of the seventeen files. (And wouldn't we all love to be
able to do that with an actual suitcase on our next
vacation?)

Once you've created the archive file, you can delete the
seventeen letters from your hard disk and copy the archive
file to a floppy.

One day, three months down the road, you suddenly
realize you need to use one or more of those letters in the
LAFF file. To access the files packed into the LAFF file, you
need to first *extract* (unpack) them. As you extract the files,
they'll be automatically restored to their original size.

Whew!

■ XTREEPRO GOLD Let's try this in a real-life example,
step by step. This time we'll be using Lotus 1-2-3 spreadsheet files.

Create an archive file You've created spreadsheets named JAN90.WK1,
FEB90.WK1 and so forth for the entire year. However, the
year is over, and now you want to store the files together a
single **1990** Arc file.

First, tag the files you want to archive. In Screen A-1, we
used the filespec of ***.wk1** to isolate the spreadsheet files,
and tagged them. Then we press **<CTRL>F5** to archive the
tagged files.

```
 Path: C:\LOTUS                              8-09-90  2:44:11 pm

┌ APR90   .WK1◆                          FILE  *.WK1
│ AUG90   .WK1◆
│ DEC90   .WK1◆                          DISK  C:POWER USER
│ FEB90   .WK1◆                          Available
│ JAN90   .WK1◆                           Bytes   2,088,960
│ JUL90   .WK1◆
│ JUN90   .WK1◆                          DIRECTORY Stats
│ MAR90   .WK1◆                          Total
│ MAY90   .WK1◆                           Files             36
│ NOV90   .WK1◆                           Bytes      1,026,979
│ OCT90   .WK1◆                          Matching
│ ▌SEP90  .WK1◆                           Files             12
│                                         Bytes         81,340
│                                        Tagged
│                                         Files             13
│                                         Bytes         94,949
│                                        Current File
│                                         SEP90    .WK1
│                                         Bytes          8,377

Archive all tagged files
to:
Enter archive file name            ↑ history  ←┘ ok  F1 help  ESC cancel
```

Screen A-1

XTreePro Gold is asking for the name you want to assign
the archive file. As you type in the file name, follow the
normal file-naming rules. However, *do not* type a file name
extension; XTreePro Gold will automatically add the ARC
extension.

In our example, we entered the name **1990** and hit
<ENTER>.

Now we get Screen A-2. Whenever you're *creating* an arc

```
 Path: C:\LOTUS                              8-09-90  2:44:53 pm

┌ APR90   .WK1◆                          FILE  *.WK1
│ AUG90   .WK1◆
│ DEC90   .WK1◆                          DISK  C:POWER USER
│ FEB90   .WK1◆                          Available
│ JAN90   .WK1◆                           Bytes   2,105,344
│ JUL90   .WK1◆
│ JUN90   .WK1◆                          DIRECTORY Stats
│ MAR90   .WK1◆                          Total
│ MAY90   .WK1◆                           Files             35
│ NOV90   .WK1◆                           Bytes      1,000,917
│ OCT90   .WK1◆                          Matching
│ ▌SEP90  .WK1◆                           Files             12
│                                         Bytes         81,340
│                                        Tagged
│                                         Files             13
│                                         Bytes         94,949
│                                        Current File
│                                         SEP90    .WK1
│                                         Bytes          8,377

ARCHIVE file: C:\LOTUS\1990.ARC
         Compatibility (PKarc)  Encryption (off)  method (archive)
                                      ←┘ ok  F1 help  ESC cancel
```

Screen A-2

file, XTreePro Gold asks for more information.

■ COMPATIBILITY. Believe it or not, there are a *number* of archiving schemes. XTreePro Gold offers you the choice of using either of two types. Each of the two types has an "up side" and a "down side."

When this menu first comes up, the compatibility format listed is "XTree." XTree's own archive format preserves the directory structure of the file(s) being archived. When the files are restored, the path will also be restored (if it has been deleted). The disadvantage is that you must own XTreePro Gold to extract the archived files.

The other archiving format is called PKarc and is widely available (even to non-XTreePro Gold users). That means that if you give an arced file to someone, they might be able to extract the files whether they do or do not own XTreePro Gold.

Typing **C** for compatibility at this point will let you toggle back and forth between the two file formats. Let's stay "mainstream" and use the PKarc format.

■ ENCRYPTION. Encryption adds a level of security to your archive file. Normally, when you create an arc file, *anyone* can extract the contents as long as they use the correct program.

Encryption allows you to add a password to your arc file. Then, only those with the right password can have access it. A password can be up to 32 characters long. (However, don't outsmart yourself with bizarre and difficult-to-type passwords. If you forget the password, you're out of luck.)

By default, encryption is turned off. Typing **E**, however, allows you to turn encryption on. For now, let's leave encryption off. (Despite the fact that we are not encrypting the file, XTreePro Gold will ask us for a password anyway. If you're not using the encryption option, just ignore the question by tapping **<ENTER>** whenever it asks for the password.)

(**Note:** "Method" is an option for adding to an existing arc file. Therefore, since we're creating a new archive, "method" is unavailable. That's why the "m" is in lowercase. Later, we'll get to look at "method.")

To recap, so far we typed **C** to set compatibility to PKarc and left encryption off. Now, press **<ENTER>** to create the Arc file.

```
 Path: C:\LOTUS                                   8-09-90  2:45:13 pm

  123     .CMP      JUL90   .WK1          FILE  *.*
  123     .CNF      JUN90   .WK1
  123     .EXE      JZZLOTUS.XLT          DISK  C:POWER USER
  123     .HLP      LOTUS   .COM          Available
  123     .SET      MAR90   .WK1          Bytes    2,080,768
  1990    .ARC      MAY90   .WK1
  APR90   .WK1      NOV90   .WK1          DIRECTORY Stats
  AUG90   .WK1      OCT90   .WK1          Total
  BURNDEV .SYS      SEP90   .WK1          Files              36
  DBF2    .XLT      T       .             Bytes       1,023,225
  DBF3    .XLT      TRANS   .COM          Matching
  DEC90   .WK1      UPTIME  .COM          Files              36
  DIF     .XLT      UTIL    .COM          Bytes       1,023,225
  FEB90   .WK1      VCWRK   .XLT          Tagged
  INSTALL .DVC      WR1WKS  .XLT          Files               0
  INSTALL .EXE      WR1WRK  .XLT          Bytes               0
  INSTALL .LBR      WRKWR1  .XLT          Current File
  INSTALL .SCR                            1990        .ARC
  JAN90   .WK1                            Bytes          22,308

 FILE         Attributes  Copy  Delete  Edit  Filespec  Invert   Log disk  Move
 COMMANDS     New date  Open  Print   Rename  Tag  Untag  View   eXecute  Quit
 ◄┘ tree  F7 autoview  F8 split     F9 menu  F10 commands      F1 help  ESC cancel
```

Screen A-3

After XTreePro Gold is finished, you might delete your "original" files, because they've all been neatly packed in the archive file "suitcase."

Let's look at the **1990.ARC** file to make sure everything is there. To look inside an arc file, all you have to do is highlight the archive file you want to examine (in this case **1990.ARC**, as in Screen A-3) and strike **<ALT>F5** to open the file.

Open archive

Using the open archive command will net you a list of all files archived inside (see Screen A-4, next page). It looks a lot like a full file display, with one important addition: the percentage of compression. The statistics box on the right now deals solely with the current arc file. You can see that the size of the 1990.ARC file is 22,308 bytes. However, the total size of the files in the arc file (when extracted) is 81,340 bytes. That's quite a savings, space-wise.

When you are looking at an arced file like this, you'll see some familiar command options: Extract, Filespec, Print, Tag, Untag, and View.

Though these options work as expected, they work only on the archive file in current view.

If you want to extract a single file, type **T** to tag it. Then type **E** to extract it. If you want to extract all the files, type

```
Compatibility (PKarc)                              8-09-90  2:45:27 pm

 APR90  .WK1    4,889  74% .a..  4-30-90  1:25:04 pm    FILE *.*
 AUG90  .WK1    8,377  73% .a..  8-31-90  3:37:10 pm
 DEC90  .WK1    8,377  73% .a.. 12-26-90 12:06:30 pm    ARCHIVE File
 FEB90  .WK1    4,889  74% .a..  2-25-90  1:52:10 pm      1990     .ARC
 JAN90  .WK1    4,889  74% .a..  1-30-90  5:35:26 pm      Bytes      22,308
 JUL90  .WK1    6,633  73% .a..  7-30-90  4:27:10 pm
 JUN90  .WK1    6,633  73% .a..  6-30-90  6:52:46 pm    ARCHIVE Statistics
 MAR90  .WK1    4,889  74% .a..  3-31-90  4:57:02 pm    Total
 MAY90  .WK1    6,633  73% .a..  5-30-90  6:53:18 pm      Files          12
 NOV90  .WK1    8,377  73% .a.. 11-30-90  5:01:00 pm      Bytes      81,340
 OCT90  .WK1    8,377  73% .a.. 10-31-90  7:02:54 pm    Matching
 SEP90  .WK1    8,377  73% .a..  9-30-90  3:45:42 pm      Files          12
                                                         Bytes      81,340
                                                       Tagged
                                                         Files           0
                                                         Bytes           0
                                                       Current File
                                                         APR90    .WK1
                                                         Bytes       4,889

ARC FILE  Extract  Filespec  Print  Tag  Untag  View
COMMANDS
                                                       F1 help  ESC exit
```

Screen A-4

<CTRL>T to tag all files and then **<CTRL>E** to extract all tagged files.

From this point on, the process works just like copying or moving. XTreePro Gold asks you for a destination, and whether you wish to replace existing files.

Modify an existing Arc file   After you create an Arc file (and copy it to a floppy disk), you don't have to delete the source files from your hard disk. You can continue using them. Then, when it's time to back up again, you can just *update* or *freshen* the existing Arc file. (Updating and freshening are quicker than creating the Arc file from scratch.)

In our current example, we've worked on some of the files, but can't remember which ones. Also, we've created another file (TOTAL90.WK1) which needs to be included in 1990.ARC.

What we need to do is add the new file (TOTAL90.WK1), and make sure we have the most current version of the other files (JAN-DEC.WK1) in our 1990.ARC file.

First, tag the files that were originally archived plus the new one. Press **<CTRL>F5** (just as if we're creating a new archive). When asked for the name of the archive file, type the name of the Arc file we want to modify (**1990** in our example) and **<ENTER>**.

```
Path: C:\LOTUS                                      8-09-90  2:46:51 pm

  123    .CMP      JUL90   .WK1+          FILE  *.*
  123    .CNF      JUN90   .WK1+
  123    .EXE      JZZLOTUS.XLT          DISK  C:POWER USER
  123    .HLP      LOTUS   .COM          Available
  123    .SET      MAR90   .WK1+         Bytes     2,080,768
  1990   .ARC      MAY90   .WK1+
  APR90  .WK1+     NOV90   .WK1+         DIRECTORY Stats
  AUG90  .WK1+     OCT90   .WK1+         Total
  BURNDEV.SYS      SEP90   .WK1+           Files            36
  DBF2   .XLT      TOTAL9  .WK1+           Bytes     1,023,225
  DBF3   .XLT      TRANS   .COM          Matching
  DEC90  .WK1+     UPTIME  .COM            Files            36
  DIF    .XLT      UTIL    .SET            Bytes     1,023,225
  FEB90  .WK1+     VCWRK   .XLT          Tagged
  INSTALL.DVC      WR1WKS  .XLT            Files            13
  INSTALL.EXE      WR1WRK  .XLT            Bytes        94,949
  INSTALL.LBR      WRKWR1  .XLT          Current File
  INSTALL.SCR                            1990     .ARC
  JAN90  .WK1+                           Bytes        22,308

ARCHIVE file: C:\LOTUS\1990.ARC
              compatibility (PKarc)  Encryption (off)  Method (update)
                                     ◄┘ ok   F1 help   ESC cancel
```

Screen A-5

At the bottom of the screen the word "compatibility" is in
lowercase, indicating that it is not a current option ("compatibility" is chosen only at the time of creation). As a
consolation prize, however, now we get to use "Method."

■ MODIFY. There are three ways (methods) of altering an
existing Arc file.

1. "Updating" an Arc file means that the tagged files are
   compared with the files in the Arc file. If a tagged file is
   newer, then it replaces the older file in the Arc file. If a
   tagged file is not in the Arc file, it is added to the Arc file.
   (This is what we want to do in our example.)

2. The second method is called "Freshen." It simply
   compares the dates of the tagged files to the dates of the
   files in the Arc file, replacing the newer files as needed. No
   additional files are added to the Arc file. (In our example,
   then, it would not add TOTAL90.WK1 to 1990.ARC.)

3. The third method is called "Archive." It just means everything that's tagged gets put in the Arc file. No questions
   asked.

To cycle through Update, Freshen and Archive, press **M**.

If Arc
doesn't
work

It is possible that your version of XTreePro Gold does not have the Arc module. Please contact the XTree Company (see page 286) about either getting your module, or just upgrading to XTreeGold.

■ **XTREEGOLD** The major difference in XTreeGold is the adoption of another archiving scheme. In addition to the Arc method, Gold also uses the "Zip" method. The difference between Arc and Zip is their efficiency and compatibility with other users. If you don't specify a choice, XTreeGold uses the Zip format — which is the recommended way to go.

If you have Arc, Zip, or even files compressed using XTree's own archiving scheme, XTreeGold will recognize and handle them appropriately.

Create a Zip
(or Arc) file

In this example, we've got a series of reports created in Microsoft Word entitled JAN.DOC, FEB.DOC, etc. The year is over, and now you want to store the files together in a single **1991** Zip file.

First, tag the files you want to Zip together. Then press **<CTRL>F5**. You'll get the prompt, as in Screen A-6, asking you to name the "compressed" file. As you type in the file name, follow the normal file-naming rules.

```
Path: C:\WORD\REPORTS                           2-09-91  7:20:30 am

  APR    .DOC◆                          FILE  *.*
  AUG    .DOC◆
  DEC    .DOC◆                          DISK  C:POWER USER
  FEB    .DOC◆                          Available
  JAN    .DOC◆                            Bytes  16,670,720
  JUL    .DOC◆
  JUN    .DOC◆                          DIRECTORY Stats
  MAR    .DOC◆                          Total
  MAY    .DOC◆                            Files           12
  NOV    .DOC◆                            Bytes       24,064
  OCT    .DOC◆                          Matching
  SEP    .DOC◆                            Files           12
                                         Bytes       24,064
                                       Tagged
                                         Files           12
                                         Bytes       24,064
                                       Current File
                                         APR      .DOC
                                         Bytes        2,048

COMPRESS all tagged files
      to:
Enter path and file name          ↑ history  ↵ ok  F1 help  ESC cancel
```

Screen A-6

Note: This is where you select the "compression method" for your file. If you type in a file name *without* an extension (i.e. "REPORTS"), XTreeGold will assume you want to create a Zip file. If you type in a filename with the "ARC" extension (i.e. "REPORTS.ARC") XTreeGold will use the Arc method.

In this situation, however, let's make a Zip file. So we just type in **REPORTS** and hit **<ENTER>**.

Whenever you're *creating* a Zip (or Arc) file, XTreeGold asks for more information as at the bottom of Screen A-7.

■ PATHS. You may select "paths full" or "paths none." This means that you can also record the paths as well as the files themselves. Later, when you restore the files, you can opt to restore the paths as well. You'll have to judge for yourself whether this is for you or not. In any case, the default is "full," and typing **P** will change it to "none."

■ ENCRYPTION. Encryption adds a level of security to your archive file. Normally, when you create an archive file, *anyone* can extract the contents as long as they use the correct program.

Encryption allows you to add a password to your compressed file. Then, only those with the right password can have access it. A password can be up to 32 characters long.

```
Path: C:\WORD\REPORTS                        2-09-91  7:20:30 am

APR     .DOC◆                        FILE  *.*
AUG     .DOC◆
DEC     .DOC◆                        DISK  C:POWER USER
FEB     .DOC◆                        Available
JAN     .DOC◆                          Bytes  16,670,720
JUL     .DOC◆
JUN     .DOC◆                        DIRECTORY Stats
MAR     .DOC◆                        Total
MAY     .DOC◆                          Files          12
NOV     .DOC◆                          Bytes      24,064
OCT     .DOC◆                        Matching
SEP     .DOC◆                          Files          12
                                       Bytes      24,064
                                     Tagged
                                       Files          12
                                       Bytes      24,064
                                     Current File
                                       APR     .DOC
                                       Bytes       2,048

Zip file: C:\WORD\REPORTS\REPORTS.ZIP
Paths (Full)     Encryption (off)  Method (add)      Speed/size (size)
                                          ↵ ok  F1 help  ESC cancel
```

Screen A-7

(However, don't outsmart yourself with bizarre and difficult-to-type passwords. If you forget the password, you're out of luck.)

By default, encryption is turned off. Typing **E**, however, allows you to turn encryption on. For now, let's leave encryption off.

■ METHOD. "Method" is used when *adding* to an existing compressed file. Since we're creating a new archive, "method" is not an option (you can hit **M**, but nothing will happen. (We'll discuss "method" when it comes up later.)

■ SPEED/SIZE. Even *within* the compression methods there are different levels of compression. The smaller the size of the compressed file, the longer it takes to create it (we're talking a difference of seconds, not minutes). You can hit **S** to toggle between speed and size.

■ FINALLY... Press **<ENTER>** to create the Zip file.

After XTreeGold is finished, the name of your Zip file appears on screen (Screen A-8) along with your other files. You may delete your "original" files because they've all been neatly packed in the archive file "suitcase."

Open Looking inside a compressed file is called "opening an
archive archive." Let's open the newly-created **REPORTS.ZIP** file to make sure everything is there. First, highlight the name

```
Path: C:\WORD\REPORTS                        2-15-91 12:26:37 am

 APR      .DOC♦                        FILE  *.*
 AUG      .DOC♦
 DEC      .DOC♦                        DISK  C:POWER USER
 FEB      .DOC♦                        Available
 JAN      .DOC♦                        Bytes   12,910,592
 JUL      .DOC♦
 JUN      .DOC♦                        DIRECTORY Stats
 MAR      .DOC♦                        Total
 MAY      .DOC♦                          Files           13
 NOV      .DOC♦                          Bytes       34,089
 OCT      .DOC♦                        Matching
 REPORTS  .ZIP                           Files           13
 SEP      .DOC♦                          Bytes       34,089
                                       Tagged
                                         Files           12
                                         Bytes       24,064
                                       Current File
                                       SEP       .DOC
                                       Bytes        2,048

FILE       Attributes  Copy  Delete  Edit  Filespec  Invert  Log disk  Move
COMMANDS   New date  Open  Print  Rename  Tag  Untag  View  eXecute  Quit
↵ tree   F7 autoview  F8 split   F9 menu  F10 commands   F1 help  ESC cancel
```

Screen A-8

```
 ┌─────────────────────────────────────────────────────────────┐
 │ Path: REPORTS.ZIP: \                          2-09-91  7:24:55 am │
 │                                         ┌─────────────────────┐ │
 │ \                                       │ FILE  *.*           │ │
 │  └─WORD                                 ├─────────────────────┤ │
 │     └─REPORTS                           │ ZIP File            │ │
 │                                         │ REPORTS .ZIP        │ │
 │                                         │ Bytes      10,025   │ │
 │                                         ├─────────────────────┤ │
 │                                         │ ZIP Statistics      │ │
 │                                         │ Total               │ │
 │                                         │   Files         12  │ │
 │                                         │   Bytes     24,064  │ │
 │                                         │ Matching            │ │
 │                                         │   Files         12  │ │
 │                                         │   Bytes     24,064  │ │
 │                                         │ Tagged              │ │
 │                                         │   Files          0  │ │
 │ No Files!                               │   Bytes          0  │ │
 │                                         │ Current Directory   │ │
 │                                         │   A:\               │ │
 │                                         │   Bytes          0  │ │
 ├─────────────────────────────────────────────────────────────┤ │
 │ ZIP DIR   Branch  Filespec  Print  Showall  Tag  Untag       │
 │ COMMANDS                                                      │
 │ ◄┘ file                          F10 commands  F1 help  ESC exit │
 └─────────────────────────────────────────────────────────────┘
```

Screen A-9

of the file you want to look at (in this case **REPORTS.ZIP**) and strike **<ALT>F5** to open the file (Screen A-9).

When you first open a compressed file, what you see may be a little disconcerting. Why no files? Remember, the "paths" option was kept at full, and the opened file reflects this. (You can use the Branch command to consolidate everything into one list, or just highlight the directory where the files were stored to get a list of all files inside the archived file, Screen A-10.)

Screen A-10 looks a lot like a full file display, with one important addition: the percentage of compression. The statistics box on the right now deals solely with the current Zip file. You can see that the size of the REPORTS.ZIP file is 10,025 bytes. However, the total size of the files in the Zip file (when extracted) is 24,064 bytes. That's quite a savings, space-wise.

When you are looking at a Zipped file like this, you have some familiar commands available: Extract, Filespec, Print, Tag, Untag, and View (and F10). These options work as expected on the currently-open, compressed file.

If you want to extract/restore a single file, type **T** to tag it. Then type **E** to extract it. If you want to extract all the file, type **<CTRL>T** to tag all files and then **<CTRL>E** to extract all tagged files.

```
Path: REPORTS.ZIP: \WORD\REPORTS                      2-09-91  7:25:46 am

 APR    .DOC   2,048  63%  .a..  11-18-90  6:33:22 pm   FILE  *.*
 AUG    .DOC   2,048  65%  .a..  12-22-90  3:45:02 pm
 DEC    .DOC   2,048  63%  .a..   1-19-91  8:02:56 am   ZIP File
 FEB    .DOC   2,048  62%  .a..   9-12-90  8:54:32 am     REPORTS .ZIP
 JAN    .DOC   1,536  70%  .a..  12-01-90  7:09:16 am     Bytes      10,025
 JUL    .DOC   2,048  62%  .a..  12-03-90 10:27:46 am
 JUN    .DOC   2,048  65%  .a..  12-01-90  7:05:36 am   ZIP Directory Stats
 MAR    .DOC   2,048  66%  .a..   5-04-90  2:04:58 pm   Total
 MAY    .DOC   2,048  63%  .a..  12-01-90  7:03:30 am     Files          12
 NOV    .DOC   2,048  66%  .a..   1-19-91  8:01:00 am     Bytes      24,064
 OCT    .DOC   2,048  65%  .a..   1-17-91 10:15:40 am   Matching
 SEP    .DOC   2,048  66%  .a..  12-23-90 10:45:54 am     Files          12
                                                         Bytes      24,064
                                                       Tagged
                                                         Files           0
                                                         Bytes           0
                                                       Current File
                                                         APR     .DOC
                                                         Bytes       2,048

ZIP FILE  Extract  Filespec  Print  Tag  Untag  View
COMMANDS
← tree                                    F10 commands  F1 help  ESC cancel
```

Screen A-10

From this point on, the process works just like copying or moving. XTreeGold asks you for a destination, and whether you wish to replace existing files.

Modify an existing compressed file After you create a Zip file (and copy it to a floppy disk), you don't *have* to delete the source files from your hard disk. You can continue using them. Then, when it's time to back up again, you can just *update* or *freshen* the existing Zip file. (Updating and freshening are quicker than creating the arc file from scratch.)

In our current example, we've re-worked some of the monthly files, but can't remember which ones.

We have to make sure REPORTS.ZIP has current version of the other files.

First, tag the files that were originally compressed (you can also tag any new files you wish to add to the compressed file). Then, press the traditional **<CTRL>F5** (just as though we're creating a new file). When asked for the name of the file to compress, type the name of the file (**REPORTS.ZIP** in our example) and **<ENTER>**. You'll get something like Screen A-11.

At the bottom of the screen are our old pals Paths, Encryption, Method, Speed/size. However, now we can actually use "Method."

```
Path: C:\WORD\REPORTS                           2-09-91  8:17:39 am

 APR    .DOC◆                               FILE *.*
 AUG    .DOC◆
 DEC    .DOC◆                               DISK  C:POWER USER
 FEB    .DOC◆                               Available
 JAN    .DOC◆                                Bytes  16,609,280
 JUL    .DOC◆
 JUN    .DOC◆                               DIRECTORY Stats
 MAR    .DOC◆                               Total
 MAY    .DOC◆                                Files           13
 NOV    .DOC◆                                Bytes       34,089
 OCT    .DOC◆                               Matching
 REPORTS .ZIP                                Files           13
 SEP    .DOC◆                                Bytes       34,089
                                            Tagged
                                             Files           12
                                             Bytes       24,064
                                            Current File
                                            REPORTS .ZIP
                                             Bytes       10,025

 Zip file: C:\WORD\REPORTS\REPORTS.ZIP
 Paths (Full)    Encryption (off)  Method (update)    Speed/size (size)
                                            ↵ ok  F1 help  ESC cancel
```

Screen A-11

■ METHOD. There are three ways (methods) of altering an existing compressed file.
1. "Updating" a Zip file means that the tagged files will be compared with the files in the existing Zip file. If a tagged file is newer, then it replaces the older file in the Zip file. If a tagged file is not in the Zip file, it is added to the Zip file.
2. The second method is called "Freshen." It simply compares the dates of the tagged files to the dates of the files in the Zip file, replacing the newer files as needed. No additional files are added to the Zip file.
3. The third method is called "Add." Everything that's tagged gets put in the compressed file. No questions asked.
To cycle through Update, Freshen and Add, press **M**.
When you're all set, **<ENTER>**.

Don't forget about using the Pull-down menus (or your mouse) to accomplish all these tasks. Also, don't forget History (if you forget History, you're doomed to repeat your typos).

Final reminder

Appendix

■ Insider Info From XTree Tech Support:

The Most Commonly Asked Questions About XTree/Pro/ProGold/Gold/Net

Straight from the XTree tech support team, here are the most commonly-asked questions (and their answers, of course) about XTree, XTreePro, XTreePro Gold, XTreeGold, and there's even a section on XTreeNet. Although most of these questions are explored in depth elsewhere in this book, maybe you can get a quick answer to *your* burning question right here! (Or maybe get an answer to a question you didn't know you had.) You may want to browse through *all* of the questions because there are some questions that can apply to more than one program.

■ XTree

■ How do I install XTree to my hard drive?

You can use XTree to install XTree. Put your XTree master disk in your floppy drive (let's assume it's the A drive). Type **A: <ENTER>** to log onto the A drive. Type **XTree <ENTER>**. Once you get the XTree screen, hit **L** (for log) **C** (for your hard drive — or D or E or whatever the letter is for the hard drive you want to put it on). Press **M** (for Make directory) and type **XTREE <ENTER>**. Press **L** then **A** to get back to your floppy. Press **<ENTER>** to get into the small files window. Now press **<CTRL>T** to tag all the files (a diamond appears next to the file names) and **<CTRL>C** to copy all tagged files and, finally, type **C:\XTREE <ENTER>** when you're asked for the destination path. After the files have been copied, you can exit XTree. Type **C: <ENTER>** to get back to your hard disk. (Make sure you edit your AUTOEXEC.BAT file to include XTree in your path statement — see page 186.)

■ When I try to log my 80mb hard drive with 4300 files, XTree doesn't log all of my files.

The original XTree can only read in 2500 files. The easiest thing to do is upgrade to one of our more powerful programs. However, you can use the DOS SUBST command and log *parts* of your directory tree. (See page 168 for details.)

■ How can I find my serial number?

Finding your serial number is a test of skill and manual dexterity — sort of the "video game" portion of XTree. First, get XTree up and running. Press **L** for Log drive then put one finger on the C key and one on the F1 key. Right after you press **C**, hit **F1** as fast as you can to freeze the logo screen, where you will find this elusive number displayed.

■ XTreePro

■ I get a message on the screen when I first load XTreePro.

It's probably because you have recently upgraded to a higher version of DOS. You need to run the configuration program (XTPROCFG.EXE) and change the disk logging method under option 1 to "standard." (See page 68.)

■ When I try to Edit a file I get "Can't find file XTPRO.X01."

One of two things on this one. You either deleted that file somehow, or you have moved (or renamed) the XTPRO directory. If you did the first, get out your original disk and re-install. If you did the latter, simply run the configuration program (XTPROCFG.EXE) and change the program path under option 1. (See page 68.)

■ After running XTreePro, I run out of memory while trying to run some of my programs.

Hold the **<Ctrl>** and **<Alt>** key down at the same time to see what version you have. It's probably version 1.0; if so, call XTree to receive version 1.1 — that will solve this problem.

■ XTreePro Gold

■ How do I collapse Gold to a 7K wedge?

First, make sure you start Gold by using **XTGOLD.COM**, not **XTG.EXE**. Then, instead of using **X** to execute a program, use **<ALT>X**. (Or use **<ALT>O** instead of **O** to open a file.) Also, in the configuration program, there are "memory utilization" options on page 3 of "Modify configuration items" which can be set to "All Memory" (collapse) or "Available Memory" (no collapse). (See page 68 for how to run the configuration program.)

■ How do I use the instant logging feature?

Let's say you have drives C:, D:, and E: logged while in a split window with 100 files tagged at midnight and you want to go to sleep but do not want to lose your work. Use **<ALT>Z** to quit, and the next time you start Gold, you'll be right back where you left off!

■ How do I find, on my hard disk, a file that contains the word "cash"?

Go into Showall mode (or Global for all drives), and do a **<CTRL>T** to tag all files. Now, do a **<CTRL>S** to search all tagged files and enter the word **cash**. Gold will untag all files which do not contain **cash**. After Gold finishes, hit **<ESC>** and press **<CTRL>S** to give you a list of all the remaining tagged files (i.e. those files containing the word "cash"). You can use View to find the specific file you want.

■ Does XTreePro Gold Support VGA? A mouse?

Yes, it supports both.

■ How can I see two directories?

Use the split window command (**F8**) to split the display in two. Each side of the display operates independently so that you may view two directories, two drives, or any other combination you wish.

■ Can I log on to my CD-ROM drive?

But of course!

■ I know Gold can edit my ASCII files, but can it edit in Hex mode?

Yes. View the file in Hex mode and press **E** for edit.

■ What is the difference between Prune and Graft?

Prune allows you to quickly delete an entire branch from your directory tree. Because Prune is such a powerful feature, Gold double-checks your action before files are deleted. Graft is a feature that lets you quickly move an entire branch of a directory tree, including all subdirectories, to a different location on the tree.

■ What does Wash Disk do?

Wash Disk makes all deleted files unrecoverable. Technically, it zeroes out (writes over) everywhere on the disk where there are no files.

■ Does XTreePro Gold run under DOS 4.0 or 4.01?

Yes. The main feature of DOS 4.0/4.01 is that it allows disk partitions to be larger than the previous 32MB boundary. XTreePro Gold, as well as other XTree products, can read a disk past the 32MB boundary. The only limit is the number of files and directories a user has on the disk.

■ Does XTreePro Gold run under OS/2?

No. We do not have a version yet that will run under the

OS/2 operating system. However, XTree *will* run under the DOS portion of OS/2 (the DOS compatibility box).

■ How much memory does XTreePro Gold use?

The program requires 256K of RAM for Gold to function properly. When running other programs from Gold, Gold's memory usage will shrink down to only 7K-8K of memory, thus allowing large programs to run. Memory usage also depends on the number of files and directories on disk. Each file or directory entry will occupy 32 bytes of computer memory, so the more files you have, the more computer memory you will use. (One K is 1024 bytes.)

■ How large of a file can I edit with the editor (1WORD)?

A user may edit text files up to 64K with 1WORD. If the user has another editor that can edit files greater than 64K, or prefers it over 1WORD, the user can configure XTreePro Gold to use that editor instead.

■ Will XTreePro Gold run under DESQView?

Yes, as long as you give it enough memory. 425K is suggested.

■ Will XTreePro Gold run under Windows?

For a program to run properly under Microsoft Windows, a special set of instructions about that program must be created for Windows. These instructions are saved in a file with the extension of PIF. A PIF file (XTGOLD.PIF) is provided on your disk to run under version 2.XX of Windows. New PIF files are being created for Windows version 3.0. If you need a PIF file for version 3.0, call tech support for the latest info.

■ How do I return to a previously- logged drive without relogging?

Use the + or − key to cycle through all logged drives.

■ XTreeGold 2.0

■ The XTreeMenu is a bit tedious to edit, is there an easier way?

You bet! All the commands used by the menus system are hot keys. To Add an item press **A**, to Delete press **D**, to Move press **M**, to Rename press **R**, etc.

■ I used to use the + or the - keys to switch between drives with XTreePro Gold, and I don't like using the < or > instead. Is there a way to switch back to my old ways?

Yes. When you start XTreeGold, use the undocumented /XT command switch. In other words, start the program with **XTGOLD /XT <ENTER>**.

■ Where are the pull-down menus?

Everywhere! To invoke the pull-downs, either press **F10,** or use the mouse to click the cursor on the top row of the screen. Even if you don't normally use pull-downs, there are some occasions where they come in handy. For example, while viewing or autoviewing you can change the view mode, set bookmarks, gather text, etc., more easily from the pull-downs.

■ Is there any way to easily find duplicate files on my computer?

There are a number of ways... but a new way in XTreeGold is to go into a Showall mode by pressing the "S" key and then press **<ATL>F4** to invoke the Showall/Global Compare facility. Press **D** for duplicates.

■ Can I Graft across drives?

Not directly — but the Branch command and the **<ALT>M**ove can accomplish the same thing. Highlight the parent of the branch you want to Graft. Press **<CTRL>T**, **<ALT>M**, enter destination, then select partial branch paths for the Source Paths prompt.

■ *I run out of memory when I try to run some of my programs.*

Make sure you start XTreeGold with XTGOLD.COM and not XTG.EXE. Then use the **<ALT>X** instead of just plain X to eXecute a program.

■ *How do I switch between windows in split windows mode?*

Use the **<TAB>** key, or point with the mouse.

■ *When I go to view my WordPerfect (MS Word, etc.)files, I get garbage instead of the document.*

You need to press the **F** key for a formatted view.

■ *My mouse doesn't work.*

In order to conserve memory, XTreeGold does not have its own mouse driver — it just knows how to use the mouse driver you should already have loaded in memory. The first step is to make sure your mouse is functioning properly in other programs. If it isn't, then find MOUSE.COM (or MOUSE.SYS) and make sure it is properly installed before entering XTree.

■ *XTree (General)*

■ *What's the difference between Showall and Global?*

Showall lists all files on the *currently* logged drive where Global lists all files on *all* logged drives.

■ *Can I print to a file?*

Yes. Start up your XTree product with a redirection. Example: **XTGOLD > filename /ps**. The "/ps" specifies standard output.

■ *How can I print to LPT2:?*

Use the same technique as above but use the term LPT2: instead of a filename.

■ Can I rename my XT????.COM to X.COM for easier access?

You can, but if you later want to configure your XTree product, you will run into some problems. Instead, make a batch file called X.BAT that calls up your program.

■ When XTree comes up I want to be high- lighting the same directory that I was in before I started the program.

In the above X.BAT example you could have the file say: C:\XTREE\XTREE (instead of having the batch file switch to C:\XTREE first).

■ How can I quit XTree and be in the directory I was last pointing at?

Use the **<ALT>Q** command while quitting to end up in the highlighted directory.

■ How do I create a new text file with XTree products?

In all products except the original XTree, simply highlight the directory you want the new file to be located and press **E** for edit. When prompted, type in the name you want to call your new file (and hit **<ENTER>**).

■ XTreeNet

■ Greg just got fired(!). Is there an easy way to find all of his files?

Do a Showall or a Global and press **<ALT>T** to tag by attribute. Now press **O** (for owner) and type in Greg's name.

■ When I've logged a couple of volumes and go to log a third, I run out of memory. Is there a way to find out how many more files I can read in?

If you start up XTreeNet with a /XM option there will be a number located just above the available bytes number in the upper right of the screen, indicating the number of files and directories you can still read in. You can increase this

number by releasing branches from memory with the minus
("-") key

■ What is the easiest way to find the owner of a directory or file?

By hitting **<ALT>I**, the statistics box on the right side of the
screen will change and allow you to get detailed information
on each file and directory.

■ Mail directories in Novell are always some number that doesn't mean anything to me. Is there a way in XTreeNet to easily see who these directories belong to?

If you press **<ALT>I** for a second time the statistics box
changes to show Trustee information. Now you can scroll
through these directories to find out.

■ How do I log my entire volume instead of just the first level of directories?

If you press the asterisk ("*") key, it will log from the cursor
down. You can also use **<ALT>L** which will automatically
read the whole volume.

■ Can I set up a default configuration for users who don't do any configuring for themselves?

Yes. When saving the Configuration, select **C** for Change
path and enter the path to your XTreeNet program.

■ Can I add trustees while in XTreeNet?

Yes. You can add, delete, and modify trustees by highlighting
the appropriate directory and pressing **A** for Attributes and
T for Trustees.

■ I set the X attribute for a file in XTreeNet and I can't remove it.

The X attribute is an unchangeable attribute in Novell once
set. You can re-install the affected program to remove this.

Appendix

C

■ *Where To Go From Here*

Just in case you've become intrigued by DOS (well, stranger things have happened), or some of the products mentioned sound like they might lighten your load, here's a list of where you can find what.

Company names are given as a point of reference. Most of these products are available (at a discount) from your local friendly computer store.

The books are available either in mainstream bookstores or computer stores that carry books.

■ *XTree Company*

The makers of XTree can be contacted by phone, fax, or mail as listed below.

The purpose of XTree's technical support lines is to answer your questions. To get the most out of your technical support experience, however, please call when you are in front of your computer with your program running.

Also, if you own a previous version of XTree, you can upgrade to XTreeGold for $35. (Call 800/282-5003.)

If you have a version of XTreePro Gold that doesn't have the "Archive" module, simply fill out and return your warranty registration card and you'll receive the current version of Gold (including the Archive module) within a couple of weeks.

Note: If you own an Epson Equity, Western Digital, Tallgrass Technologies, or Headstart Technologies computer, the version of XTree that came with your computer is computer-specific. That means you cannot copy it to another computer system and expect it to be fully functional. You can discover the version number of Pro and Gold by simultaneously pressing **<CTRL>** and **<ALT>**. In XTree, the version number is displayed when you call up the program. Also available is a version of XTree for local area networks and one for the Macintosh.

Mailing
Address
XTree Company
4330 Santa Fe Road
San Luis Obispo, CA 93401

Technical
Support
805/541-0604

FAX
805/541-8053

BBS
805/546-9150

■ *Other Software*

■ *Disk Technican*
Prime Solutions
1940 Garnet Ave.
San Diego, CA 92109
800/847-5000

■ *Norton Utilities*
Symantec
10201 Torre Avenue
Cupertino, CA 95014
Customer service:
408/252-3570

■ *PC-Kwik*
Multisoft Corp.
15100 S.W. Koll Parkway
Beaverton, OR 97006
800/234-KWIK

■ *OPTune*
Gazelle Systems
42 N. University Ave. #10
Provo, UT 84601
800/233-0383

■ *Fastback*
Mace Utilities
Fifth Generation Systems
10049 N. Reiger Rd.
Baton Rouge, LA 70809
Sales: 800/873-4384
Tech support:
504/291-7283

■ *PC Tools*
Central Point Software
15220 N.W. Greenbrier
Pkwy #200
Beaverton, OR 87006
Sales: 503/690-8090
Tech support:
503/690-8080

■ SpinRite II
Gibson Research
22991 LaCadena
Laguna Hills, CA 92653
Sales: 714/830-2200
Tech support:
714/830-2500

■ VOPT
Golden Bow Systems
P.O. Box 3039
San Diego, CA 92103
Sales: 800/284-3269
Tech support:
619/298-9349

■ Other Books on MS-DOS And Hard Disks

■ The Official SpinRite II & Hard Disk Companion
By John Goodman
Published by
IDG Books Worldwide
800/28BOOKS

■ Microsoft Quick Reference MS-DOS Commands
By Van Wolverton
Published by
Microsoft Press
800/677-7377

■ Managing Your Hard Disk
By Don Berliner
with Chris DeVoney
Published by Que
800/428-5331

■ Peter Norton's DOS Guide
By Peter Norton
Published by Brady
800/624-0023
from New Jersey:
800/624-0024

■ Running MS-DOS
By Van Wolverton
Published by
Microsoft Press
800/677-7377

■ PC World's Complete DOS Handbook
By John Socha
Published by
IDG Books Worldwide
800/28BOOKS
(Available June 1991)

D Appendix

■ *Pop Quiz Answers*

From Part 1:

Page 23 ■ What are the three things DOS can mean?
1. Disk Operating System.
2. A place on a disk for storing DOS files.
3. You are not in a program (as in "go to DOS").

Page 24 ■ What does the colon mean in "A:" and "C:"?
It means "drive." As in the A drive and the C drive, which is how we refer to them in this book.

Page 26 ■ What is the purpose of directories?
Directories are storage areas for files and programs.

Page 28 ■ What are the two things the system prompt tells you?
1. The computer is ready for a command.
2. The current disk and directory.

Page 33 ■ What do these mean?
*.txt
Any file that ends in TXT.

1*.doc
Any file that begins with L and ends with DOC.

chap?.doc
Any file that begins with CHAP and has one character after CHAP and ends in DOC. (**Note:** this would include chap1.doc and chap9.doc, but *not* chap11.doc).

.
All files.

■ If you can't delete a file, what does that tell you about   **Page 35**
the file's attributes?
    The file has been set to be "read only."

■ Is it okay to delete "system" files?
    Never.

■ Which one of the attributes would tell you whether
you've backed up the file or not?
    The archive bit.

■ Do all computers have the same CONFIG.SYS and
AUTOEXEC.BAT files?
    All computers should have CONFIG.SYS and
    AUTOEXEC.BAT files, but the contents of each
    CONFIG.SYS and AUTOEXEC.BAT files are
    different on different computers.

From Part 4:   **Page 185**
■ The root should not be used as a storage area.
    True. The root should only be used as the
    entryway or gateway to the rest of your computer
    system.

■ Give directories long and complex names.
    False. The less you have to type, the better.

■ Keep the file count under 200 in each directory.
    True. Having too many large directories inhibits
    your performance and the machine's!

■ Index

Instructions for an Index? Well, not exactly. This Index may not work precisely like other Indexes. It is not a mindless cataloging of every single mention of a particular word or phrase. Instead, it's designed to help you find what you're looking for. (Novel concept, no?)

Each idea or phrase is listed as many ways as possible to help you locate an entry, whether you know the correct term or not. For instance "read-only" files are mentioned a dozen or more times throughout the book. If you look at the "Read-only" entry in the index, you'll see only the two places listed (the definition and an example) that are worth looking up. On the other hand, you'll find the term "Read-only" cross-referenced in this index under File and under Attributes as well as under just plain "Read-only." (And remember, the Table of Contents lists each command alphabetically.)

.	109	undo	212
+	55, 92, 93, 138, 222	Arc: see Archiving	
-	55, 138, 222	Archive attribute	33
<	222	Archive bit	34
<ENTER>	42	Archiving	263
>	222	Arc (PKarc)	266
?	166	Zip	271
^ symbol	42	compatibility	266
1Word	97	extract Arc files	268
commands	98	extract Zip files	273
print	151	modify Arc files	268
7K Wedge	137, 139	modify Zip files	274
All files on the disk: see Showall		method	269, 275
Alphabetical order	161	freshen	269, 275
Application	51	updating	269, 275
Application menu	50, 205	open Arc file	267
command (F9)	51	open Zip file	273
edit	52	ASCII	30
update	206	Editor	97
auto install	206	file	101
collapse	207	Associate	105
command (F9)	206	Associated batch file	105
edit	207	Asterisk	31
edit script	210	Attribute	33, 193

+/-   55
archive   33
command   53
add   55
remove   55
hidden   33
read-only   33
system   33
tag/untag   174
AUTOEXEC.BAT   35, 186
edit   98
print   148
Automatically replace...   71, 78
AutoView   181
Avail   213
Backup   36, 191, 216
by date   194
incremental   194
keep track of   193
daily   192
incremental   192
system   192
disks required   192
in six steps   193
BAK   30
Basics   41
BAT   30
Batch files   36, 55
associated   105
creation   56
1Word   101
MS-DOS   57
edit   97
execute   102
variables
Gold   59
MS-DOS   58
Books mentioned   287
Branch   213
Built-in text editor   97
Bypass log   152
Cache   189
Can't find file XTPRO.X01   278
Can't Update Parent
Directory   80, 90
Cancel   60, 121
Cassette: see Floppy drive
Catalog of tagged files   148

CD-ROM   148, 279
Change
configuration   66
the colors   66
the setup   66
volume label   154
Character   29
Child directory   24
CHKDSK   36, 39, 184
Clock   80
Cluster   184
Collapse
+   92
update   207
display   91
Color   66
COM   30
Command central   46
Command Shell   46, 61, 102
exit   62
COMMAND.COM   34
Commands
1Word   98
command keys
XTree   245
XTree Easy   256
XTreeGold   252
XTreeNet   235, 258
XTreePro   247
XTreePro Gold   249
CTRL & ALT   243
edit   98
function keys
XTree   122, 246
XTree Easy   257
XTreeGold   254
XTreeNet   260
XTreePro   122, 248
XTreePro
Gold   123, 251
history   130
mouse   50, 61, 65, 106, 140
repeat   130
Common extension   30
Compare   214
Branch/Showall/Global   215
directory   164
directory/files   214

files   164
  XTree Programs   39
Compress (archive)   267
  Zip   272, 273
CONFIG.SYS   34, 186
  edit   98
  print   148
Configuration   66
  for laptops   133, 217
  Main Menu   67, 69
  system   186
Conserve disk space   133
Copy   35, 70
  automatically
    replace...   71, 78
  file and directory
    structure   78, 88, 216
    to a directory   72
    to another drive   70
  file as   71
  history   74
  many files   75
  to a floppy   70
Copy file to   71
Create
  an association   105
  Arc file   264
  batch file   101
  directories   25
  directory   86
  Zip file   270
Cross-linked cluster   184
CTRL   42
Current commands   42, 45
  directory   42, 141
  drive   24
  file   43, 141
  filespecs   46
  statistics   165
  window   45
Customize   66
Data file   28
Date & time display   81
Date and time stamp   80
Decompress
  Arc   267
  Zip   273
Delete   82
  BAK files   196

directory   83, 87
duplicate files   195
file   82
from floppy   82
several   82
old files   196
unneeded files   195
DESQView   280
Destination
  path   74
  window   74
  Window   138, 144
Dir Empty   225
Dir Not Logged   225
Directories   24
Directory   86
  child   25
  collapse   91
  copy structure   78, 88, 216
  creation strategies   185
  current   43
  delete   83, 87
  delete via Gold   90
  destination   74
  hide/unhide   93
  make   86
  management   86
  move   90
  parent   25
  print   148
  Prune (Gold)   84
  rename   86, 153
  root   24
  security   157
  structure   24
  subdirectory   25
  tag/untag   171
  when to create more   25
  window   96
Directory Statistics   165
Directory window   42, 44, 108
Disaster recovery   189
Disk tag/untag   172
Disk wash   84, 159
Disk Statistics   42, 165
Disk window   42
Display
  attributes   106
  date & time   81

EGA/VGA   70
  extended   70
  help   124
  split/unsplit   163
Display color selection   67, 69
DOS: see MS-DOS
DOS Shell   46, 61, 102
Double-density   118
Drive   23
  current   24
  names   23
Duplication   35, 70
Edit
  Autoexec.bat   98
  Config.sys   98
  with your word processor   101
Edit Script   210
EGA   70
Ending, file   30
Enter   42
Erase: see Delete
Error messages
  Can't Update Parent
     Directory   80, 90
  insufficient memory   64, 65,
                               139
  too many files   148
Exclude files   112, 174
EXE   30
EXecute   46, 102
Exit the Command Shell   62
Exit the program   151
Expanded file window 43, 44, 108
  mouse   141
Extended display   70
Extended Statistics   165
Extension   30, 105
Extract
  Arc files   267
  Zip files   273
F10 Commands   228
File   28
  archiving   263
  ASCII   101
  attributes   33, 53
  automatically
     replace...   71, 78
  average size on disk   166
  branch window   213

copy   35
file & directory
  structure   88
  to floppy   70
copy files & directory
  structure   78, 216
copy more than one   75
copy to a directory   72
current   43
data   28
date & time stamp   80
delete   82
  from floppy   82
  several   82
different versions of
  the same file   71
display
  attributes   106
  date & time   106
  size   106
duplication   35
  ending, see extension   30
  extension   30
  commonly-used   30
filespec   45
find   114, 213
  duplicates   114
  on floppies   114
  text   116
hide/unhide   156
matching   109
move
  more than one   145
  to another directory   143
naming   28
print   149
program   28
remove:
  BAK files   196
  duplicates   195
  rename   152
  while copying   71
  while moving   143
retrieval   84
retrieve deleted   225
specification   109
statistics   165
storage   196
tag/untag   171

text   101
undelete   225
view   177
window   108
File display   106
  date & time file   106
  file size   106
  1, 2, 3 columns   106
  sort criteria   161
File specification   45, 108
File Window   108
  mouse   141
File/Directory Limit   68
Filespec   45, 108, 217
  all files (*.*)   147
  exclusionary   112, 174
  history   112, 131
  Gold   113
  invert   113
  keep   115
  window   46
  with tag/untag   172
Filters   179
Find   114
  directory   114
  duplicate files   114
  file   114
  on floppies   114
  text in a file   116
Floppy disk format
  Gold   119
  MS-DOS   117
  high/low-density   118
  log   137
Floppy drives   23, 118
Format a floppy disk: see Floppy
  disk format
Formatted view   178, 232
Function keys   120, 217
General Read error on drive C: 277
Global   113, 123, 282
  Statistics   165
Go to DOS   22
Graft   79, 90, 146, 279
Graphics Toggle   208
Hard disk   23
  backup programs   187
  caching   189
  chkdsk   184

disk defraggers   188
disk scrubbers   188
five guidelines   183
house cleaning   195
log   137
maintenance   183
name   154
optimization   183
strategies   185
system configuration   186
total files   165
unerase/disaster recovery 189
Help   46, 124
  Gold   127
  Quick Reference   128
  XTree/Pro   125
Hex mode   279
Hidden   34
Hidden attribute   33
Hide/unhide directory   93, 157
Hide/unhide file   156
High-Density   118
History   130, 217
  filespec   112, 131, 217
  Gold   113
  labels   132
  mouse   140
  permanent/saved
    commands   132
How many files are in
  this directory   165
How many files are on
  this disk   165
IBMBIO.COM   34
IBMDOS.COM   34
In DOS   22
Initialize disk: see Format
Instant Log   139
Insufficient memory 64, 65, 139
Invert   113, 174
  file specification   113, 174
  file tags   113, 174
  see also Filespec, Tag/Untag
Keep filespec   115
Labels, history   132
LAN   235
Laptop   190
  configuration   133, 217
Launch a program: see Execute

Lines down the page 49
Link: see Open
List
  1Word Commands 98
  files needed 133, 217
  function keys 217, 254
  Gold's batch files
    variables 59
  mouse commands 140
  XTree files required 217
  XTreeGold viewers 231
Log 137, 222
  a directory as a drive 168
  branch 223
  bypass 139, 152
  destination window 138
  drive 223
  instant 139
  re-log 63
  current directory 138
  release 138, 225
  save 139
  snapshot 137
  switch between logged
    disks 138
  tree only 223
Lost cluster 184
Lotus 1-2-3 files 179
Low-Density 118
Lowercase letters 94
Maintenance 183
Make directory 86
Making a Batch File 56
Managing directories 86
Margins (print) 150
Matching files 109
Media 120
Memory 64, 65, 139, 222, 280
Menu
  see Application Menu
  see Pull-down Menu
Microsoft Word Files 178
Modify configuration 66, 69
Mouse 50, 61, 65, 106, 140
  driver 140
  history 140
  open 141
  scroll bar 140

  tag/untag 141
  view 141
Move 70, 141, 224
  automatically replace 143
  directory 90, 146
  file to another directory 143
  files & directory 224
  files to another drive 224
  more than one file 145
Move file as 142
Move file to 143
MS-DOS 21
  batch files 36
  Chkdsk 36
  format 36
  variables 58
  VER 36
  definition 21, 22
  version 36
  4.0/4.01 279
MS-DOS Commands
  format a disk 117
  path statement 186
  prompt 186
  subst(itute) 168
  version 190
Name a file 28
Name a hard disk (volume) 154
New Page 69
Newdate 80
No Files Match 225
No Files! 46, 109, 147, 225
Not in a program 22
Online help 46, 124
Oops! 225
Open 105
  Arc file 267
  create an Association 105
  with mouse 141
  Zip file 273
Operating system: See MS-DOS
Optimize hard disk 183
OS/2 280
Parent directory 25
Partial Untag 176
Path 25
  in Zip file 271
Path statement 99, 186, 187
Pathnames, print 148

Peek at a file 177
Peer-to-peer 236
Permanent History 132
PKarc 266
Place on the hard disk 22
Previously-used commands
  see History
Print 148
  1Word 151
  ASCII 149
  directory 148
  file 149
  form length 150
  margins 150
  tagged files 148
  tree 148
  viewed file 232
Program file 28
Prompt command 186
Prune 84, 90, 279
Pull-down menu 228
  command (F10) 228
  file window 231
Put: see Copy
Question mark 32
Quick Reference (Gold) 128
Quick Reference Guide 217
Quit 151
  command shell 62
  to another directory 152
Quit configuration program 69
Quit without saving changes 67
Re-log 63
Read permanent settings
  from disk 69
Read-only (attribute) 33
READ.ME 150
Recorded history
  see Permanent History 132
Release log 138
Remove BAK files easily 196
Remove directory 83, 87, 90
  duplicate files 195
Rename
  command 152
  directory 86, 153
  file 152
  while copying 71
  while moving 143

volume label 154
Repeat commands: see History
Replace 143
Restore default configuration 67
Retire files 196
Retrieve files 84
Return 42
Return expand display 43
Return file commands 43
Return to XTree 62
Root 24, 25
Save
  1Word file 98
  history 132
  log, tags 139
  viewed file 232
Save configuration and exit 67
Save configuration and quit 69
Scroll bar 140
Search viewed text 180
  see also Find
Security 155
  hide
    a directory 93
    a file 156
    simple precautions 155
Select Path 74
Setup 66
Shell 46, 102
Showall 110, 159, 282
  branch 213
  statistics 160, 165, 174
  tag/untag 174
  window 159
Small file window 42, 44, 108
Snapshot 137, 139, 152
Software 51
Software manufacturers
  mentioned 286
Sort criteria 161
Split/unsplit window 163
  active window 164
  merge tags 165
Stamp: see Date & time stamp
Statistics 165
  current 165
  extended 166
  global 165
  showall 160, 165, 174

total disk space 165
matching files 165
tagged files 165
Statistics window 165
Stop: see Cancel
Subdirectory: see Directory
Substitute 168
Swap 1Word with your
word processor 101
Switch to previously-logged
disks 138
System 34
System attribute 33
System backup 192
System Prompt 26, 62
elements 27
System requirements 39
Tag/untag 169
all files in a directory 171
backed up files 193
by attributes 174
file 171
with mouse 141
hard disk 172
invert 113
file specification 174
file tags 174
merge tags 165
partial untag 176
save tags 152
showall 174
tagging 45
untagging 45
with filespecs 172
Technical support Q&A 276
Text editor 97
Text file 101
Time: see Date & time
Too many files 148
Transfer tags 165
Tree 24
print 148
structure 24
Two windows: see Split/unsplit
TXT 30
Undelete 225
Unerase 84, 189
Unhide: see Hide/unhide
Unlog 225

Untag: see Tag/untag
Unwanted files 195
Variable 58
Gold 59
MS-DOS 58
VER 36
Version of DOS 36, 39
VGA 70
View 177, 231
all files on disk: see Showall
AutoView/zoom 181
contents of Arc file 267
contents of Zip file 273
dBASE 178
file size, date & time,
attributes: see File Display
formatted files 178, 232
Lotus 1-2-3 178
Microsoft Word 178
tagged files 180
text in search file 117
WordPerfect 178
XTreeGold viewers 231
Wash disk 84, 159
Wildcard 31, 32
Window 41
AutoView 181
directory 42, 44, 96, 108
disk statistics 42
expanded file 44, 108
file 108
navigation 44
small file 42, 44, 108
split/unsplit 163
statistics 165
Windows (Microsoft) 221, 280
Word processing: see Edit
XTG_CFG.EXE 68
XTPROCFG.EXE 66
XTree Company 285
XTree Programs
comparison 39
side-by-side 49
system requirements 39
XTREEINS.EXE 66
XTreeMenu: see Application Menu
XTreeNet 235
ZIP: see Archiving 263
Zoom 181

Biographies

Beth Woods

As both a writer and computer professional, Beth Woods' writing experiences range from articles in *PC Magazine* and *Comdex Show Daily* to television scripts (a member of the WGA, her recent credits include "Star Trek: The Next Generation"). Further, she has been "in the trenches" teaching novice users since 1983 as a computer instructor providing private instructions as well as designing and conducting seminars in DOS, hard disk survival, personal information management, word processing, and more.

Richard Tennant

Chicago native Rich Tennant is one of only a handful of cartoonists focusing on technology. His sketches expose a lighter side of the otherwise serious world of information technology. His self-syndicated cartoon series, "The 5th Wave," appears in the *San Jose Mercury News*, the *San Antonio Express News*, *ComputerWorld*, and in numerous corporate newsletters and publications worldwide.

Michael Cahlin

Michael Cahlin, who conceived of and helped design this book, is president of Cahlin/Williams Communications, a public relations/marketing communications agency specializing in the microcomputer industry. Since 1983, Cahlin has helped make the reputations of some of the most prominent software manufacturers in the industry; he was XTree Company's first PR firm. In 1989, he created the first "software amnesty program" in the United States, for XTree Company. Cahlin is also the founder of The Chocolate Software Company and The Financial Software Company.

Jan Altman

Editor Jan Altman, vice president of the Stanford/Palo Alto PC Users Group, is founder of The Express Train, a computer training/consulting company. She is a Microsoft Certified Trainer and a member of Microsoft's Consultant Relations Program. Jan is based in Santa Clara, CA,

About IDG Books Worldwide

Welcome to the world of IDG Books Worldwide. International Data Group (IDG) is the world's leading publisher of computer periodicals, with more than 150 weekly and monthly newpapers and magazines reaching 25 million readers in more than 40 countries. If you use personal computers, IDG Books is committed to publishing quality books that meet your needs. We rely on our extensive network of publications—including such leading periodicals as *ComputerWorld, InfoWorld, MacWorld, PC World, Portable Computing, Publish, Network World, SunWorld, AmigaWorld,* and *GamePro*—to help us make informed and timely decisions in creating useful computer books that meet your needs.

Every IDG book strives to bring extra value and skill-building instruction to the reader. Our books are written by experts, with the backing of IDG periodicals, and with careful thought devoted to issues such as audience, interior design, use of icons, and illustrations. Our editorial staff is a careful mix of high-tech journalists and experienced book people. Our close contact with the makers of computer products helps ensure accuracy and thorough coverage. Our heavy use of personal computers at every step in production means we can deliver books in the most timely manner.

We are delivering books of high quality at competitive prices, on topics customers want. At IDG, we believe in quality, and we have been delivering quality for 25 years. You'll find no better book on a subject than an IDG book.

Jonathan Sacks
President
IDG Books Worldwide, Inc.

International Data Group's publications include: **ARGENTINA'S** Computerworld Argentina; **ASIA'S** Computerworld Hong Kong, Computerworld Southeast Asia, Computerworld Malaysia, Computerworld Singapore, Infoworld Hong Kong, InfoWorld SE Asia; **AUSTRALIA'S** Computerworld Australia, PC World, Macworld, Lotus, Publish!; **AUSTRIA'S** Computerwelt Oesterreich; **BRAZIL'S** DataNews, PC Mundo, Automacao & Industria; **BULGARIA'S** Computer Magazine Bulgaria, Computerworld Bulgaria; **CANADA'S** ComputerData, Direct Access, Graduate CW, Macworld; **CHILE'S** Informatica, Computacion Personal; **COLUMBIA'S** Computerworld Columbia; **CZECHOSLOVAKIA'S** Computerworld Czechoslovakia, PC World; **DENMARK'S** CAD/CAM WORLD, Computerworld Danmark, PC World, Macworld, Unix World, PC LAN World, Communications World; **FINLAND'S** Mikro PC, Tietoviikko; **FRANCE'S** Le Mond Informatique, Distributique, InfoPC, Telecoms International; **GERMANY'S** AmigaWelt, Computerwoche, Information Management, PC Woche, PC Welt, Unix Welt, Macwelt RD; **GREECE'S** Computerworld, PC World, Macworld; **HUNGARY'S** Computerworld SZT, Mikrovilag; **INDIA'S** Computers & Communications; **ISRAEL'S** People & Computers; **ITALY'S** Computerworld Italia, PC World Italia; **JAPAN'S** Computerworld Japan, Macworld, SunWorld Journal; **KOREA'S** Computerworld, PC World; **MEXICO'S** Computerworld Mexico, PC Journal; **THE NETHERLAND'S** Computerworld Netherlands, PC World, AmigaWorld; **NEW ZEALAND'S** Computerworld New Zealand, PC World New Zealand; **NIGERIA'S** PC World Africa; **NORWAY'S** Conputerworld Norge, PC World Norge CAD/CAM, Macworld Norge; **PEOPLE'S REPUBLIC OF CHINA'S** China Computerworld, China Computerworld Monthly; **PHILLIPPINE'S** Computerworld Phillippines, PC Digest/PC World; **POLAND'S** Komputers Magazine, Computerworld; **ROMANIA'S** Infoclub; **SPAIN'S** CIM World, Communicaciones World, Computerworld Espana, PC World, AmigaWorld; **SWEDEN'S** ComputerSweden, PC/Nyhetherna, Mikrodatorn, PC World, Macworld; **SWITZERLAND'S** Computerworld Schweiz, Macworld; **TAIWAN'S** Computerworld Taiwan, PC World, Publish; **THAILAND'S** Computerworld; **TURKEY'S** Computerworld Monitor, PC World/Turkiye; **UNITED KINGDOM'S** Graduate Computerworld, PC Business World, ICL Today, Lotus UK, Macworld UK; **UNITED STATES'** AmigaWorld, A+, CIO, Computerworld, Digital News, Federal Computer Week, GamePro, InfoWorld, Lotus, Macworld, Network World, NextWorld, PC Games, PC World, Portable Office, PC Letter, Publish!, Run, SunWorld Journal; **USSR'S** MIR PC, Computerworld, Computer Express, Network, Manager Magazine; **VENEZUELA'S** Computerworld Venezuela, Micro Computerworld; **YUGOSLAVIA'S** Moj Mikro.

Introducing XTreeGold 2.0

The World's favorite file and disk manager just got better. We've kept all the great things you loved in XTreeGold 2.0, and added important new features that make XTreeGold 2.0 better and easier to use than ever.

- With XTreeGold 2.0, you can choose between our original keystroke command line or
  - └ our new **pull-down menus**.
- You can **"un-delete"** files that have been accidentally erased.
- Add **PKZip compatibility** to our file compression system, to get more out of your hard disk.
- Create an **application menu** automatically with Autobuild, which searches your disk for more
  - └ than 700 popular applications.
- View more data files than ever with our newly **expanded viewer list**.
- What's more, we've made many of our standard features faster, better, and easier.

To upgrade for just $35 use the order form below. Or call **800-282-5003** to order by phone.

XTreeGold 2.0 Upgrade Order

Send to: XTree Upgrades, 14 Inverness Drive East, Building E, Suite 104, Englewood, CO 80112-9725

Today's Date	Phone Number
Your Name	
Company Name	Title
Address	
City	State ZIP
Disk Format desired (Check one) ☐ 5.25" ☐ 3.5"	**REQUIRED:** *Serial number:*

X TREE COMPANY

The world leader in disk management.

XTree is a registered trademark and XTreeNet and XTreeGold
are registered trademarks of XTree Company,
a division of Executive Systems, Inc.

METHOD OF PAYMENT

☐ Check ☐ Money Order

☐ Visa ☐ Mastercard ☐ American Express

Card Number

Expire Date

Signature

CA and CO residents must add appropriate sales tax.

MAKE PAYABLE TO: XTree Company

	AMOUNT
Upgrade	$35.00
CA Sales Tax	$ 2.10
CO Sales Tax	$ 1.30
TOTAL	

HardDrive Overlord!

Peace of mind in one powerful package.

Overlord! *employs three sophisticated techniques to discover damaging viruses. Virus eradication is now made affordable!*

PROTECTION SYSTEM

HardDrive Overlord! is a full-time virus protection system. It contains all three types of virus protection — scanning, filtering and authenticating.

SPECIAL OFFER

$69⁹⁵ Regularly $99⁹⁵

COMPUTER VIRUSES

Computer viruses are harmful or irritating programs that stay in memory or spread themselves from one executable program to another, waiting for a trigger before doing its damage.

With **HardDrive Overlord!** you will detect viruses before they can damage your system. You will also learn how to eradicate them.

VIRUS SCANNERS

Overlord! scanners look into your system for known viruses. When they find or suspect a virus, they halt the operation and notify you.

Footutil ♦ is the automatic **Hard-Drive Overlord!** scanner. It goes to work when you install the software and is available to scan any diskette or hard drive on command.

VIRUS FILTERS

Overlord! filters examine operations that viruses may be causing.

And they are fast, sure, and non-intrusive — setting **HardDrive Overlord!** apart from any other anti-virus software.

Overlord ♦ If OVERLORD detects an operation caused by a virus, it will alert you immediately. You will

have the opportunity to prevent the executing program from damaging your system.

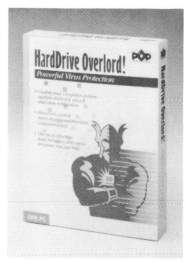

Watcher ♦ monitors your Random Access Memory (RAM) to detect programs that are attempting to remain in memory.

FILE AUTHENTICATORS

Footpad ♦ is a run-time authenticator; it checks a program's footprint against one on file. If they don't match, and a file which has been changed by a virus will have a different footprint, **Hard-Drive Overlord!** stops the operation and alerts you.

Check ♦ is the on-demand authenticator. It gives you a strong last line of defense against viruses. When you see something suspicious, run CHECK to search for known viruses and footprint the file.

POP Computer Products, Inc.
P.O. Box 1389
Evergreen, CO 80439
(303) 674-0200

Logo is the registered trademark of POP Computer Products, Inc.

Reminders!

An electronic calendar and day book.

Here's a program that automates the chores you struggle with or just cannot do in a day book or executive scheduler. **Reminders!** *combines to-do lists, notepads, and phonebooks with calendars and schedules to give you a program so personal, it sets off alarms to keep you out of trouble!*

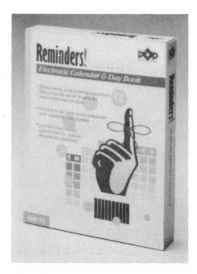

SPECIAL OFFER

$69⁹⁵ Regularly
$99⁹⁵

Pops Up ◆ Here's how versatile **Reminders!** is. If you want to look at your schedule while you're working on a large spreadsheet, simply press a hot-key combination. Up pops **Reminders!**. And it's fully functional. Exit **Reminders!** and you'll discover the spreadsheet right where you left it.

ADDITIONAL FEATURES
AutoDial
Dates Displayed
Category
Log
Print
Mouse Support
Automatic Scheduling
Word Search
Conflict Warning
Memory Jogger

REMINDERS! MAIN FEATURES
Reminders ◆ Our program controls your never-ending list of notes regarding things to do.

Alarms ◆ Set an alarm. When the date arrives, your alarm will sound and put your reminder on the screen in any text-based program.

Calendar ◆ Scroll through the calendar to any date and press a key. There's your schedule.

Phonebook ◆ Our Phonebook lets you refer to names, notes, or anything important you need to remember.

Options ◆ As if **Reminders!** wasn't flexible enough, its options allow you to "fine-tune" the program. Change the 14 system defaults or any of the screen colors to configure **Reminders!** in a unique and practical way.

POP Computer Products, Inc.
P.O. Box 1389
Evergreen, CO 80439
(303) 674-0200

Logo is the registered trademark of POP Computer Products, Inc.

GET YOUR HARD DISK UP TO SPEED.

And keep it that way with...

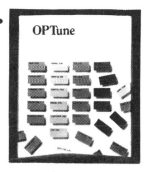

OPTune

You may not notice it but your hard disk is gradually slowing down. And the more you use it the slower it may become. That's why it's so important to have a hard-disk optimizer that will allow your system to operate at its peak performance level – that optimizer is OPTune.

File Defragmentation

As you know, DOS is extremely inefficient when it comes to storing files. Routine erasing and saving of files can cause them to become located in several different places on your disk (or fragmented). OPTune combines those scattered file pieces into complete, sequential files which means your hard disk may respond up to four times **faster** and **last longer** too!

Hard-disk Tuning

OPTune will also "fine-tune" your drive by performing a low-level, non-destructive reformat of the hard disk. Doing so ensures synchronization between the hard disk and the rest of the system which means a **permanent increase** in drive responsivness...up to 500%!

Speed

With OPTune you can automatically optimize your hard disk every day in mere seconds! Once you have completed the initial optimization, include OPTune as part of your AUTOEXEC.BAT file and start each day with a fine-tuned, defragmented hard drive.

SPECIAL PRICE!

As a purchaser of the Official XTree MS-DOS Hard Disk Companion you are entitled to OPTune at a

30% discount of

$69.95

To order OPTune at this special price, call Gazelle Systems at 800-233-0383 and mention this ad.

PC W●RLD

BEST BUY

GAZELLE · 42 North University Avenue Provo, Utah 84601 (801)377-1288

Co/Session lets you use your office PC as though you were there...

Co/Session remote access communications software enables you to do everything you previously had to do at the PC in your office— *but* from the location of your choice and at your own convenience.

Via modem, you can access (even transfer) files, run programs, print reports, use on-line network resources, and more, just as though you were seated at the keyboard in your office...

even when you're not

Even when you're at home...before dinner...when you get back from the health club...after you read the kids a story. Even when you're on the road...in your hotel room...at a branch office...calling on a client. Co/Session can help you accomplish all you have to do while allowing you to enjoy the things you want to do. To find out more about how, call us toll-free, at 800- 322-9440.

Special Offer! Two PC Package only $129: Save $66 when ordering a CO/Session Two PC Package by mailing this ad to Triton at the above address. Please enclose payment by check or money order plus $10 shipping for each package ordered.

CO session ™·

a product of Triton Technologies Inc
200 Middlesex Turnpike, Iselin, New Jersey 08830
(201) 855-9440 • Fax (201) 855-9608

THOW TO MANAGE WHEN
T**IME IS MONE**Y

"Most Impressive" -Business Week

Just how much is your time worth? 30 minutes a day to prioritize. 5 hours a week to report and review. Cash in on this and more!

On Time & On Track

Here's the best-selling PC software system used by busy executives to automate their work. Tracks your 3 most vital business areas - - People, Projects & Time. Each entry cross-references automatically. A winner! A great gift for your office manager!

Total Management System

Appointment Calendar with Alarms • Conflict Checking •Prioritized To-Do Lists • Office Scheduler Group Names • Project Schedules • Milestones & Deadlines • Time Charts (GANTT) • Card File Categories • Client & Contact Histories • Delegations & Follow-Ups Intelligent Dates • Auto Dialer • Memo Pad • Hot Keys & more!

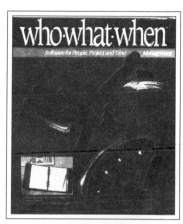

who·what·when
Software for People, Project and Time Management

Reports Fit Day Runner™ Day-Timer™ Franklin™ etc

New!!!
One Month Calender
Report on a Single Page

"Practical, easy and useful. From box to computer in less than an hour."
New York Times

$195
Save $100

CHRÔNOS

800-777-7907

555 De Haro Suite 240 • San Francisco, CA 94107 • Fax: (415) 626-5393

Why stick with second-rate communications software when upgrading is this easy?

Did you know that the best communications software is not Crosstalk, Procomm or Smartcom? It's HyperACCESS/5 from Hilgraeve.

Seeing is believing. So we're making a very special offer to owners of Crosstalk™, Relay™, Smartcom™, Mirror™, Procomm, Telix and Qmodem. For a limited time, you can step up to HyperACCESS/5, normally $199, for only

$49⁹⁵

"A must-have for those interested in telecommunications..."   John C. Dvorak - PC Magazine, 12/12/89

"A new standard in performance of communications software has arrived, and its name is HyperACCESS/5."
PCResource, 8/90

"The graphics and user interface are top notch and visually impressive."   InfoWorld, 6/11/90

"...makes all other communications software positively obsolete...enough goodies to keep a super-power-user interested and busy for a long time."
REMark, 6/90

transfer files through your modem at up to 5 times the modem's speed. And now that we've put HyperProtocol in the public domain, you can get the same fast transfers when you call BBSs or friends with other comm software.

Automating communications is a breeze

HyperACCESS/5's Discerning Learning™ watches you, learning not just your keystrokes, but your intentions. Quickly, easily, and without writing scripts, you can automate every facet of your communications, even entire calls!

Upgrade to the experts' choice now!

The computer industry's top software evaluators have unanimously chosen HyperACCESS/5. Isn't it worth $49.95 to find out why?

There's NO RISK. If within 60 days you're not completely satisfied, return HyperACCESS/5 for a full refund.

Some programs lack important features like: Zmodem, PC-to-PC power, strong script language, or terminal emulators you need. Others may have what you need, but are slow, awkward or unreliable. HyperACCESS/5 gives you everything you need, with the speed, agility, and reliability you deserve!

Guaranteed results in 10 minutes or less

We guarantee you can install and make your first call in 10 minutes or less. HyperACCESS/5 is Hardware Aware™ —it adapts itself to your PC and 70 specific modems, plus generic types—so you can place and answer calls *immediately*. And its slick Sliding Windows™ interface is more than intuitive, it's obvious!

HyperProtocol sends files faster

HyperACCESS/5's HyperProtocol has on-the-fly compression and lets you

Editor's Choice   Best Overall   Best Overall
July 1988 & May 1987   April 1990   September 1986

Attention Procomm, Crosstalk and Smartcom owners!

Step up to HyperACCESS/5 for DOS for only $49.95 risk-free. Proof of ownership is required.

TO ORDER:

CALL TOLL-FREE: 800-826-2760, 8am-6pm EST
OR BY FAX: 313-243-0645. See info below.
OR BY MAIL: See info below.

Hilgraeve Inc.

To order by mail or fax, please send your name, company, address, phone number, credit card number, expiration date, and signature (or send certified check or money order) to Hilgraeve Inc., HyperACCESS/5 Upgrade, 111 Conant Ave., Suite A, Monroe, MI 48161. Price is $49.95 plus $6.00 shipping. Offer good in US and Canada only. Limited time offer. Limit of one per customer.

Cut Your Support Time With System Sleuth Analyzer

With the passive analysis capabilities of System Sleuth Analyzer you can explore the inner working of your system and resolve conflicts that arise from installing new hardware and software. System Sleuth Analyzer features:

I/O Port address availability: Finds used/unused space for add-in boards. **Memory resources:** Lists EMS/XMS, conventional memory statistics and status of memory managers and large-frame EMS detection for multi-tasking systems. **General system information:** Shows CPU type, ROM-BIOS version. **Hard disk information:** Determines space used, available, partitions, etc. **Hardware interrupt status:** Find IRQs available, in use. Discover the video adapter installed and video modes available. Provides a user-definable menu to allow additional functionality. Displays motherboard and virtual configuration switch settings. Boot-time status shows the results of POST tests. System Sleuth Analyzer includes on-line help a hardcopy report generator and **Installation Assistant**, a new feature that makes the location of unused I/O addresses, DMA channels and IRQs easier than ever before.

SPECIAL! Fill out and return this coupon today and receive System Sleuth Analyzer (a $79.95 value) for **only $40.00**, plus $5.00 shipping and handling. **Save over $35.00** by taking advantage of this offer now! **Limit: one unit per coupon.** CA residents add tax.

System Sleuth Analyzer $40.00

Sales Tax ....

Shipping and handling $5.00

Name _____

Company _____

Address _____

Address _____

City _____ State _____ Zip _____

Phone # _____

Visa/MasterCard # _____ Exp. Date _____

 DARIANA TECHNOLOGY GROUP, INC.

6945 Hermosa Circle Buena Park, CA 90620

(714) 994-7400 (714) 994-7401 Fax

Get Control of Your Finances!

Get

Finance10™

To Order, call
1-800-332-2983

Finally, an easy-to-use software program that helps you make "cents" out of complex financial information.

Finance10 is a collection of ten, easy-to-use financial calculators that puts you in complete control of financial information. Complicated financial calculations are made *in seconds*, while input data is checked automatically for tax law limitations and other special considerations.

With **Finance10** you can quickly estimate the affordable price for property. Evaluate whether it makes sense to lease or purchase a car or finance a house. Compare financial benefits of a pension plan. Determine sums for tax returns and financial statements. Calculate bank balances at the end of a series of deposits, and much, much more. **Finance10** even prints customized reports in seconds!

Only **Finance10** has two modes of operation. Use it as a stand alone application or as a handy pop-up utility (using a thrifty 8K of RAM)! Great for consultants working on laptops.

No accounting or computer experience is required. Simply choose the calculator you need, enter the facts you know, and *ba-bing*, **Finance10** does the rest! No other financial software is as fast, comprehensive, or easy to learn.

Only **Finance10** includes all of the following calculators: ❶ Bond Yield to Maturity; ❷ Depreciation; ❸ Financial Managers Rate of Return; ❹ Individual Retirement Account (IRA); ❺ Internal Rate of Return; ❻ Lease vs. Purchase Analysis; ❼ Loan Amortization Schedule; ❽ Personal Financial Statement; ❾ Present Value/Future Value; ❿ Statistics.

Special Offer: Normally, **Finance10** retails for $69.95. But you can get yours for only $39.95 (and save $30!), just by mentioning *The Official XTree Companion.* Want more? Order today and you'll get more than $1,000 in money-saving discount coupons on name-brand, award-winning hardware and software products. **Finance10** even has a 60-day NO RISK money-back guarantee. No other financial software offers this unbelievable combination of price, value, support and savings!

P.O. Box 481290   Los Angeles, CA 90048

To order by mail, please send your name, company, address, phone number, VISA or MC credit card number, expiration date, and signature (or send certified check or money order) to The Financial $oftware Company. Price is $39.95 + $6.00 shipping and handling per copy. (CA residents add $2.50 sales tax per copy. Limit of one per customer.) The entire ten program package requires DOS 3.0 or later and 130K RAM (8K in pop-up mode).

More from the New World of Computer Books...
IDG Books Worldwide

The only *in-depth*, complete guides to buying software & computers!

InfoWorld Test Center Software Buyer's Guide
▲ More comprehensive, up-to-date, and authoritative than any other guide
▲ Covers: word processors, spreadsheets, databases, desktop publishing (high-end and low-end), and Windows 3!
▲ With definitive, unbiased reviews that really help you evaluate the right software for the job you need done
$14.95
from the Editors of *InfoWorld* Magazine, with a special preface by Michael Miller, Editor-in-Chief, *InfoWorld* Magazine
1-878058-11-8, 356 pp., 5 1/2 x 8 1/2"

InfoWorld Test Center Computer Buyer's Guide
▲ From InfoWorld's $3 million Test Center--the industry's most respected testing facility
▲ Covers: 16 MHz '386s, 33 MHr '386s, '486 supermachines, and portable computers, too!
▲ With definitive, unbiased reviews that really help you evaluate the right computer for your needs and budget
$14.95
from the Editors of *InfoWorld* Magazine, with a special preface by Michael Miller, Editor-in-Chief, *InfoWorld* Magazine
1-878058-12-6, 254 pp., 5 1/2 x 8 1/2"

Another authorized edition--for a bestselling hard disk utility!

The Official SpinRite II & Hard Disk Companion
▲ The authorized, inside guide to SpinRite, from Gibson Research
▲ With valuable, "insider" tips never before revealed
▲ With a section on how hard disks die--and how to prevent those problems on your computer
$14.95
by John M. Goodman, Ph.D., with a foreword by Steve Gibson, President of Gibson Research
1-878058-08-8, 280 pp., 5 1/2 x 8 1/2"

▲▼▲
Available at your local bookstore or computer/software store.
Or call (800) 28BOOKS.
(That's 800-282-6657)

Other Valuable Guides from the New World of Computer Books...IDG Books Worldwide

Finally--a practical guide to portable computing!

Portable Computing Official Laptop Field Manual

▲ A complete, take-it-with-you-on-the-road-manual:
with printer codes, software keystroke references,
on-line access phone numbers, individual hardware
references, DOS summaries, and more

▲ Leave your manuals at home--everything you need is in this
one handy-sized book!

▲ From Portable Computing Magazine--the mobile professional's
monthly bible

$14.95

by Sebastian Rupley, with a foreword by Jim McBrian, Publisher,
Portable Computing Magazine
1-878058-10-X, 224 pp., 5 1/2 x 8 1/2"

The powerful programming tool you need for Paradox 3.5!

PC World Paradox 3.5 Breakthrough Power Programming

▲With hundreds of programming tips and techniques not found in
any other book

▲ Definitive coverage of the Paradox engine, PAL, and SQL Link

▲ Includes one 3 1/2" disk of valuable software, including a ready-to-
run accounting system, an advanced program editor, and utility scripts--
fully customizable and worth $$ hundreds!

$39.95, includes one 3 1/2"disk with over 2 Mb of program code,
condensed onto a 1.44Mb disk
by Greg Salcedo & Martin Rudy, with a foreword by Richard Swartz, Borland International
1-878058-02-9, 750 pp., 7 3/8 x 9 1/4"

Available at your local bookstore or computer/software store.
Or call (800) 28BOOKS.
(That's 800-282-6657)

IDG Books Worldwide Registration Card
THE OFFICIAL XTREE MS-DOS & HARD DISK COMPANION, 2ND EDITION
Please take the time to fill this out—and you'll be sure to hear about updates to this book and new information about other IDG Books Worldwide products. Thanks!

Name _____

Company/Title _____   _____

Address _____   _____

City/State/Zip _____

What is the single most important reason you bought this book? _____

Where did you buy this book?
- ❏ Bookstore (Name _____   _____   )
- ❏ Electronics/Software Store (Name _____   )
- ❏ Advertisement (If magazine, which?_____   )
- ❏ Mail Order
- ❏ Other:

How did you hear about this book?
- ❏ Book review in: _____
- ❏ Advertisement in: _____
- ❏ Catalog
- ❏ Found in store
- ❏ Other: _____

How many computer books do you purchase a year?
- ❏ 1
- ❏ 2-5
- ❏ 6-10
- ❏ More than 10

How would you rate the overall content of this book?
- ❏ Very good
- ❏ Good
- ❏ Satisfactory
- ❏ Poor

Why? _____

What chapters did you find most valuable? _____

What did you find least useful? _____

What kind of chapter or topic would you add to future editions of this book?

_____

Please give us any additional comments. _____

❏ Check here if you need additional infomation on XTree products. Add specifics:

Thank you for your help.

❏ I liked this book! By checking this box, I give you permission to use my name and quote me in future IDG Books Worldwide promotional materials.

Fold Here

Place
stamp
here

IDG Books Worldwide, Inc.
155 Bovet Road, Ste. 730
San Mateo, CA 94402

Attn: Reader Response